P9-AGS-777

WELCOME TO THE LAND

. . . where Stephen Donaldson's extraordinary characters challenge Lord Foul the Despiser's remorseless attempts to corrupt the magic of this complex and compelling world.

From the awesome, windswept height of Kevin's Watch to the dim and brooding menace of Garroting Deep, each part of the Land breathes its own unique, distinctive life. A special part of Donaldson's genius is to create places so vivid and beautiful that their memory stays with the reader: the Hills of Andelain, the beautiful heart of the Land; the Plains of Ra, where Ramen tend the great free horses, the Ranyhyn; the Isle of the One Tree . . . and so much more.

When the idea for *The Atlas of the Land* was first suggested, the task seemed overwhelming—but there was no question that Karen Fonstad was the one to do it. Her skill as a cartographer, her strict attention to detail, and her own love of the Land all combine within these pages to bring the Land to life.

"In practice, the crucial point is that Karen Fonstad has done everything humanly possible to make this Atlas accurate and valid. I won't mention her hundreds of hours of meticulous and diligent work; but I will mention the dozens of hours of work *I've* done at her request, explaining my ideas, verifying hers, and checking the finished product.

"The result is not what I would have done—it is much better."

Stephen R. Donaldson

Also by Karen Wynn Fonstad

Published by Ballantine Books:

THE ATLAS OF MIDDLE-EARTH
THE ATLAS OF PERN

THE ATLAS OF THE LAND

Karen Wynn Fonstad

A Del Rey Book

Ballantine Books • New York

A Del Rey Book
Published by Ballantine Books

Library of Congress Cataloging in Pubication Data
Fonstad, Karen Wynn.
The atlas of the land.
"A Del Rey book."
I. Title.
PS3556.047A8   1985   813'.54   85-6203
ISBN 0-345-31431-X (hdcvr)
ISBN 0-345-31433-6 (pbk)

Manufactured in the United States of America

First Edition: November 1985

10   9   8   7   6   5   4   3   2   1

Designed by Gene Siegel
Cover design by James R. Harris
Hand lettering by Richard Nebiolo

To Mother

—My Atiaran—

*Whose straight back has been a
lifelong inspiration.*

ACKNOWLEDGMENTS

Although the quality and accuracy (or inaccuracy) of the product within these pages rests entirely with the author, the work could never have been completed without the encouragement and assistance of many people.

Foremost, Stephen Donaldson, who offered the hospitality of his home while we spent several grueling days going through my preliminary sketches and notes; then spent even more time and effort reviewing the final maps and text.

The editors and staff of Del Rey books who provided helpful suggestions and assistance on layout and revisions.

My husband, Todd, Associate Professor of Geography, who not only lent emotional support, but also provided references and guidance during the evaluations of the physical geography. My children, Mark and Kristina, and my mother, Estis Wynn, who kept up my spirits whenever necessary.

The University of Wisconsin-Oshkosh Department of Geography for allowing me use of cartographic equipment.

The Oshkosh, Wisconsin, and Norman, Oklahoma, Public Libraries for providing source materials.

UW-Oshkosh faculty member Dr. Lurton Blassingame, who introduced me to the series.

CONTENTS

INTRODUCTION

The Land—is it real? Or is it a dream? By the end of the First Chronicles of Thomas Covenant the Unbeliever, the question almost ceases to be important even to Covenant. But real or not, readers can glimpse the Land through Covenant and appreciate the oneness which can result from Earthpower: the totality of experience that makes each part of the Land function in communion with the rest. During the Sunbane, we can also grieve with Covenant over the loss of that consummate glory.

The experiences of Earthpower and the Sunbane are beyond any ability of pen and ink to portray; so this atlas can never hope to show more than a pale image of the Land. Yet if "Joy is in the ears that hear," it may also be in the eyes that see—if we can reach beyond our earthbound imaginations.

The Geography of the Land

From the snowy mountains and highlands of the far Northern Climbs to the heat of the Gray Desert, from the soaring peaks of the Westron Mountains to the sucking delta muds of Lifeswallower, the Land is varied in clime, topography, and vegetation. It covers a vast area—over three million square miles, spread almost two thousand miles east-west from the western marge of the Westron Mountains to the Sunbirth Sea, and almost as far north-south, with unknown lands beyond.

Although the previously published maps of the Land do not include a scale, the numerous references to distance given during the course of Covenant's travels verify the expanse of the Land:

300 leagues (lgs.) from Mithil Stonedown to Revelstone[1]
200 lgs. from docks on Soulsease to Revelstone[2]
Confluence of Rivers White and Grey[3]:
    100 lgs. to Guards Gap
    150 lgs. to Last Hills and Garroting Deep
    70 lgs. to Revelstone
500 lgs. to Landsdrop (Southron Range to Northron Climbs)[4]
300–400 lgs. Revelstone to Plains of Ra[5]
50 lgs. across the Plains of Ra[6]
270–300 lgs. Revelstone to Doom's Retreat[7]
40 lgs. Doom's Retreat to Cravenhaw[8]
60–65 lgs. Revelwood to western edge of Trothgard[9]
150+ lgs. Rivenrock to the confluence of the Black and Mithil Rivers[10]
50 lgs. Rivenrock to Gallows Howe[11]
400 lgs. Revelstone to Seareach[12]
40 lgs. north edge of Lifeswallower to The Grieve[13]
360 lgs. Soulbiter to Revelstone[14]

The Land is not only varied in its physical attributes, but also in its populace. Tall Woodhelvennin, stocky Stonedowners, massive Giants, tiny Wraiths of Andelain, snow-hardened *Haruchai*, nomadic Ramen, lore-wise Demondim-spawn ur-viles and Waynhim, trembling *jheherrin,* mindless Stone- and Sunbane-warped creatures of Lord Foul all inhabit the Land. The Woodhelvennin and Stonedowners are relatively few—still recovering from the Ritual of Desecration—even after millennia; but Foul's breeding dens produce masses to fight his battles.

This atlas details maps and descriptions of both the physical features of the Land and many of the inhabited sites.

The Format of the Atlas

Covenant journeys through the Land four times. Each of those times he reaches new destinations; yet he visits some locations repeatedly—notably Kevin's Watch, Mithil Stonedown, Andelain, Revelstone, and Mount Thunder. Instead of chronologically, the Land has been divided roughly into quarters and within each region are included site maps of important locations.

Over the millennia between the two Chronicles there are dramatic differences in vegetation due to the Sunbane; and drastic social changes associated with the corruption of Earthpower and the rise of the Clave. Physical changes of landforms are relatively few, however, and even local sites are more aged than altered. Therefore, the sequence within each section is locational, moving from the Central Hills to the margins of the Land—from Kevin's Watch to *Melenkurion* Skyweir, Andelain to Revelstone, Mount Thunder to The Grieve, and Morinmoss to Foul's Creche.

Beyond the Land there are still no locational maps: the Unhomed could not return to Home, and neither the *Haruchai* nor the Giants had knowledge of the location of the Isle of the One Tree, except for the Guardian. Estimates could be based on the voyage of Starfare's Gem. However, even that voyage yields insufficient knowlege of the Sunbirth Sea to map its shores. Only the Giantship and the locations visited on the voyage are sufficiently described for illustration.

In addition to the regional and site maps, chronologies and pathway maps are given for each of Covenant's sojourns. Journeys of the Warward and other important characters are also included. As distances listed in the Chronicles are consistently given in leagues, most maps show this unit measure on the scale. A league is equal to 3 miles, or about 4.8 kilometers. For ease of comparison all the major regional and pathway maps are of equal scale. Site maps and subregion maps vary.

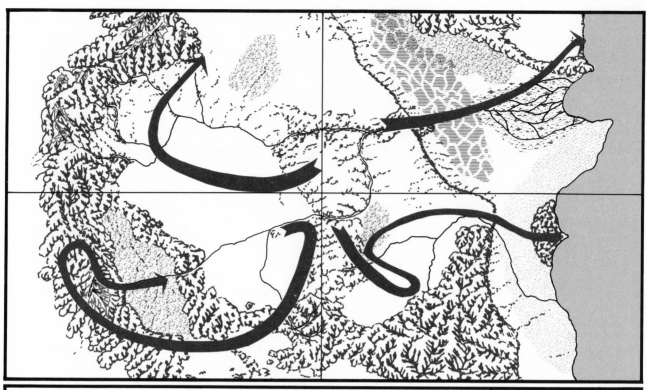

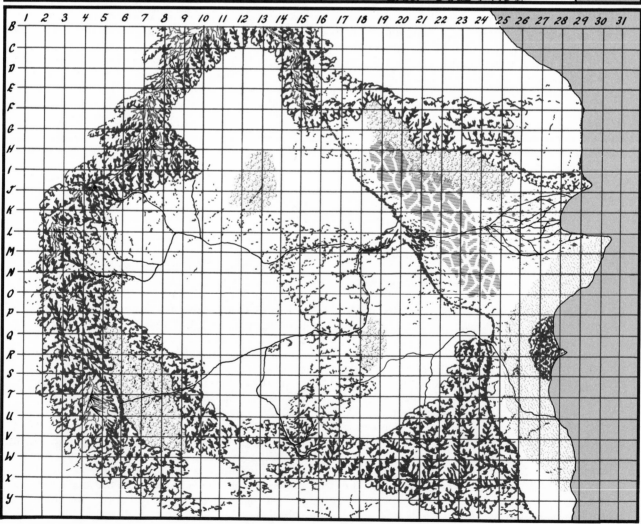

Although not extensive, the locations revealed in the Chronicles have been indexed for easy reference. The grid is a simple combination of alphabetical reference points for the north-south axis, and numerical divisions for the east-west axis. Each grid square equals twenty leagues (sixty miles) between reference points.

Symbols used to represent various physical and cultural phenomena are kept fairly constant, although some variations are necessary (notably in the pathway maps). A legend is included with most maps for easier reference, but the symbols usually fit one of the following categories:

Physical

▭	Damaged Plains
▭	Low Hills
▭	Escarpment
▭	Ravine
▭	Snowcapped Mountains
▭	Ice Floes
▭	Ocean
▱	Lake
⌇	Perennial Stream
⌇	Intermittent Stream
⌇	Waterfall
▭	Forest (absent under Sunbane)
▭	Forest (continues under Sunbane)
▭	Marsh

Cultural

○	Community
○	Individual's Habitation
▲	Temporary Abode or Camp
——	Road
—=—	Bridge
→)(←	Ford

Site Maps

▭	Courtyard
□◻□	Assorted Buildings
▭	Window
▭	Door
🌳	Tree
▭	Pier

Pathways

→	Covenant's Path
⇢	Secondary Character's Path(s)
➜	Warward
➤	Foul's Army
□	Encounter
▲	Campsite
—+→	No Night Camp
2	Date (as of midnight)
○	Full Moon
●	Dark of the Moon
●	Sun of Rain
●	Fertile Sun
●	Sun of Pestilence
●	Desert Sun

While the maps on the following pages will help the reader draw closer to the Land, they cannot fully portray those portions which were not understood by Covenant—or even the Lords. No illustration can convey the process involved in Damelon's Door, Lady Alif's access to Kemper's Pitch, or the vision of *Elemesnedene*. Such things must be left to the mind's eye.

HAVEN FARM

When Thomas Covenant's first novel becomes a bestseller, he and his wife Joan are able to purchase Haven Farm, which they have been renting.[1] The farm fronts on a highway which runs between a town two miles east, and another ten miles beyond the farm.[2] The nearest farmsteads are a half mile away.[3] Trees line the edge of the property next to the highway, but Covenant's white frame house can be clearly seen across the fields, silhouetted against the black woods behind. A sign and mailbox stand at the entrance of the drive.[4]

The old farm is ideal for their needs. Joan had supported them in the lean days by breaking horses, and the farm includes a stable near the house.[5] For Convenant's work, a tiny hut—complete with hearth—nestles in the woods behind the house, close enough for easy access along a wooded path; but quiet and secluded, overlooking a small stream known as Righters Creek.[6]

Then come the wrenching changes: leprosy and divorce. Covenant burns his work at the hut's hearth, then locks the small building. Joan's stables, too, are abandoned, until finally they are destroyed in the conflagration set by an arsonist.[7] The Covenants' abandonment is not the first the farm has seen. Past history can be glimpsed via the wandering dirt side road which serves three vacant houses.[8] It is this road that is taken by Linden Avery in the Second Chronicles, when she returns at dusk in an attempt to watch Covenant without his knowledge.[9]

When Covenant first returns from the leprosarium, he clears the house of all but the barest necessities, locking the excess in the guest room.[10] Thus the living room, although carpeted, is bare of all but book cases, telephone, clock, and the long couch and coffee table which Covenant places in the middle of the room—far enough from the wall to walk around.[11]

Later, as Linden walks through the house, she glimpses the other rooms. Behind the living room lies the kitchen, with table and two straight chairs. Turning down a hall, she passes Covenant's room, the bath, and comes to the guest room—which temporarily houses Joan.[12] It is from this room that Foul's servants take Joan, returning later to summon Covenant. Tracked by Linden, he accompanies the summoner and they pass arrow-straight through the woods to a hollow in the hills.[13]

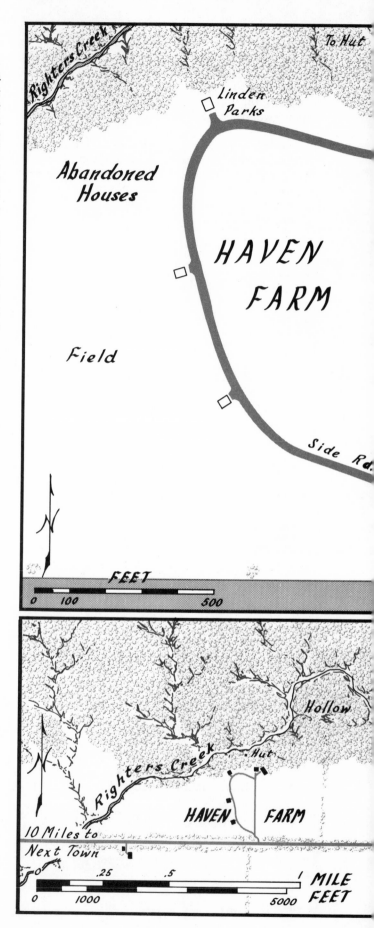

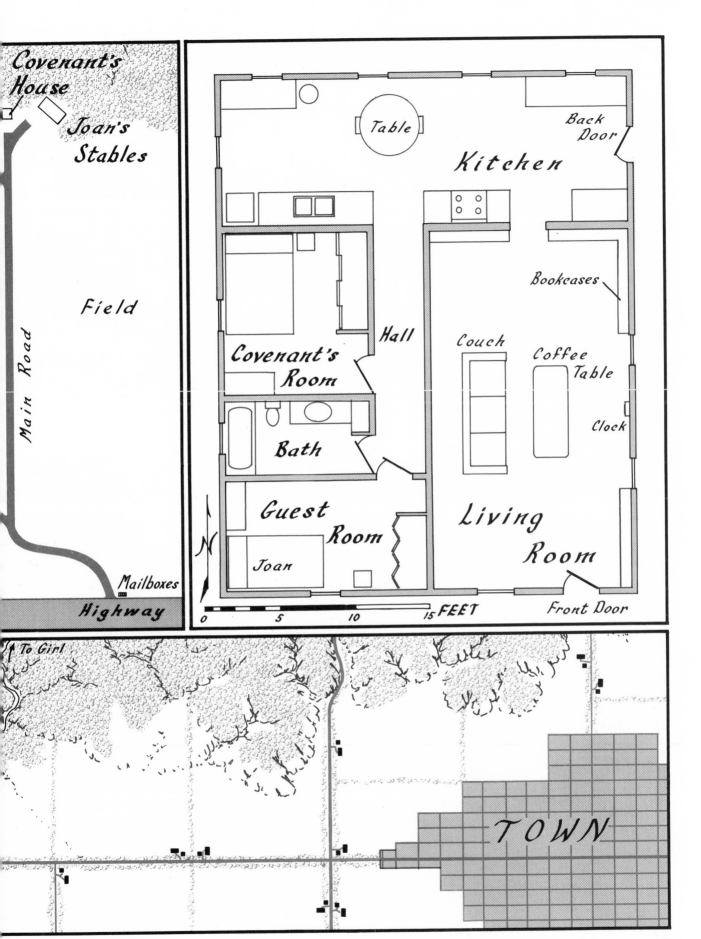

THE TOWN

Two miles east of Haven Farm is the closest town—small and stagnant, with only about 5,000 inhabitants[1]; yet it is the county seat and holds both the courthouse and the county hospital.[2] Half-rural in nature, the town is surrounded by farmland except in the northwest where the hills and woods lie close enough for Covenant to reach almost to the outskirts without crossing farmland.[3] On the far side of the town from Haven Farm is a vacant field utilized for parades and similar community activities. On one occasion Covenant finds a revival tent there.[4]

Around the business district is an area of the oldest homes, and on the side of town passed by Covenant on one of his wandering visits those older homes extend all the way to the outskirts. Linden's apartment is upstairs in an old frame house close to the business district.[5] Its unkempt yard and grubby paint are typical of many commercial fringe area houses which eke out an income as rental property.

Like most small towns it centers around the one intersection busy enough to require a traffic stoplight,[6] with a commercial area, strung out along the major road through town, and only a few stores fronting on to nearby side streets. When Covenant chooses to challenge the town's ostracism by walking in to pay bills, he must travel almost the full length of the business district to reach his destination: the Bell Telephone office. He passes in turn several smaller stores, the grocery store, the courthouse, the department store, and the electric company office before reaching (a half block later) the telephone office.[7] The electric and telephone offices are small, requiring only a small amount of space for a few displays and room for the staff work area and records. The department store occupies one of the largest buildings in the area, as does the grocery store. The pseudo-Greek courthouse stands at the heart of the town.[8] Across from it is an office building—that of Covenant's attorney.[9]

When the Chronicles open Covenant passes in front of the department store, bumping into an old beggar, but he does not speak.[10] At the telephone office a boy delivers the beggar's note[11]; but it is not until Covenant returns from the telephone office and is walking once again past the courthouse that he actually speaks to the beggar.[12] Angered at his situation, Covenant decides to visit his attorney. Stepping into the intersection as the light changes, he falls as the police car comes screaming through.[13] Thus begins the saga . . .

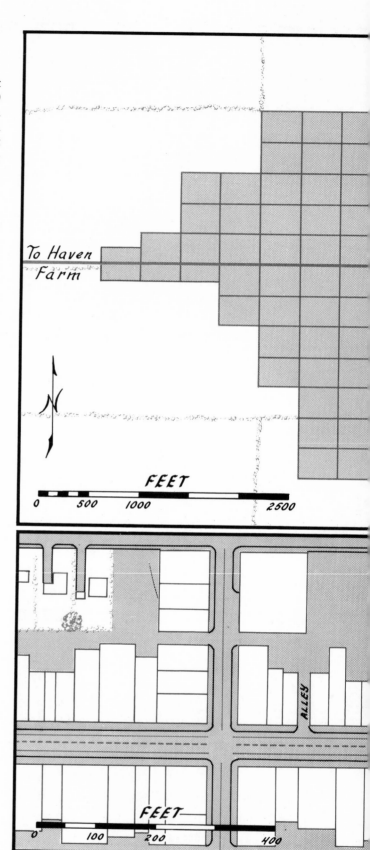

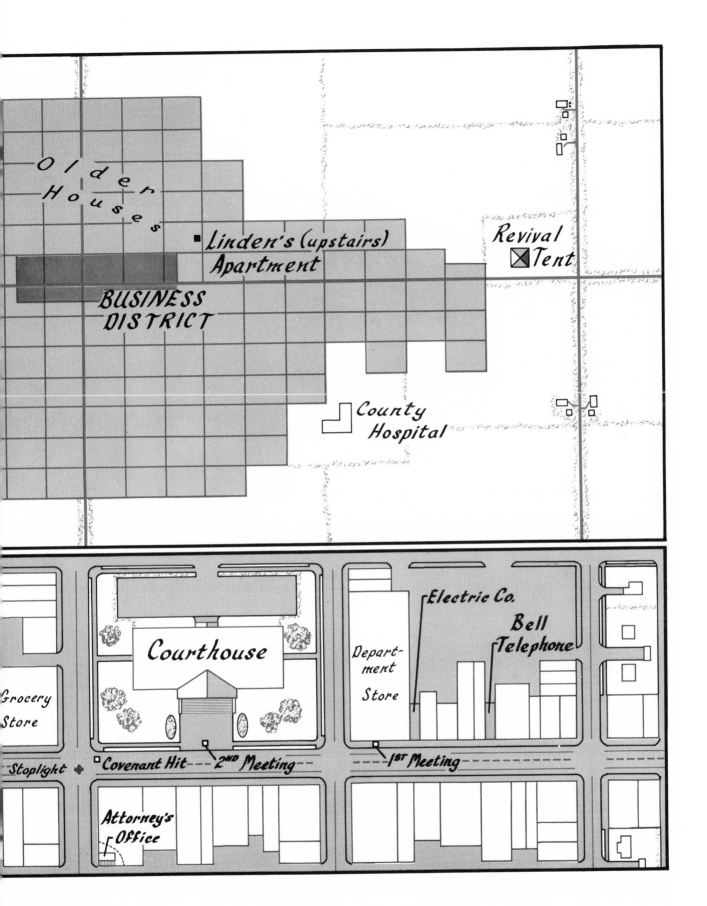

Older Houses

Linden's (upstairs)
Apartment

BUSINESS
DISTRICT

Revival
Tent

County
Hospital

Courthouse

Electric Co.

Bell
Telephone

Department
ment
Store

Grocery
Store

Stoplight

Covenant Hit - - - 2ᴺᴰ Meeting - - -

- - - - - 1ˢᵀ Meeting - - - -

Attorney's
Office

THE LAND
THE SOUTHWEST

THE LAND

The people of the Land use that term to refer to the area between the Westron Mountains and the Sunbirth Sea, and from the Northron Climbs to the Southron Range.[1] The villages of the *Haruchai* lie within the western valleys of the Westron Mountains and so are peripheral,[2] as are the Gray Desert and the Waste near the Last Hills. The Land is slightly smaller than the United States (ca. 3 million versus 3.6 million square miles).[3] Though Covenant did not traverse the full length or breadth of the Land, he certainly covered the major areas—among them: 900 miles (300 leagues) from Mithil Stonedown to Revelstone, almost as far to *Melenkurion* Skyweir, and 1200 miles (400 leagues) from Revelstone to The Grieve.[4]

The Land is almost encircled by mountains. Giant Woods merge in the west with the Northron Climbs, and the Climbs veer west, then south into the massive Westron Mountains. The Last Hills arc past the defile of Doom's Retreat into the hills west of the Mithil River, and beyond these build the peaks of the Southron Range. Only by the Sunbirth Sea is the Land open to the outside world, but even there stand seaside cliffs at both Foul's Creche and The Grieve.[5]

The Land is almost bisected by Landsdrop—that massive east-facing escarpment which runs fifteen hundred miles (five hundred leagues) from within the Northron Climbs to the Southron Mountains. The configuration of the Land prior to the cataclysmic faulting was probably much the same as it is now. Mount Thunder already stood, for in its bowels the banes were buried which caused the break[6]; and if it still survived after withstanding such forces, then those physical features more distant are probably even less altered. Landforming processes are, by man's standards, almost infinitesimally slow. The delicate pinnacle of Kevin's Watch overlooks the Land for Covenant's and Linden's use as it did for Kevin's nearly six thousand years earlier.

THE SOUTHWEST

The southwestern quadrant encompasses some of the most major physical and cultural features of the Land: *Melenkurion* Skyweir, the highest mountain; Garroting Deep, the mightiest of the remnants of the One Forest; Doriendor Corishev, capitol of the birth-land of Berek Halfhand[1]; Mithil Stonedown, gateway to Kevin's Watch (an insignificant village which produces very significant people); and a portion of Andelain, the heart of the Land.

Near the confluence of the Black and Mithil Rivers an outcrop of resistant crystalline rock produces the Crystal Hills. They stand just south of the river, and the faceted weathering of the crystalline rock produces the *barranca* (a sheer-walled ravine) which holds Crystal Stonedown during the Second Chronicles.[2]

To the south and east, Kevin's Watch stands four thousand feet above the surrounding countryside, and is backed by peaks which rise even higher.[3] Below it the foothills are steep and involuted, and lie in the drainage basin of the Mithil River, their west-running valleys constantly turn Covenant and Atiaran from the northeast-trending path.[4] Only the narrow stream valley beginning near the base of Kevin's Watch cuts north through the hills for several leagues before turning west like the others.[5]

The South Plains lie south of the Black River and north of the rugged topography which runs from the Last Hills to Andelain. Under the desert sun, with all vegetation destroyed, the full extent of the Plains can be sensed: "Except for the ragged weal of the Mithil, the Plains were nearly featureless. They spread north and west as far as he could see, marked only by the faint undulations of the terrain—bare even of shrubs or piles of rock."[6]

Near the southwest corner of the South Plains lies the narrow gap of Doom's Retreat. South beyond its rubble-strewn ravine are the Wastes which grew green and rich before the destruction of the watershed with the felling of the One Forest.[7] The encroachment of the Gray Desert produced the arid landscape of "jagged hills, gullies, arroyos."[8] Doriendor Corishev, which once had stood as the "masterplace" was abandoned; its remnants still stand on its south-running ridge for the use of the Warward in its retreat to Cravenhaw at the south end of Garroting Deep.[9]

West and north of Garroting Deep stand the great Westron Mountains. The gorge of the Rill can be traversed by a bridge to reach the southern part of the range.[10] The mountains are typical of any great range—alpine glacial features in the upper elevations contrasting with "sheltered glens and coombs and gorges" cut by swift-running snow-fed streams.[11] Rockfalls, such as the one encountered by Covenant and Elena, are common.[12] A final valley, descending from the pass formed by a col leads the travelers to the plateau of Rivenrock—a narrow band encircling the east face of the twin peaks of *Melenkurion* Skyweir—peaks which stand fifteen to twenty thousand feet above the plateau and are capped by glaciers. At the juncture of the twin peaks a cleft allows the passage of the Black River. Strengthened by the EarthBlood, the river flows with such power that it never tolerates a permanent bridge or ford.[13] Its rushing waters race from Rivenrock to Garroting Deep four thousand feet below.[14]

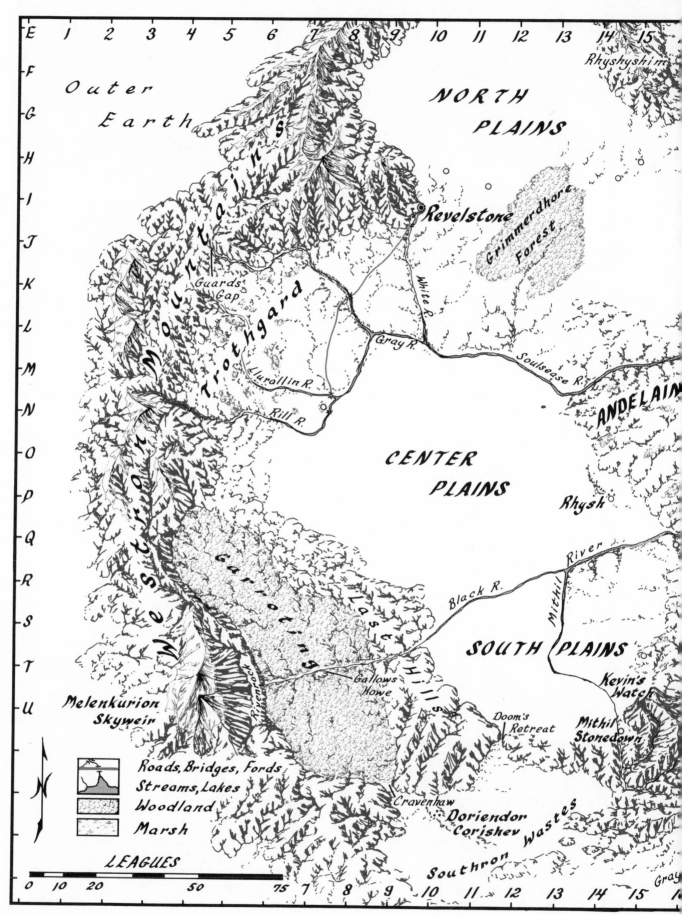

E 1 2 3 4 5 6 7 8 9 10 11 12 13 14 15

F

G   *Outer*   NORTH

H   *Earth*   PLAINS   *Rhyshyshim*

I   ⊙ *Revelstone*   *Grimmerdhore*

J   *Forest*

K   *Guards*   *White R.*

L   *Gap*   *Trothgard*

M   *Llurallin R.*   *Gray R.*   *Soulsease R.*

N   *Rill R.*   ANDELAIN

O   CENTER

P   PLAINS   *Rhysh*

Q   *River*

R   *Garroting*   *Black R.*   *Mithil*

S   SOUTH   PLAINS

T   *Melenkurion*   *Rivenrock*   *Gallows*   *Kevin's*
          Skyweir   *Howe*   *Watch*

U   *Doom's*   *Mithil*
                                           Retreat   *Stonedown*

              N   Roads, Bridges, Fords
                         Streams, Lakes
                         Woodland   *Cravenhaw*   *Doriendor*
                         Marsh   *Corishev*   *Wastes*

              LEAGUES   *Southron*   *Gray*

         0 10 20   50   75 7   8   9   10   11   12   13   14   15

4

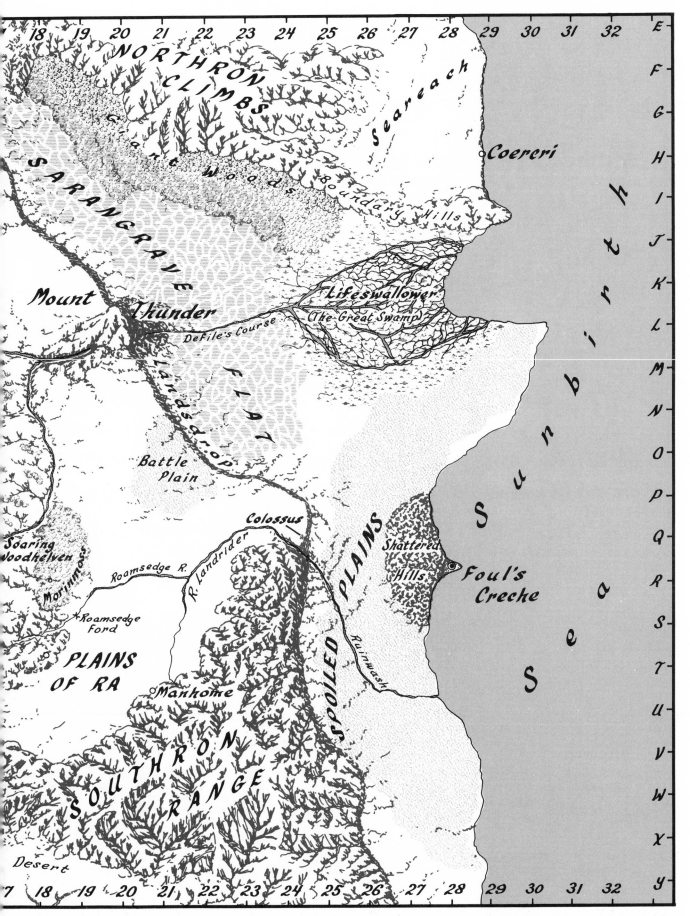

NORTHRON
CLIMBS

Seareach

F

G

Coercri

H

SARANGRAVE

Giant

Woods

Boundary Hills

I

J

K

Lifeswallower
(The Great Swamp)

Mount

Thunder

DeFile's Course

L

Sunbirth

M

N

FLAT

Landsdrop

O

P

Battle
Plain

Colossus

Shattered
Hills

S

Foul's
Creche

Q

R

S

e

a

S

Soaring
Woodhelven

Morinmoss

Roamsedge R.

R. Landrider

SPOILED PLAINS

Rainwash

T

U

V

Roamsedge
Ford

PLAINS
OF RA

Manhome

W

SOUTHRON

RANGE

X

Desert

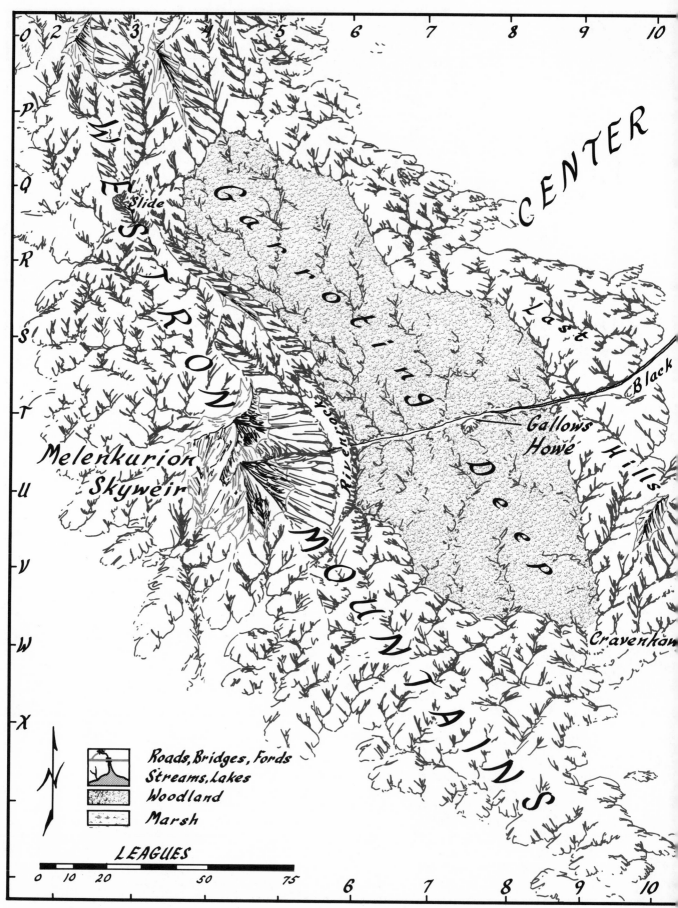

CENTER

WESTRON

Garroting

Slide

Melenkurion
Skyweir

River Soulsease

Garroting Deep

Gallows
Howe

Last

Black

Hills

Cravenhaw

MOUNTAINS

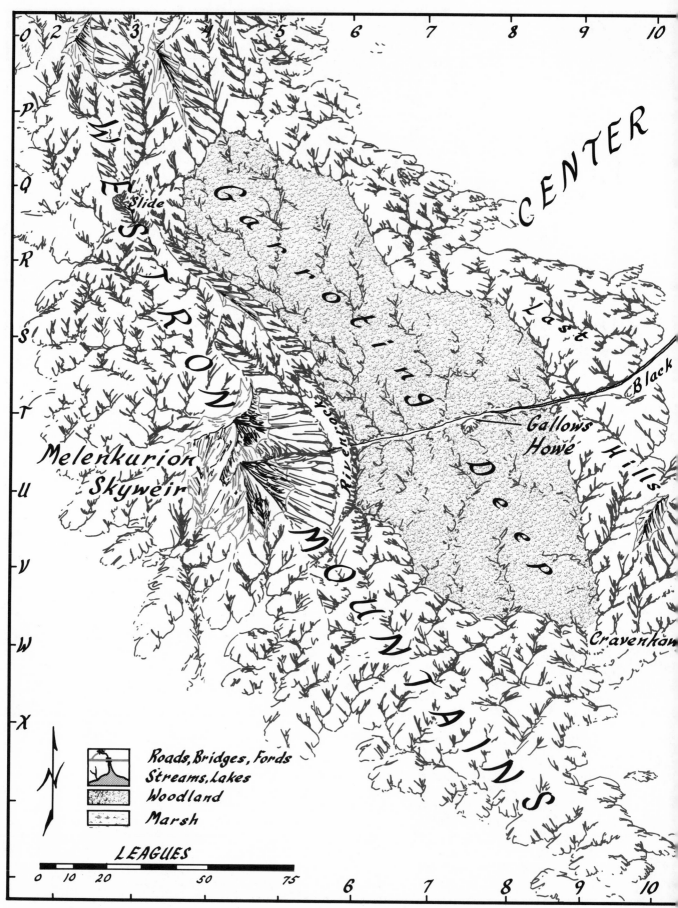

N

Roads, Bridges, Fords
Streams, Lakes
Woodland
Marsh

LEAGUES

0 10 20   50   75

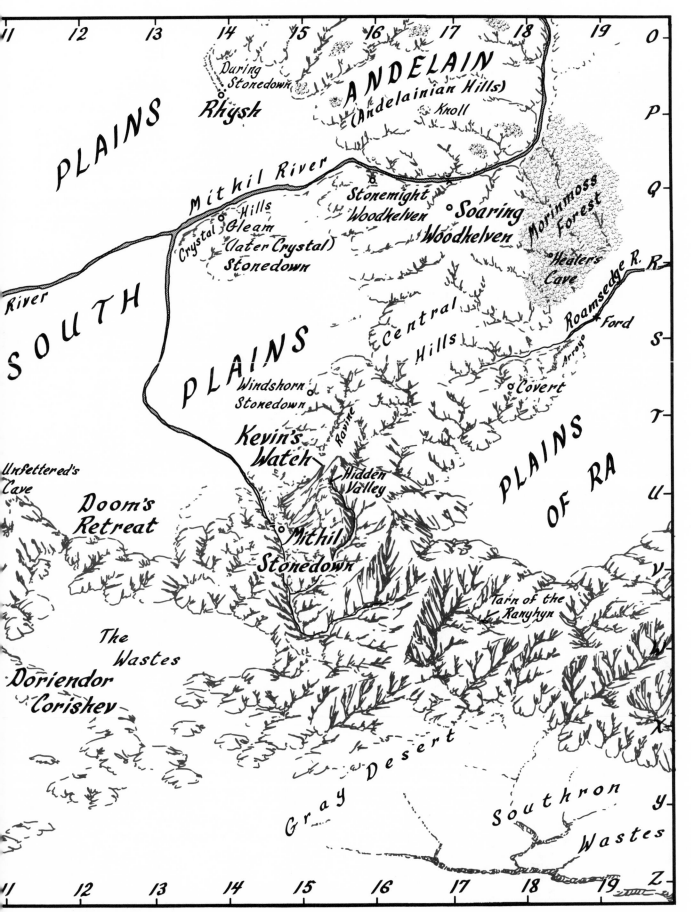

THE SOUTHWEST

T Black R.

9

10

11

U

Garroting

Deep

Cave of
Unfettered
One

V

W

Cravenhaw

Doriendor
Corishev
(Masterplace)

Ridge

N

The

LEAGUES

0   10   20   30

10

11

SOUTH

PLAINS

Mithil River

13   14   15   T

Ravine

Kevin's
Watch

U

Doom's
Retreat

Mithil
Stonedown   o

V

W

Wastes

13   14   15   Y

SOUTH PLAINS AND SOUTHRON WASTES   9

CRYSTAL STONEDOWN

East and south of the confluence of the Black and Mithil Rivers stands an outcropping of crystalline rock—bedrock for the undulating Crystal Hills. In a ravine within the hills a stonedown lies hidden. During the time of the First Chronicles, the stonedown is known as Gleam Stonedown, and is only casually mentioned when Triock recalls his visit there after the entire population had been destroyed by *kresh*.[1] At some later time the village was resettled, and renamed Crystal Stonedown.

The ravine which enclosed the village is sheer-sided like a *barranca*, a Spanish term which describes a deep ravine or gorge, commonly one which develops in arid lands.[2] The cut of the ravine reveals the nature of the bedrock of the Crystal Hills, for the walls "were formed of faceted crystal which caught the light and returned it in delicate shades of white and pink."[3] The colors and crystalline form of the hills reveals they are probably formed of quartzite—a dazzling natural substance which weathers in such stark, crisp angles that it seems almost to have been quarried.

The ravine reaches the river at a shelving bank, but rises as it twists into the hills. Within the ravine the village is close enough to the river for easy access, but far enough for even the reflection of its central bonfire to be hidden until Sunder and Linden reach a point midway between the shore and the homes.

As in most stonedowns, the houses face in toward the central open space—each vying for a view to the interior of the village. The village holds only about one hundred sixty people in forty stone houses, for during the time of the Sunbane, populations are necessarily small.[4]

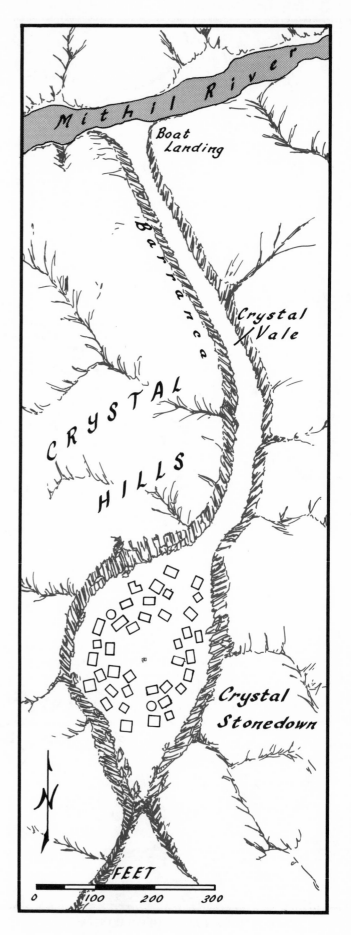

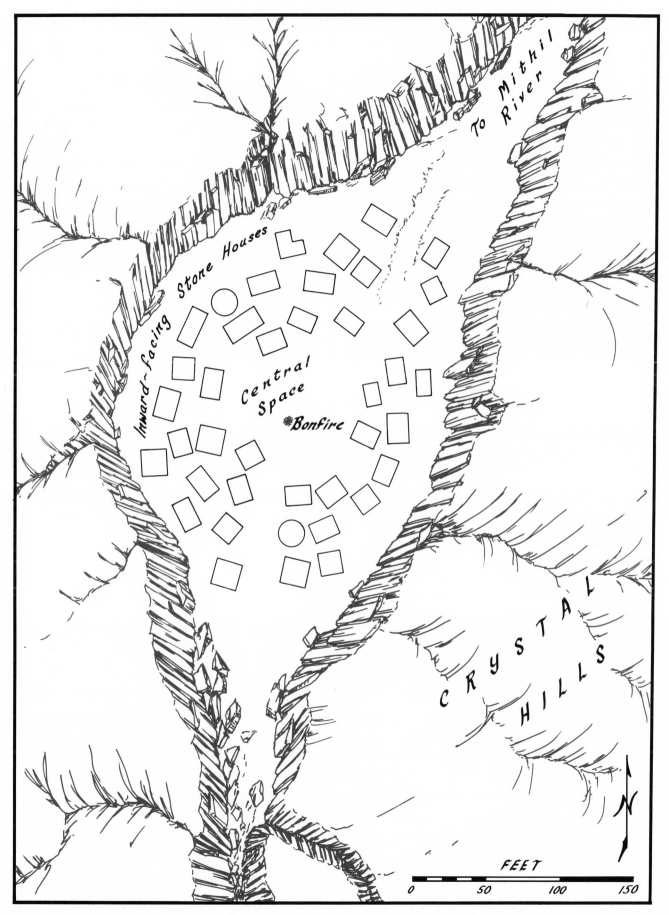

To Mithil River

Inward-facing Stone Houses

Central Space

Bonfire

CRYSTAL HILLS

N

FEET

0   50   100   150

STONEMIGHT WOODHELVEN

Some leagues east of Crystal Stonedown lies another village discovered by Covenant during the Second Chronicles—Stonemight Woodhelven. The Woodhelven is also concealed in a ravine, but one of quite different nature from the Crystal Vale. Almost opposite the most southwest corner of Andelain the land has become blasted and desolate—worse than the Sunbane alone produces. For here, during Quaan's valiant stand against Foul's Army (during the time of Covenant's second summoning), a sliver of the Illearth Stone fell. Over the millennia its presence has damaged both the surrounding countryside and the people of the area.[1]

The nature of the ravine is different in bedrock and form, as well. It is almost a small canyon, hardly more than a league in length and only thirty feet at its deepest point,[2] with its "upper edges . . . like dark teeth silhouetted against the sky."[3] In the usual manner of dry land canyons, the edges are often cut with smaller gullies and gashes through the more dense caprock into the less resistant layers below. It serves as a local drainageway during rain, so its floor is strewn with sand and stones left after each onslaught.[4] As the canyon twists north toward the Mithil, the walls close in. At last even the open sky disappears, for the caprock roofs the last stretch forcing rainwaters to pour through a natural tunnel to reach the river beyond.[5]

At the widest point of the canyon the Woodhelven stands. It has been built in the millennia since the First Chronicles. Its structures are different from those of anything Covenant saw earlier, and its proximity to the site of Soaring Woodhelven suggest its presence would have been noted at the time had it been present. The houses are tiny, one-room wooden structures, built on massive stilts to lift them above the floods during the Sun of Rain.[6] They line the walls of the canyon, crouching against the shelter of the sides away from the strongest course of the water.[7] The structures are sufficiently adequate to withstand the flow, but are poorly constructed and in disrepair. Their unsophisticated building techniques do not even include gabled roofs; and the "wattle and daub" construction is exposed to constant ravages from rain, leaving many open gaps in the walls.[8]

North of the houses some fifty or sixty paces a twelve-foot post stands wedged into a crack in the stone. It is positioned in line with a gash in the opposite canyon wall, so that a victim tied to the post will receive the first rays of sun reaching to the canyon floor.[9]

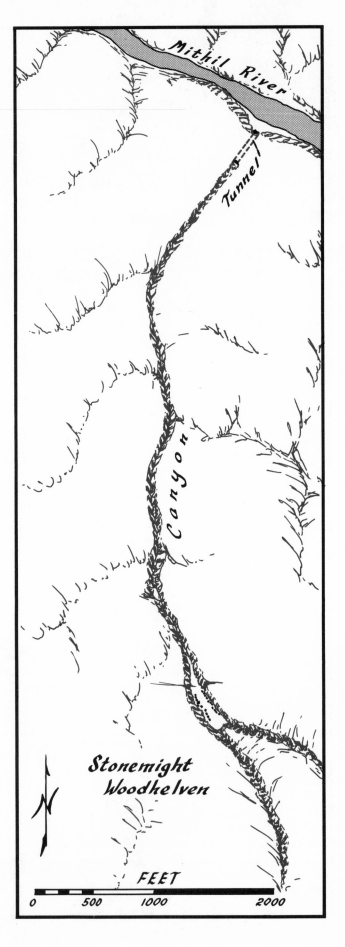

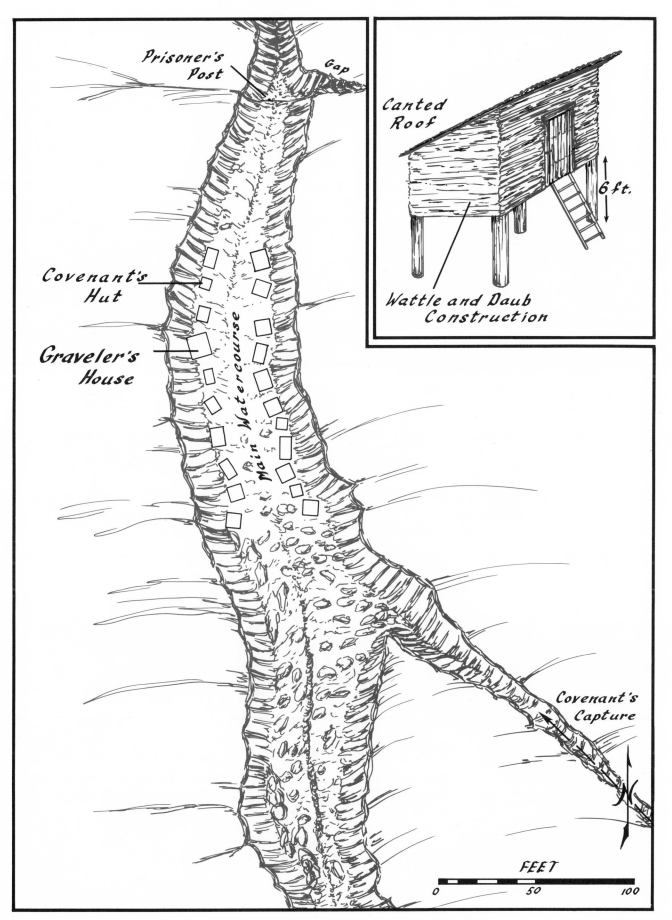

Prisoner's Post

Gap

Covenant's Hut

Graveler's House

Main Watercourse

Covenant's Capture

Canted Roof

6 ft.

Wattle and Daub Construction

FEET

0   50   100

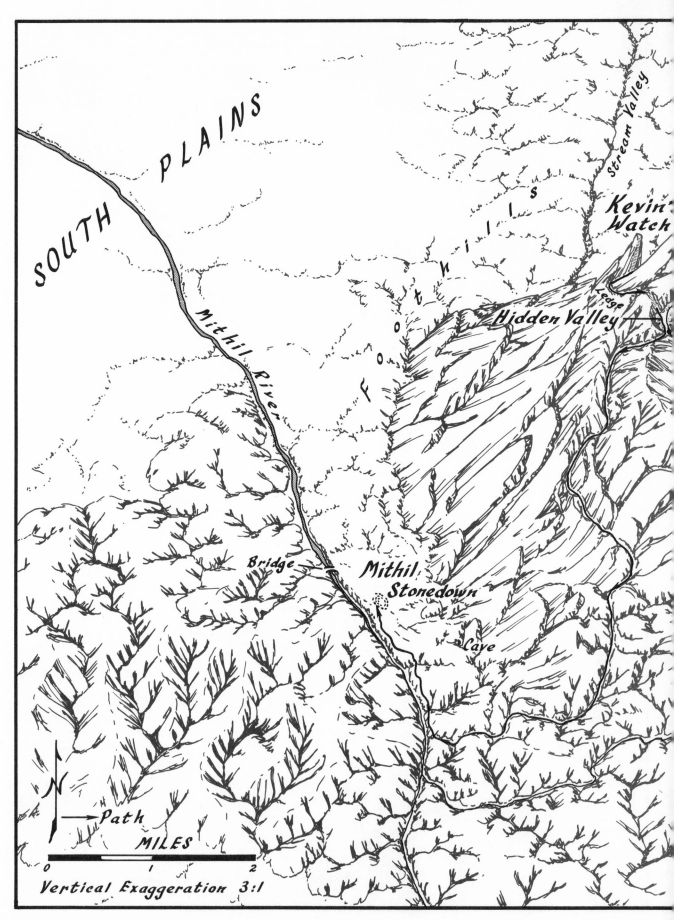

SOUTH PLAINS

Foothills

Stream Valley

Kevin's Watch

Hidden Valley

Ledge

Mithil River

Bridge

Mithil Stonedown

Cave

N

Path

MILES

0   1   2

Vertical Exaggeration 3:1

CENTRAL HILLS

SOUTHRON RANGE

MITHIL VALLEY

On all but one occasion when Covenant is summoned to the Land, he is brought to Kevin's Watch, and must make the long descent to Mithil Stonedown via a difficult mountain path. Although the way is long, it requires only a few hours to descend. Lena is able to lead Covenant down in an afternoon; and Linden and Covenant find their way after sunset, with ample time for their capture and imprisonment, and an undetermined time of unconsciousness prior to dawn.[1]

The parapet of Kevin's Watch stands four thousand feet above the surrounding foothills, and the stair to the base of the pinnacle spans five hundred feet to a ledge which edges the cliff west and south of the Watch.[2] The ledge ends at a ravine of tumbled rock which cuts into the mountain behind the Watch. Some way up the ravine a cleft cuts into the right wall, and through it a stair descends even lower to the Hidden Valley.[3]

In passing from the Hidden Valley to the Stonedown, the travelers must follow the valley downstream a short distance until the walls narrow too much to allow passage. There a cut to the west ascends, then levels, then gently descends until once again the path stands on the outer cliff of the mountain. From this vantage the village of Mithil Stonedown is visible some two thousand feet below—half the elevation from that of the Watch has already been passed. The remainder of the path cuts in and out of rugged areas of this western face, winding south, then west, until it reaches the level of the foothills. The last distance to the Stonedown is covered by a long, slow hill which slopes down to the village.[4]

The village stands not far from the Mithil River, in a sheltered rock-strewn valley. Hidden among the boulders is the entrance to a large cave which shelters the refugees during the battle with Foul's stone-warped creatures, and millennia later protects the animals of the village during those periods of the Sunbane which are unsuitable for them to be outside.[5]

A half mile downriver from the Stonedown an ancient stone bridge crosses the Mithil.[6] Beyond the river, the hills continue west to Doom's Retreat and beyond. The land north is rugged for a few leagues before leveling into the South Plains. East of the river the plains are narrow. The rolling foothills near Kevin's Watch are an intermediate zone between the flats near the river and the higher central hills which stand between the South Plains and the Plains of Ra. Atiaran leads Covenant through this moderately rolling intermediate zone north toward Soaring Woodhelven, utilizing a narrow stream valley which lies directly below Kevin's Watch.[7]

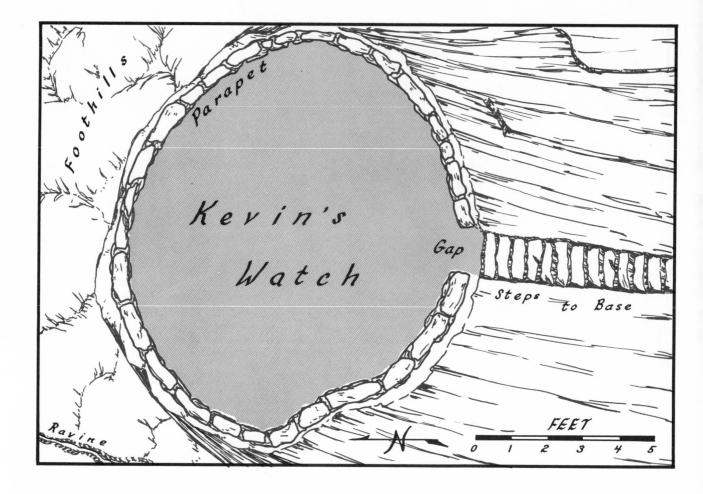

KEVIN'S WATCH

As the Southron Range swings west, a spur extends north of the bulk of the range, forming a wedge of mountains which end at Kevin's Watch.[1] From the vantage of Kevin's Watch the Land stretches east, north, and west as far as sight will reach. It is here Kevin makes his last reconnaissance prior to performing the Ritual of Desecration, and Warmark Troy comes to study Foul's Army before the encounter at Doom's Retreat.[2]

The Watch—"a smooth stone slab . . . roughly circular, ten feet broad, and surrounded by a wall three feet high"—[3] stands atop a five hundred foot high sliver of stone which leans out a "stone's throw" (one hundred feet or so) from the north face of the last mountain. Four thousand feet directly below lie the north-running central hills.[4]

On the side facing the mountain, the wall is broken by an opening—entry and exit to a narrow stair which spans the full five hundred feet of the stone pinnacle—at least a thousand steep and uneven steps.[5]

At the base of the stone spire, the steps end at a ledge—two to three feet in breadth—inching west along the main cliff face until it reaches a rock-strewn ravine.[6] Some distance up the ravine, in the south wall, a cleft veers away through the rock. A stair in the side of the cleft leads to its floor, and the walls draw ever higher until—with a sudden turn—it opens into the Hidden Valley.[7]

All this portion of the mountain—ravine, cleft, and valley—were formed ages ago by massive fallen blocks of stone. The blocks reached their present position so long ago, they have been compacted and many of the spaces between filled with smaller stones and earth.[8] The irregularity of the stone positions results in the somewhat unusual drainage patterns—the ravine gushing its waters west over the outer face, while the stream in the Hidden Valley bubbles the full length of the mountain before turning to join the Mithil River.[9] It also reveals why it is necessary to have descending steps from the ravine to the base of the cleft which connects the ravine to the valley.

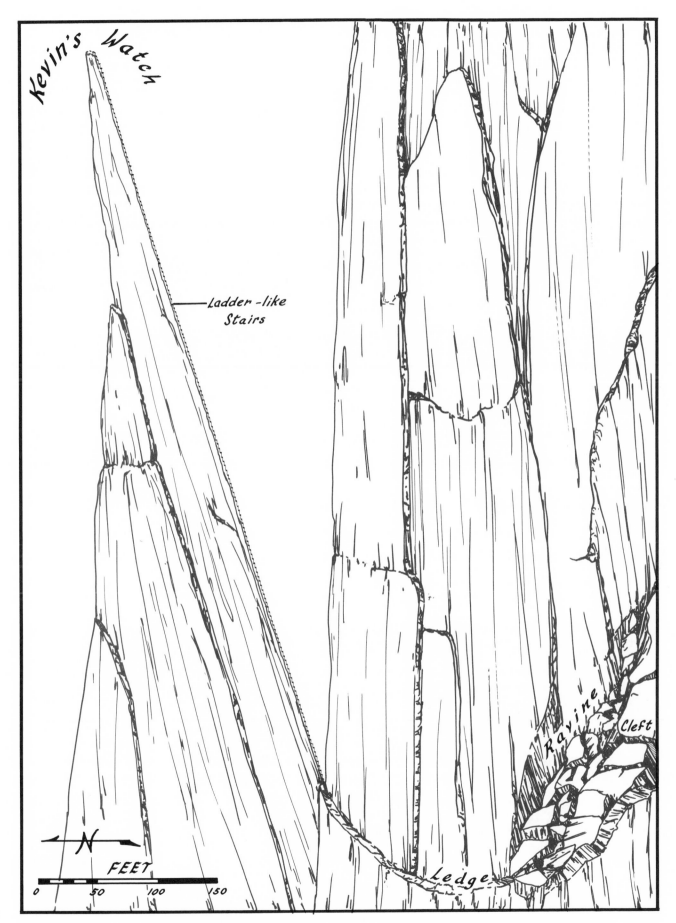

Kevin's Watch

Ladder-like
Stairs

Ravine

Cleft

N

FEET

0   50   100   150

Ledge

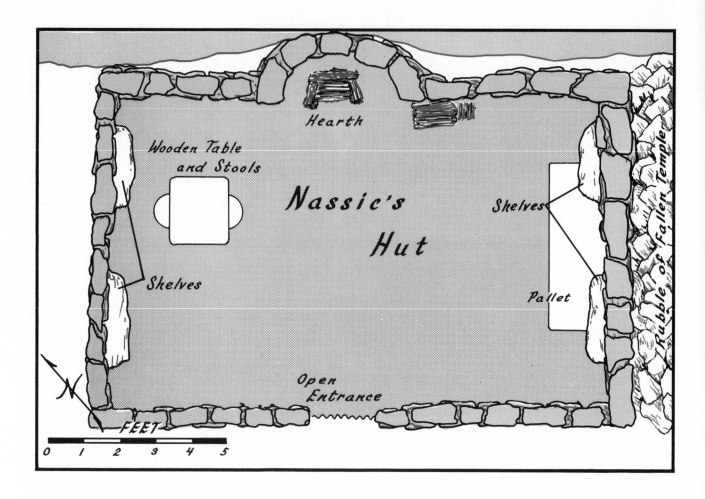

The labels within the figure read: Hearth, Wooden Table and Stools, Shelves, Nassic's Hut, Shelves, Pallet, Rubble of Fallen Temple, Open Entrance, FEET, 0 1 2 3 4 5, N

THE HIDDEN VALLEY

In the high reaches of the mountain behind Kevin's Watch is a tiny secluded dell—hidden to the outside by rocky ridges east and west and the mountain's peak to the north. The valley is no more than fifty yards long. Through its midst a stream bubbles down from the mountain's peak and at the far end turns east between sheer walls—the narrow trough formed by its passage.[1]

The valley is different each time Covenant sees it. When Lena brings him there, it is "sun-bright"—its sparkling stream running through a grassy floor, and the sheer mountain walls softened by majestic pines.[2] When he is carried to the valley by Triock and Foamfollower during Foul's preternatural winter, "only bare, wasted earth showed through the thickening snow. The pines had been stripped naked and splintered . . . and instead of water, a weal of ice ran through the valley."[3] Millennia later, during the time of the Sunbane, Covenant returns with Linden, and the dell once again has changed. The Sun of Rain has swollen the stream to a torrent, and the absence of vegetation results in a floor of mud.[4]

At the outset of the Second Chronicles, in honor of the past deeds of the Unbeliever and based upon a prophecy that the Unbeliever will return, a temple had been erected. Even in its prime the temple was no more than a few stone buildings, but as the centuries passed and the prophecy was not fulfilled; the belief fell into disrepute and the buildings into disrepair.[5]

By the time of Nassic, the ruins form a cairnlike heap of boulders. Only Nassic's stone hut—a "squat stone dwelling" without even a door—remains in usable condition, containing a single room with a hearth and chimney.[6] Within, Covenant is shocked to see the changes in lore since his earlier summonings—wood, stone, and iron mixed in use, a wood-consuming fire in the hearth. The sidewalls hold wooden shelves, and a wooden table with stools occupies one corner, laden with iron tools. The changes in small things hint of the changes in greater things he has yet to learn.

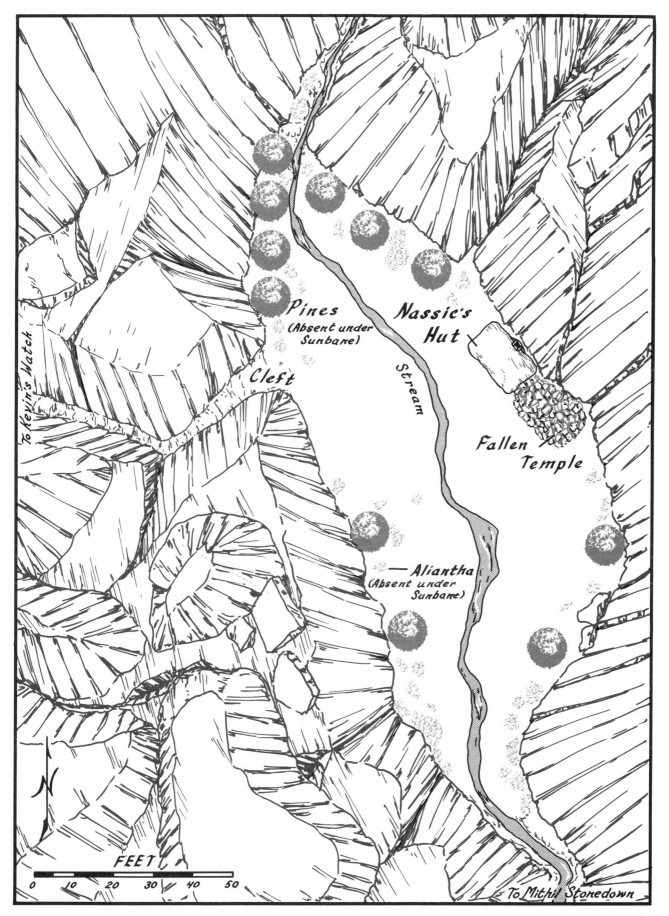

To Kevin's Watch

Pines
(Absent under Sunbane)

Nassic's Hut

Cleft

Stream

Fallen Temple

— Aliantha
(Absent under Sunbane)

N

FEET

0   10   20   30   40   50

To Mithil Stonedown

19

MITHIL STONEDOWN

Mithil Stonedown lies in the upper Mithil Valley between the peak of Kevin's Watch and the Mithil River.[1] The Stonedown is typical of the *rhadhamaerl* villages.[2] Its homes lie in roughly circular formation, facing in to gain best view of and access to the central open area—the gathering place of the people.[3] In the center of the open area is a low stone platform, which served as a stage of Atiaran.[4]

During the First Chronicles, the population of the Stonedown is five hundred,[5] requiring about one hundred fifty homes to house the villagers. By the time of the Second Chronicles, the Sunbane has taken its toll. The population is a fraction of its former size—smaller than that of Crystal Stonedown,[6] and most of the houses are abandoned.[7]

The houses are all of stone, but their construction is varied. Most are one-storied buildings, with flat roofs whose eaves reach Foamfollower's shoulders[8]; but there are three basic types. The most common type is constructed of many stones, laid without mortar, and may be round or rectangular.[9] The next type is indicative of the rock material available in the valley. Some types of granite weather in very regular patterns through the process of joint-block separation. The resultant slabs are very rectangular and appear almost to have been quarried.[10] The most massive could be used for the flat roofs, but may also be used for walls. The third (and least common) type is formed of a single massive boulder, merely hollowed out for living space.[11]

House sizes vary, also. The one in which Covenant and Linden are imprisoned is no more than a hut with a single room.[12] In contrast, Trell's house is one of the largest.[13] The prison hut stands near the central clearing, and Covenant and Linden are able to reach their judgment site directly.[14] Conversely, Trell's house stands on the outskirts of the village—nearest the river in the distance.[15]

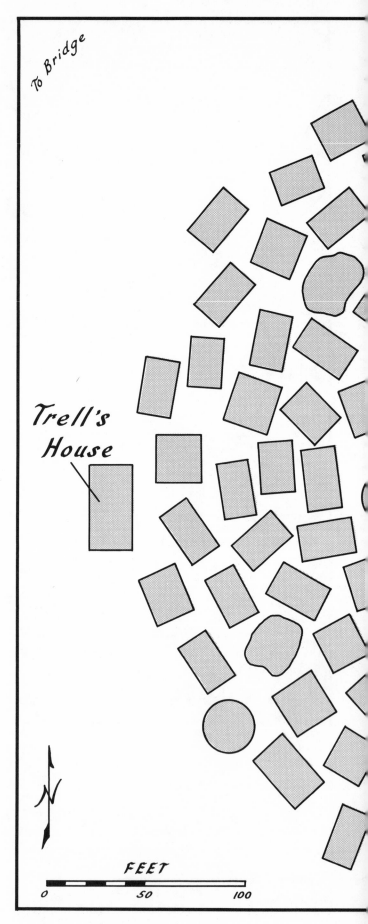

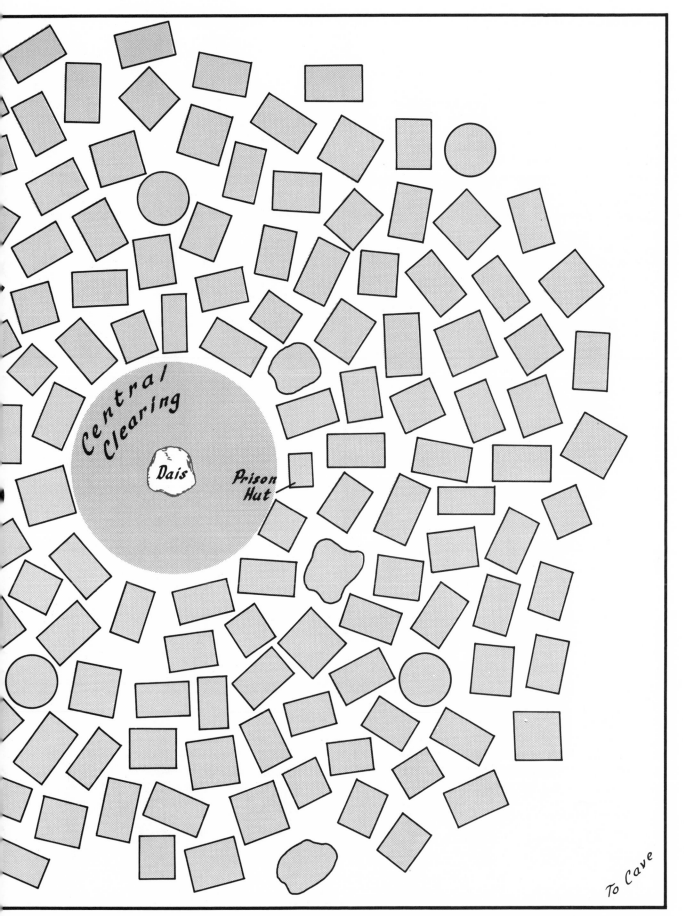

Central Clearing

Dais

Prison Hut

To Cave

Trell's House

As Gravelingas of Mithil Stonedown, Trell's family is honored with one of the largest homes in the village. Yet it is no more than comfortable. The house is rectangular, with a single door entering the center front. Inside is a room which extends to the back of the house. Its windows allow the warm light of the graveling to spill outside.

A table with bench-seating for six or eight people occupies the middle of the floor, yet does not dominate the room. Several stools stand against the walls. Against the rear wall is a slab of stone which holds the gigantic granite pot in which Trell produces the new graveling for the village. Shelves cut into the walls around the main room hold the cooking and serving utensils for the family, and a slab—heated by graveling—serves as the cooking surface.[1]

On each side of the main room are two curtained doors. Two of the side rooms serve as bedrooms for Lena and her parents, one as a workroom, and the fourth as lavatory.[2] The bathing facility has continuously running cold water, which can be diverted to either washbasin or tub. A graveling pot serves as both light and heater for drying.[3]

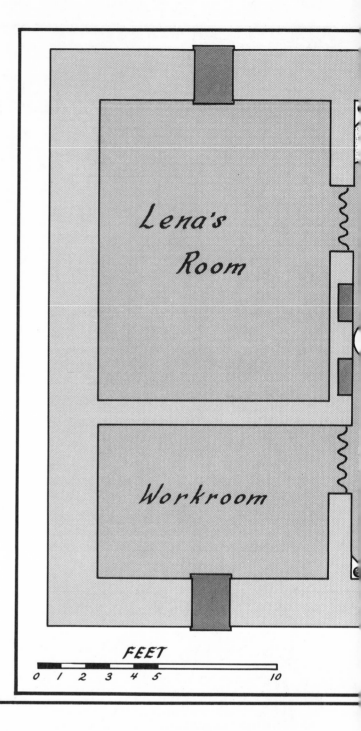

Lena's Room

Workroom

FEET

0 1 2 3 4 5 10

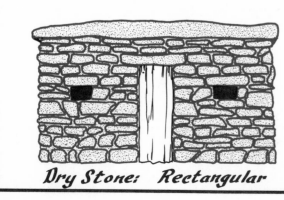

Dry Stone: Rectangular

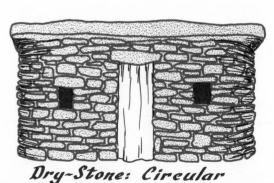

Dry-Stone: Circular

22

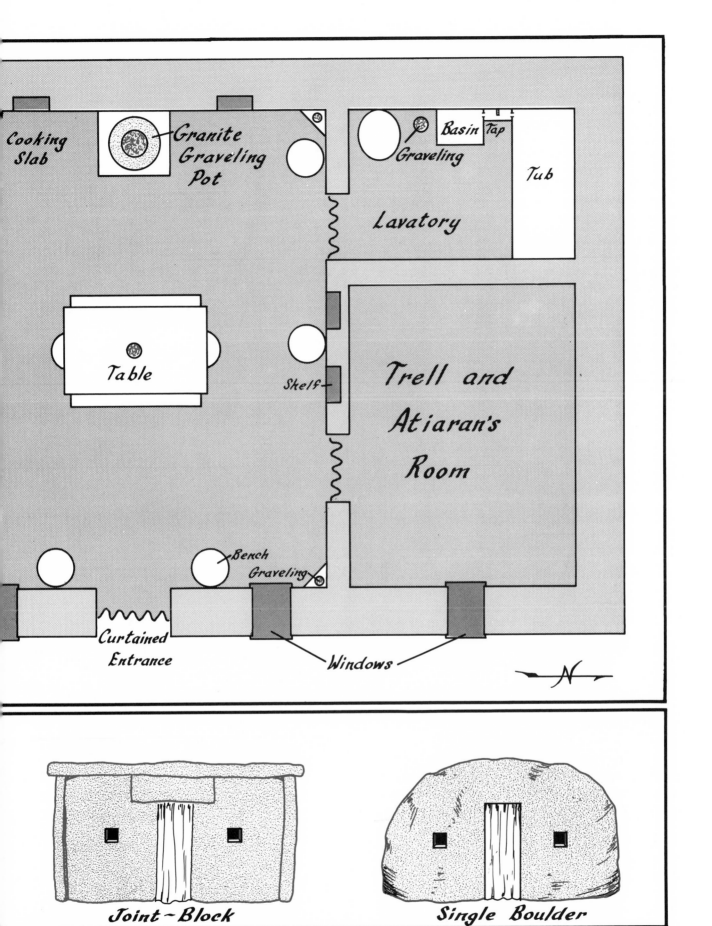

Cooking Slab

Granite Graveling Pot

Graveling

Basin Tap

Tub

Lavatory

Table

Shelf

Trell and Atiaran's Room

Bench Graveling

Curtained Entrance

Windows

N

Joint-Block

Single Boulder

DOOM'S RETREAT

Beyond the South Plains the Southron Range sends a last ridge of mountains west to join the most rugged portion of the Last Hills. Only one direct route cuts through these peaks: Doom's Retreat, the gateway to the Southron Wastes. The name is steeped in a history written in blood, for it is the traditional location of desperate last stands—the place to which defending Warwards have retreated from Landsdrop, pursued by Foul's armies. Due to its topographic configuration, however, it is eminently defensible and can be held against an army of much larger size.[1]

Doom's Retreat is not a broad gap, but a narrow defile of uncertain origin.[2] It might once have been a gorge cut by waters draining north into the Black and Mithil river basin during the time of the One Forest when the lands south of the gap were still green[3]; or it might be a fault-line running transversely across the range. The canyon runs crookedly through the most narrow spread of the mountains. Although foothills lie beyond the canyon both north and south, the Retreat itself spans a mere quarter mile.[4] South of the narrow gap is room for the defending army to wait in ambush for those attackers funneled through the canyon bottleneck.[5]

The canyon walls are steep, but the detritus broken away from the sides lie as scree, narrowing the clear portion of the canyon floor. High up onto the walls the boulders are piled. Between the tumbled rocks are hiding places for four hundred of Hile Troy's warriors to wait in ambush[6]; but the scree also serves another function. To block the canyon, Verement places a Word of Warning in the Retreat by weaving over almost the entire length of the fallen rock of the canyon. When the upper portions of the scree collapse, the sheer mass of rock piled high up the walls is sufficient to block the entire lower portion of the canyon.[7] Even a massive effort by Foul's huge army can clear a path of only thirty feet broad through the debris.[8]

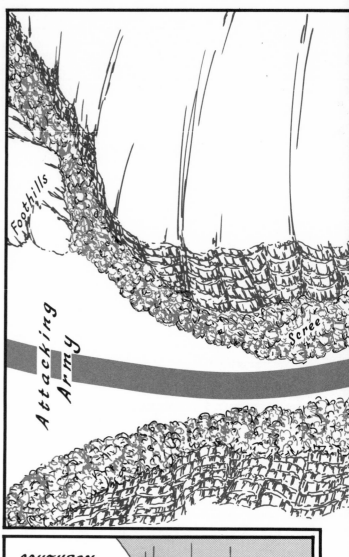

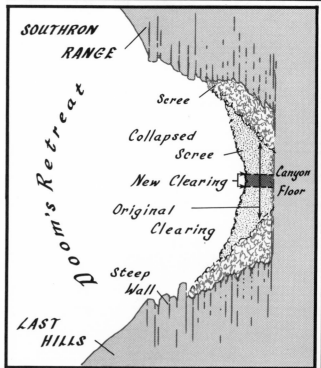

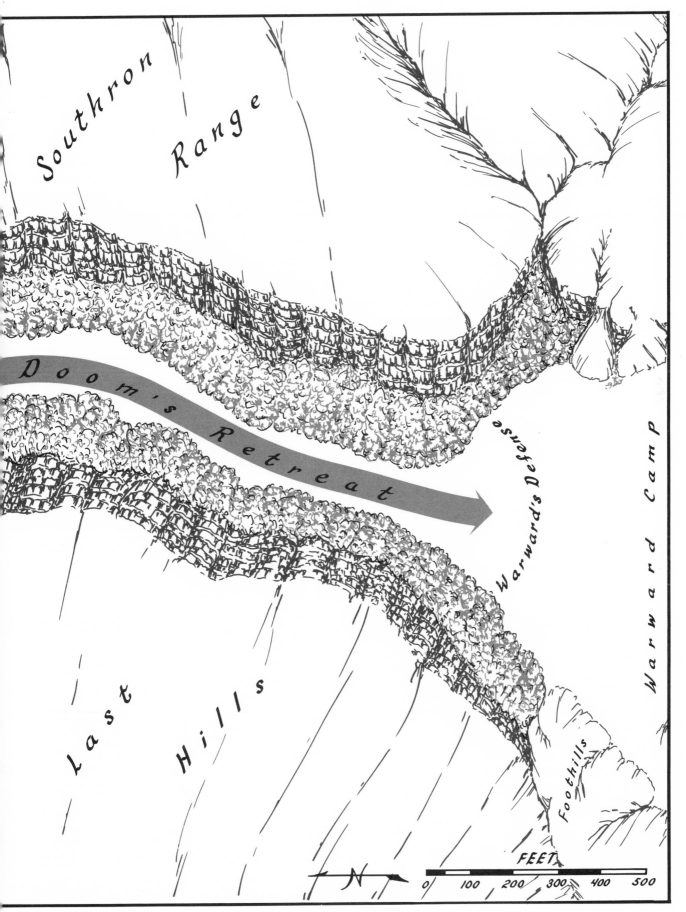

Southron Range

Doom's Retreat

Last Hills

Warward's Defense

Warward Camp

Foothills

FEET

N

0   100   200   300   400   500

DOREINDOR CORISHEV

During the time of the One Forest, the lands south of the mountains were green and thriving, and for centuries supported a great nation—the people of Berek Halfhand. The chief city of the nation was Doriendor Corishev. It stood atop a high hill which crowned a south-running ridge from the mountains, in perfect command of the northern region of the nation. This strategic location is verified by the name, which translates as "masterplace" or "desolation of enemies."[1]

When Hile Troy's Warward makes a brief stand at Doriendor Corishev during its march from Doom's Retreat to Cravenhaw, a millennia has passed since the abandonment of the city. The winds and raw weather of the Southron Wastes have gnawed at the once strong construction. The roofs and archways have long since fallen, taking with them the upper stones of the supporting walls. The walls themselves have remained relatively intact, however, forming a maze open to the sky.[2]

As a once-great city, the ruins reveal the full spectrum of room and building sizes—from tiny storerooms to great meeting halls—an intriguing puzzle to analyze. Some structures are obvious—such as the thick walls which completely surround the city. Inside the walls, all buildings were set back sufficiently to allow defenders plenty of space to operate. The walls were cut by only two massive gates—one facing east, the other west.[3] The arches of both gates have collapsed.[4] and only the opening through the rubble indicates their original position. Other piles of stones lie against the inside of the walls, remnants of what once must have been steps and fighting platforms inside the upper parapet. It is from one of these stone rubble piles that Troy observes the approach of Foul's Army.[5]

The only specific room description within the city ruins is of the meeting hall which Troy enters during his flight from the vortex of trepidation. The room is far enough within the city to be difficult to find within the labyrinth of ruined walls, yet close enough to the eastern gate for Troy to find himself meeting the vanguard of Foul's occupying troops.[6] The hall seems to be about one hundred twenty feet (forty yards) square. From his position in the center of the room Troy walks twenty yards to a wall, feels his way along the wall another twenty yards to a corner, turns, and finds an opening within a short distance. Spanning the ruined wall with his arms, he (incorrectly) decides he is at the east end of the room. He strikes out across the room, but after ninety feet is halted by quiet laughter of one of the creatures entering at the opposite end of the hall—close, but far enough for him to be uncertain of the source.[7]

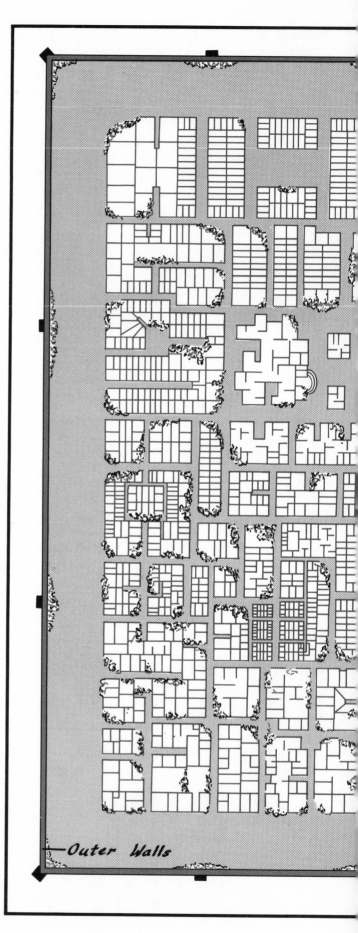

—Outer Walls

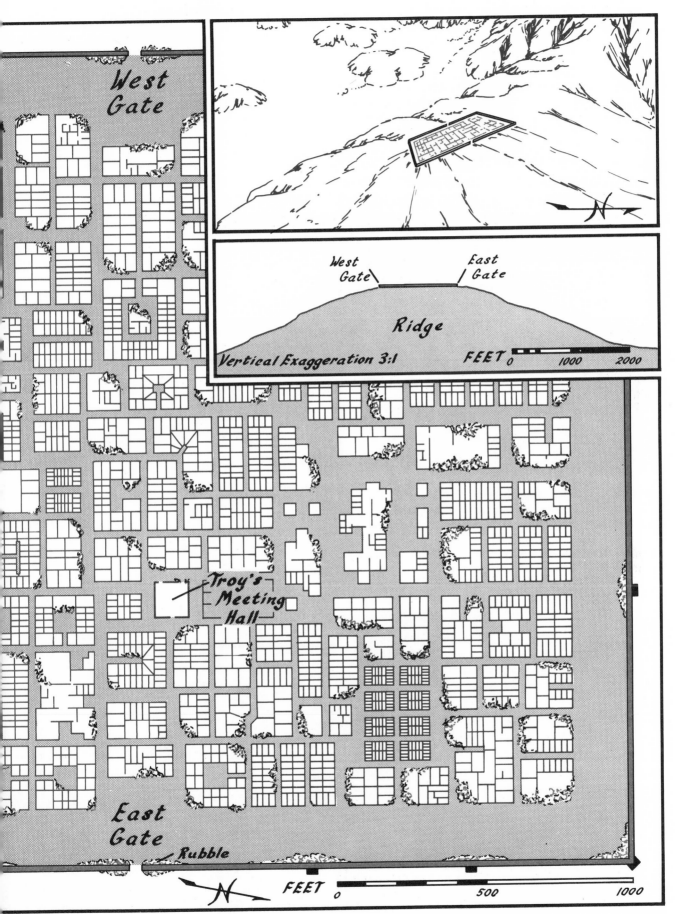

West
Gate

West
Gate

East
Gate

Ridge

Vertical Exaggeration 3:1   FEET 0   1000   2000

Troy's
Meeting
Hall

East
Gate

Rubble

N   FEET 0   500   1000

27

THE ROCKSLIDE

During Covenant's journey with Elena to *Melenkurion* Skyweir, eighteen days out of Revelwood, the company's path is blocked by a massive rockslide which has filled the mountain valley through which they are passing. Although the fall is old, new shifts within it are audible even before the travelers attempt their ascent.[1] Elena stabilizes the slide with the Staff of Law, and is successful on the north face; but the south face is far larger.

Viewed from the north the scree and larger stones form a broadly rounded "V" which stretches from cliff to cliff several hundred feet above the valley floor. Visible above the center ridge of the slide on both valley walls are huge scallop wounds—the source of the fallen debris.[2]

As the company reaches this center ridge, however, they are shocked to discover that the south-facing fall is three to four times longer than that on the north. It stretches more than a thousand feet from crest to valley floor. Prior to the avalanche, the valley descended sharply at this location. That precipice remains, but is now buried beneath tons of fallen stone.[3]

Once again Elena places a Word of Command on the face of the fall, but she knows it is not sufficient to hold. Gingerly, the company begins their descent, angling across the face. In less than a hundred feet Covenant's mustang begins to slide. In fear the horse plunges straight down the fall, worsening the avalanche. Within moments, the company is caught up in a series of desperate maneuvers. Covenant and Elena both are eventually unhorsed, being rescued by their respective Bloodguard. By this time their own movements, coupled with the speed of the slide, have carried them two-thirds of the way down the slope. Acting on its own volition, Elena's Ranyhyn valiantly assists Covenant's mustang's escape, but is buried in the new avalanche its actions produce.[4]

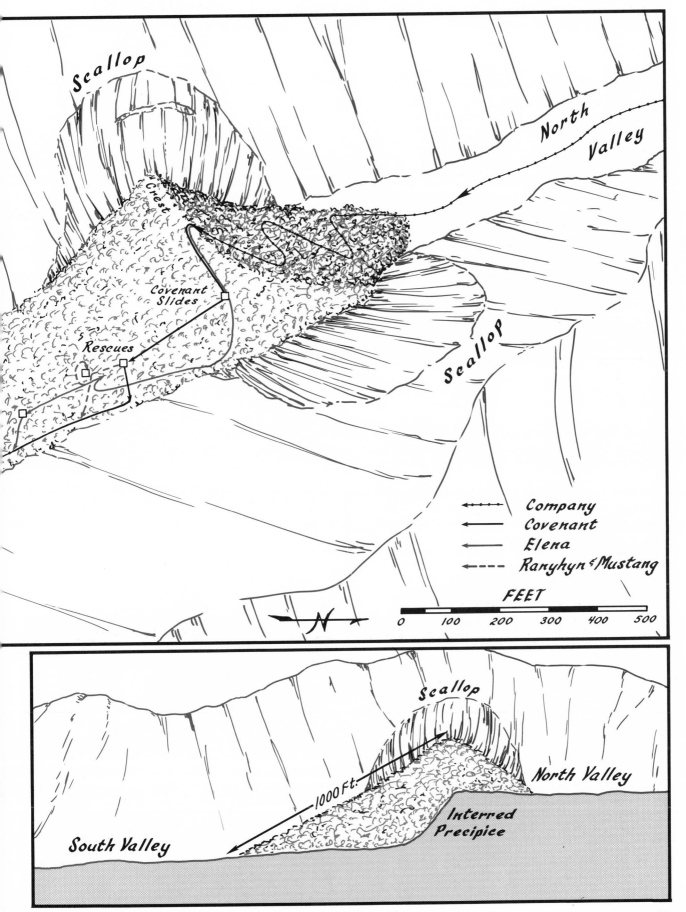

Scallop

North Valley

Crest

Covenant Slides

Rescues

Scallop

→•→•→ Company
←——— Covenant
←——— Elena
←--- Ranyhyn & Mustang

FEET

0   100   200   300   400   500

N

Scallop

North Valley

1000 Ft.

Interred Precipice

South Valley

MELENKURION SKYWEIR

In the southern Westron Mountains *Melenkurion* Skyweir towers over Garroting Deep. Along the mountain's eastern edge, it is skirted by the narrow plateau of Rivenrock. The cliff of Rivenrock rises four thousand feet above the forest, and the peaks of *Melenkurion* Skyweir reach fifteen to twenty thousand feet above the level of the plateau[1]—twenty thousand plus feet higher than Garroting Deep—the largest mountain in the Land.

The twin peaks of *Melenkurion* Skyweir are thus perpetually capped with snow, and glaciers gnaw the upper vales into sharply pointed spires.[2] The lower slopes of the great mountain join a few thousand feet above the level of Rivenrock, but the juncture is always visible—almost as if the two Matterhornlike peaks were composed of differing rock.[3]

Perfectly in line with this juncture a deep chasm splits the narrow plateau at the mountain's feet, hence the name: Rivenrock. Rivenrock extends from the northern edge of the mountain (where Covenant and Elena reach it via a southeasterly running mountain valley), around the entire eastern mountain face until it disappears rounding the southern slopes of the peak. At its widest the flatland is no more than several hundred yards.[4]

The chasm cutting through the midst of Rivenrock is the gorge of the Black River.[5] Deep within the mountain, waters of the hidden lakes join with the potent EarthBlood, and empty through unknown subterranean passages until they emerge on the eastern edge of the mountain far within the cleft of Rivenrock.[6] Although the rift is no more than twenty feet across at its broadest point, the water in its depths is not even audible; and a falling stone goes beyond hearing before reaching the floor.[7]

It is through this cleft that Amok leads Elena's company into *Melenkurion* Skyweir. At the point where the mountain begins its ascent from the plateau, the travelers jump into the ravine, falling some fifteen to twenty feet to a narrow ledge, which descends into the mountain.[8]

Glacier

Valley

Melenkurion Skyweir

Cleft

Rivenrock

Garroting Deep

Black River

MILES

0 1 2 3 4 5   10

N

Vertical Exaggeration 7:1

Interior

No analysis of the interior of *Melenkurion* Skyweir is possible without realizing the ethereal qualities of the mountain. Although the chasms, lakes, falls, chambers and passages all exist as physical entities, their specific locations are unknowable. Only the power of Kevin's lore, as utilized by Amok, gives the company the ability to pass through Damelon's Door and reach the subsequent chambers deep within the mountain. Without Amok as guide, the access would not be possible.[1]

The entrance to the mountain is clear—along the descending ledge within the cleft of Rivenrock.[2] Gradually, the ledge reaches the domed chamber which contains Damelon's Door. Beyond, only relative positions can be estimated. The cleft is absent, so the company is clearly in a very different part of the mountain. They stand within a large cavern—the Audience Hall of Earthroot.[3]

The way seems to descend beyond the cavern. Eventually, pausing to eat and sleep,[4] this long passage, called the Aisle of Approach, leads to Earthrootstair.[5] At the base of the stair is a second cavern: the site of the sunless lake of Earthroot. The lake winds through colonaded chambers until it reaches a waterfall. Hidden by the fall is the tunnel to the cave of the EarthBlood.[6]

Little else is known of the mountain's interior. The original channels feeding the Black River cannot be traced. All that can be certain is that those through which Covenant and Bannor are carried during their escape are in part new—formed by the wrenching battle between Elena and Kevin. Within a few hundred yards of the waterfall, the boat is drawn sideways toward a distant chasm which had not been present earlier. The cataract which pours into the chasm carries the boat "down the frenetic watercourse in a long nightmare of tumult, jagged rocks, narrows, sudden, heart-stopping falls . . . from cavern to cavern through labyrinthian gaps and tunnels and clefts."[7] At last the speeding waters are sucked into a side tunnel, and out into the cleft of Rivenrock and the Black River.[8]

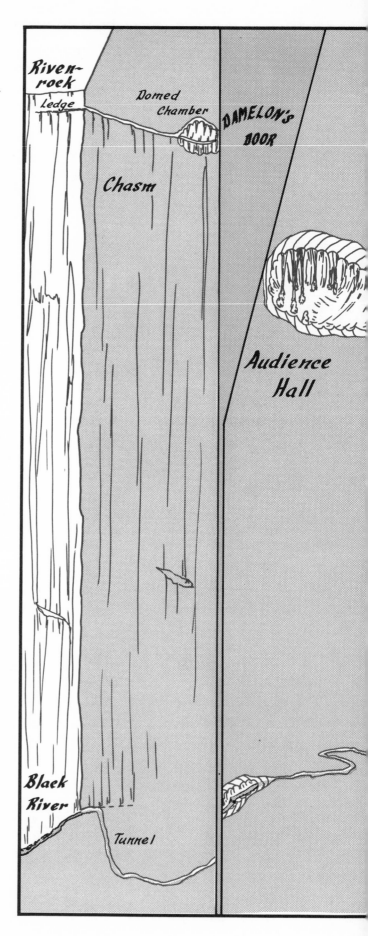

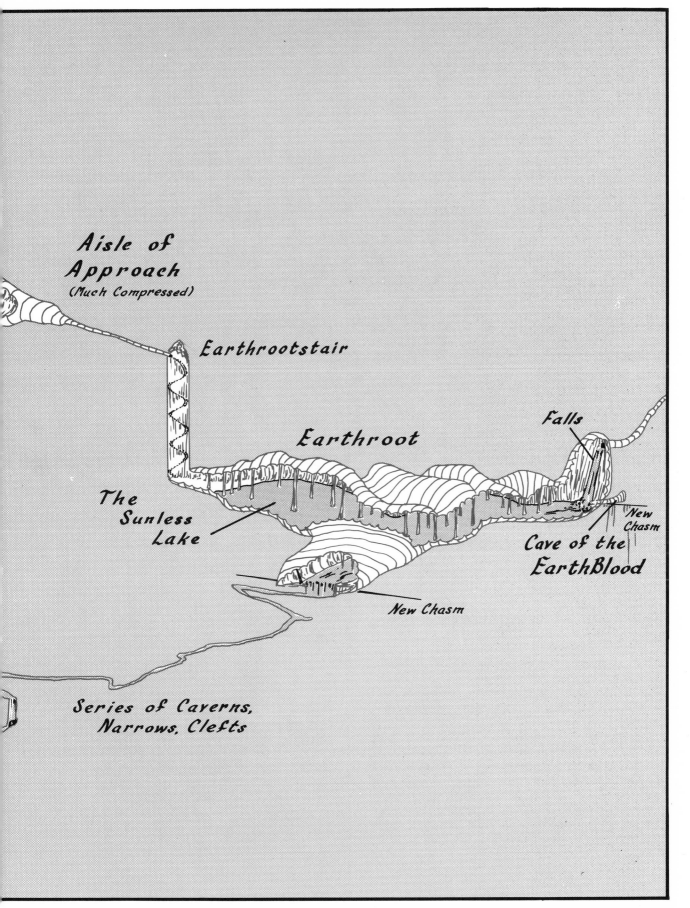

Aisle of
Approach
(Much Compressed)

Earthrootstair

Earthroot

Falls

The
Sunless
Lake

New
Chasm

Cave of the
EarthBlood

New Chasm

Series of Caverns,
Narrows, Clefts

33

Damelon's Door

Within the mountain the cleft of Rivenrock continues growing even wider, as the company travels farther and deeper toward the mountain's heart. The ledge continues along the south wall of the chasm, its two to three foot width sufficient only for walking along in single file. Gradually, as the chasm widens, the ceiling arcs higher, taking on the appearance of a cavern. The distance along the cleft is uncertain, but is long enough for Covenant to slowly become very apprehensive.[1]

As the cleft becomes more cavernous, stalactites begin to appear—only a few at first, then gradually increasing in number and size until Covenant viewed them as "a blue-lit, black, inverted forest—a packed stand of gnarled and ominous old trees with their roots in the ceiling."[2] Stalactites are formed by water which seeps through the overlying rock, carrying some of the rock's minerals with it in chemical solution. As the mineralized water passes along the rough rock surface, the minerals the liquid holds in solution are deposited on the surface of the stone. Gradually, accumulations occur in those areas where the liquid repeatedly drips, producing hanging formations. The size and shape of the formations depend upon the speed of accumulation. Where the liquid drops to the floor of a cavern, stalagmites commonly develop—more blunt and broad than the stalactites above them.[3] In the chasm through which the company travels, however, no stalagmites are visible. If any are present, they lie far below, tucked against the steep walls of the deep cleft. Most of the liquid probably falls thousands of feet until it reaches the underground river far below.

As the company reaches the widest and highest portion of the domed cavern, they find the path almost blocked by a stalactite which has angled so far down that it has attached itself to the outer lip of the ledge. Room is available for the travelers to pass through singly, and the ledge is visible continuing beyond, but Amok halts.

This is the location of Damelon's Door—a lore-made passage. Only those (such as Amok) who have the knowledge may cause the entry to be formed. Without the lore-spell, those passing this point "will wander forever lorn and pathless in the wilderness beyond."[4]

In response to Amok's touch, a "delicate web of light spread outward in the plane of the gap . . . filled the whole Door."[5] As each traveler passes beyond the lore-made portal, he finds himself able to peer back into the place just left, but the river's noise is gone. The company has been transported to a place completely removed from the chasm-cavern through which they had entered the mountain.[6]

Ledge from Rivenrock

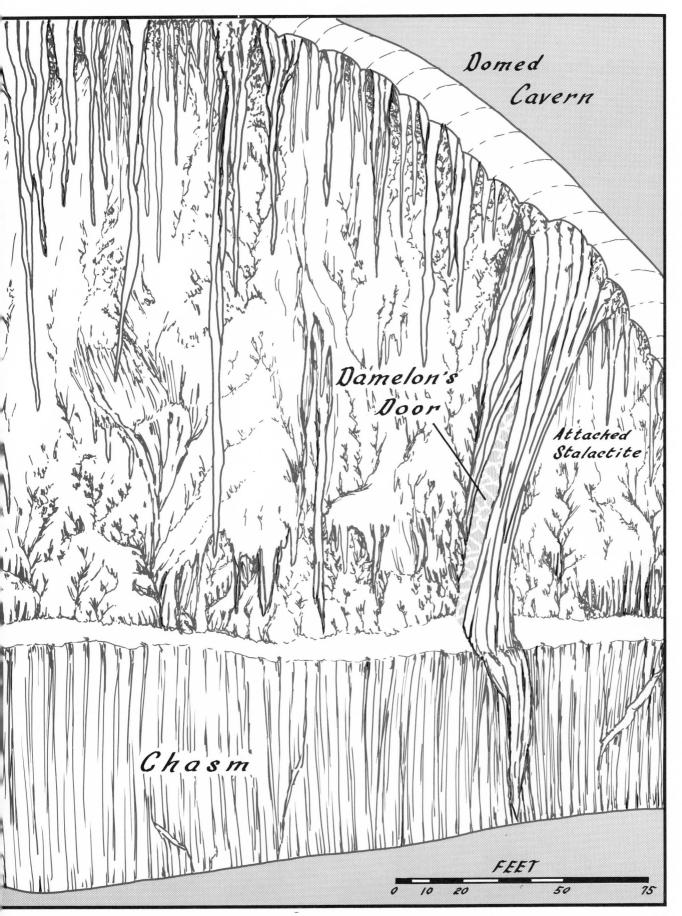

Domed Cavern

Damelon's Door

Attached Stalactite

Chasm

FEET

0   10   20   50   75

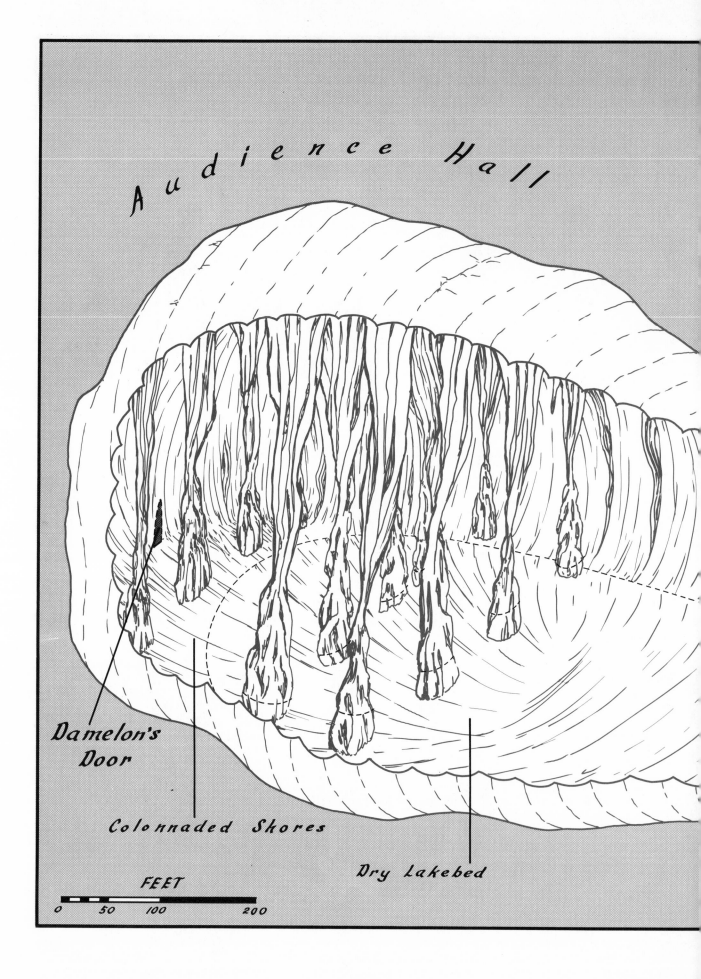

Audience Hall

Damelon's
Door

Colonnaded Shores

Dry Lakebed

FEET

0   50   100   200

The Audience Hall

After passing through Damelon's Door the company finds itself in the Audience Hall of Earthroot. It is a large cavern—large and majestic, especially when lit by the Staff of Law—crowned by hanging stalactites and dotted with the corresponding stalagmites. In places, the two features have grown sufficiently large to join and form columns. Where fissures in the dome of the cavern have allowed the inflow of mineralized water more thickly, the columns have formed fairly regular colonnades—in contrast to the random locations of other stalactites and stalagmites in the cavern.[1]

Although its floor is relatively dry now, Amok explains that in the past when Earthpower was better known, a "sunless lake would rise in season to meet those who sought its waters."[2] Thus, the company can observe what appears to be a protracted shore.

Amok leads them down the slope across the colonnaded shore, and on through the middle of the hall in what must have originally been the lakebed. The central floor should be less rugged than the beach, due to the water's solution action when the lake filled; yet the millennia since the fall of the Old Lords would have allowed time for new stalagmites to begin forming. Whether due to the new irregularities thus produced, or to the mazement which comes over him, Covenant stumbles through the Hall. Slowly, the Hall must once again become reduced in size to a mere passageway; for no note is ever made of passing from the Hall, yet upon awakening after a rest, Covenant learns that they are in the Aisle of Approach—the path to Earthrootstair.[3]

Former Water Level

Aisle of Approach

37

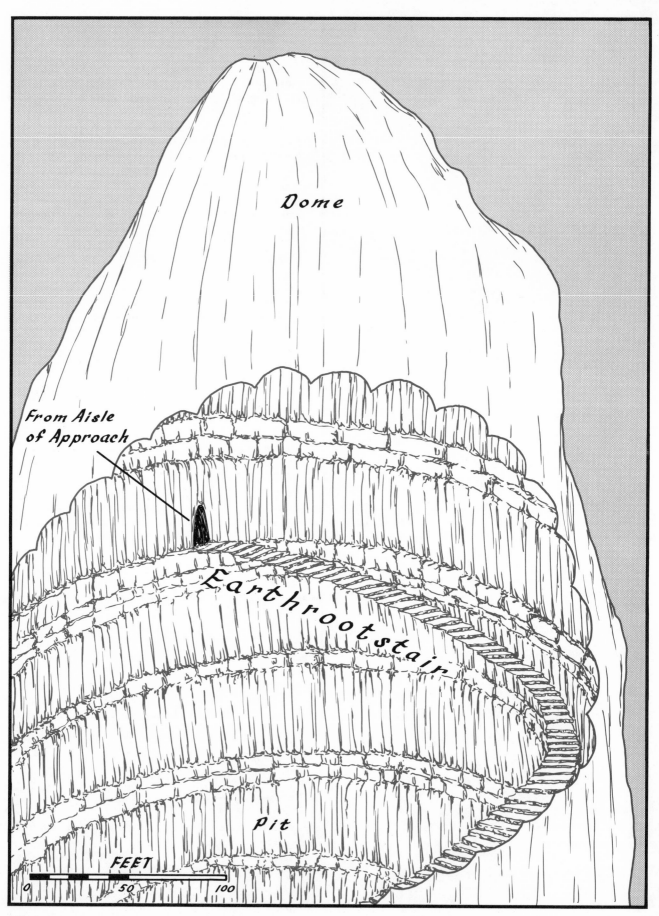

Dome

From Aisle
of Approach

Earthrootstair

Pit

FEET

0   50   100

Earthrootstair

Aisle of Approach

Stair

Pit

Earthrootstair

In cavern systems, the water which forms the caverns and the features within them always seeks an outlet. It seeps along weak beds of rock, forming horizontal caves and tunnels, such as the Audience Hall and the Aisle of Approach. When water reaches a joint or fissure in the floor of the bedrock, however, it follows gravity. Gradually the fissure is widened. As the opening grows, deep pits form. Such a feature is the site of Earthrootstair.[1]

As the Aisle of Approach reaches the pit which holds Earthrootstair, the path suddenly swings left, along a crevice. A ledge of ten feet edges along, and begins to curve down into the opening, cut as steep uneven stairs. The stairs spiral clockwise as they descend the pit.

On their right edge, a chasm plunges several hundreds of feet. Cautious peering reveals the floor of the chasm is lit by rocklight.[2] As the company nears the lower portion of the pit, the fiery rocklight is almost overpowering. One side of the pit opens into a gigantic cavern which is the source of the light—Earthroot.

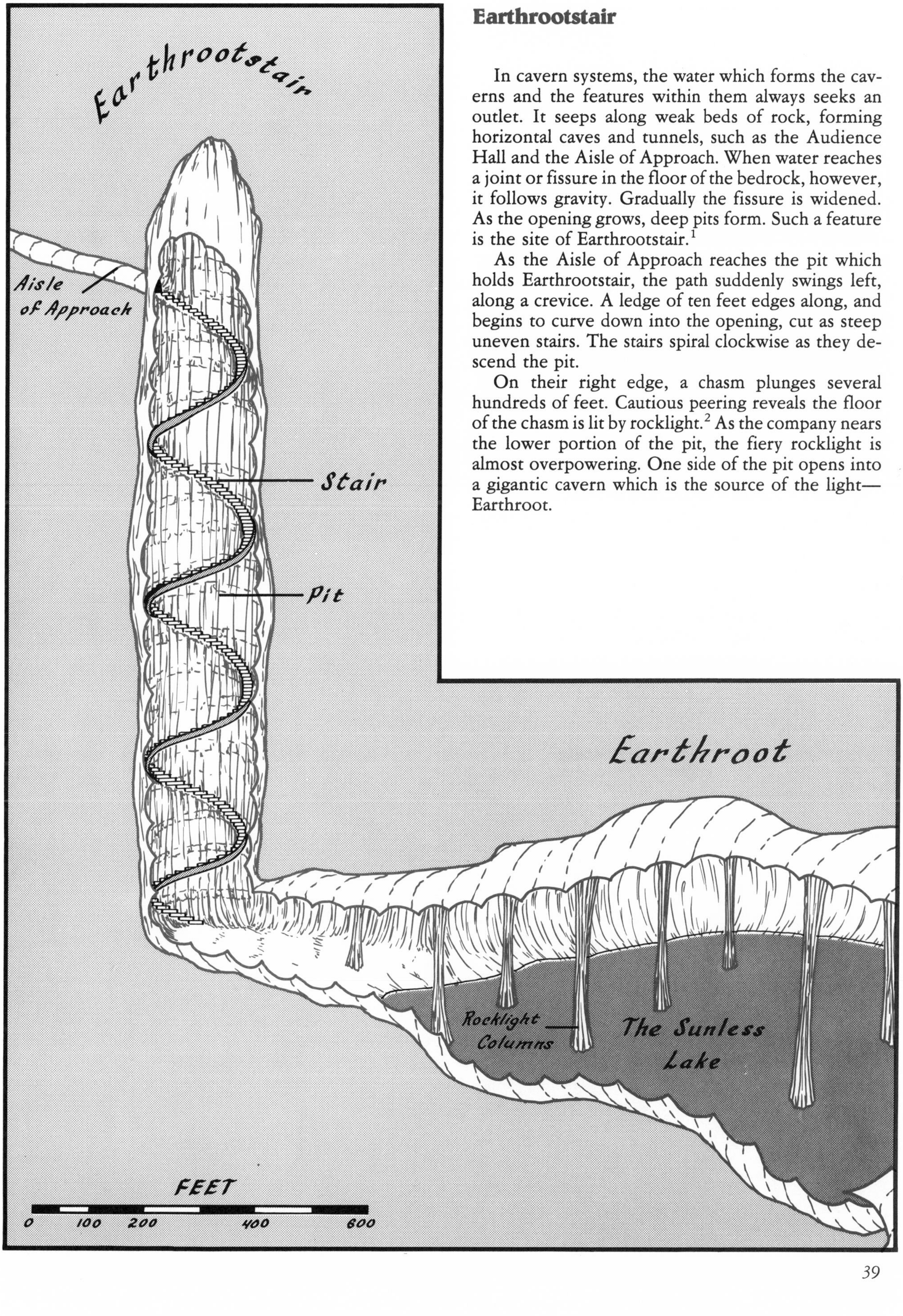

Earthroot

Rocklight Columns

The Sunless Lake

FEET

0   100   200   400   600

39

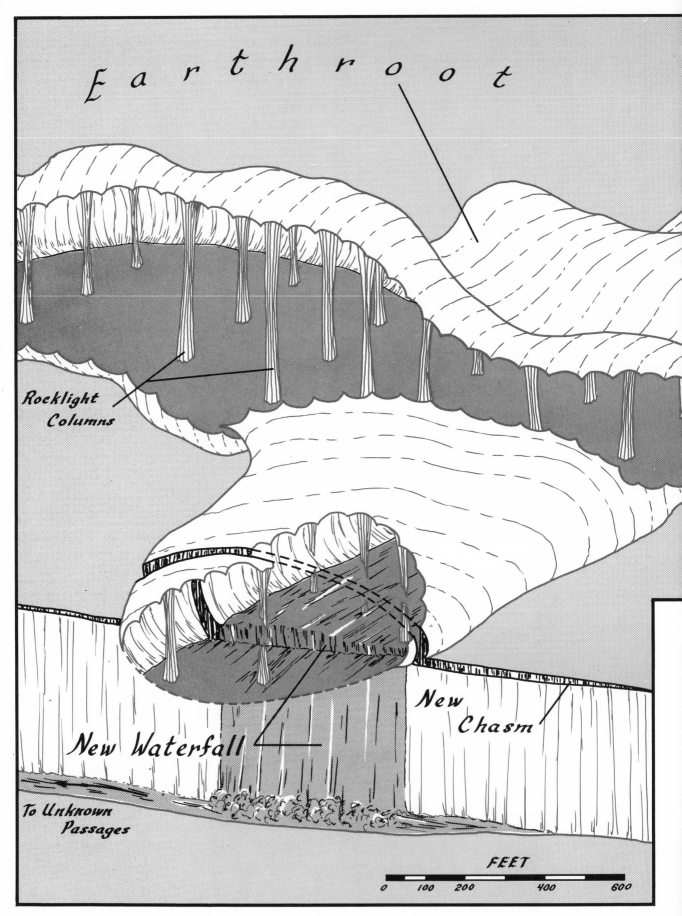

Earthroot

Rocklight
Columns

New Waterfall

New
Chasm

To Unknown
Passages

FEET

0   100   200   400   600

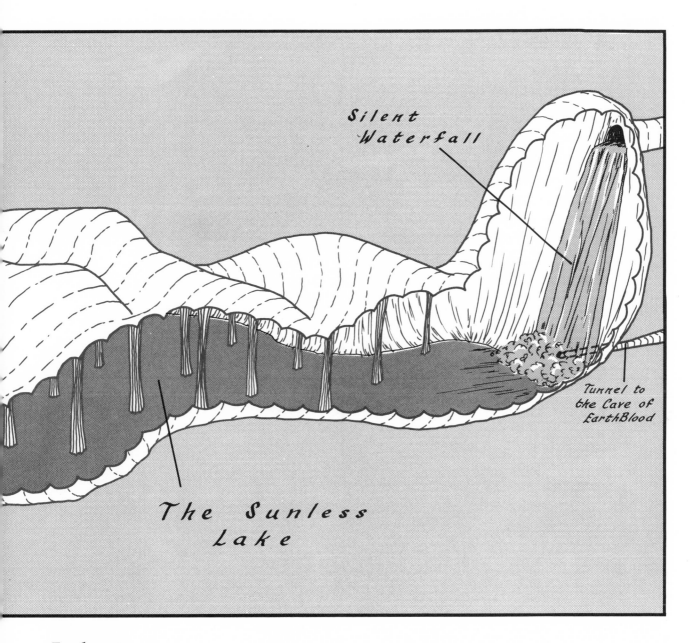

The Sunless Lake

Silent Waterfall

Tunnel to the Cave of EarthBlood

Earthroot

Within the vast cavern of Earthroot, a lake stretches as far as the eye can see. The domed ceiling looms out of sight in the shadows, but reaching down from it are columns of stone. They stand throughout the cavern, spaced regularly through the full width and length of the lake. Rocklight glows from the hearts of the columns—illuminating the lake with their fiery glow, making it appear as if a sheet of bronze.[1]

The water of the sunless lake is too powerful for mortals or for natural wood, for it combines the gathered waters of the mountains with the power of the EarthBlood. To cross the lake the company enters an enchanted boat, and the echoes of their voices power the vessel as it weaves between the columns to the far end of the cavern.[2] The source of both water and power enter the lake at this location. From a spring in the wall—so high that it is not visible—a silent waterfall pours. Beneath the fall is the tunnel which holds the stream of EarthBlood.[3]

After Amok's dissolution and Elena's fall, Bannor and Covenant attempt to regain Earthrootstair. The previously still waters of the lake are no longer immobile, however. The battle between Elena and Kevin has opened a new cleft in the floor on one side of Earthroot's cavern. The waters of the lake are pouring through it. The cleft is some distance from the company's incoming path, and the boat swings sideways toward it, captured by a powerful current. Over the cleft a massive waterfall now plunges. As the boat reaches the foot of the fall, it is again swung sideways—along the axis of the cleft—until the waters surge into other unknown passages which lie deeper still.[4]

Cave of the EarthBlood

Behind the waterfall which feeds the sunless lake of Earthroot is the way to the Seventh of Kevin's Wards. A small tunnel, probably only about ten feet wide, runs straight into the rock. Through its midst runs the stream of EarthBlood—no more than a yard wide—which fills the tunnel with a potent reek.[1]

After only a short distance the tunnel enlarges into a small cave. The far end wall is black, as if it is composed of a different rock than the rest of the cave. From top to bottom the rock seeps moisture: the Blood of the Earth. The potent fluid drips down the slope at the base of the end wall and collects in the rude trough which leads out through the tunnel.[2]

No seam or fissure is visible when the company first reaches the cave, but during the battle between Kevin and Elena a crack appears directly below Elena's feet. Quickly it widens into a chasm and the High Lord falls.[3]

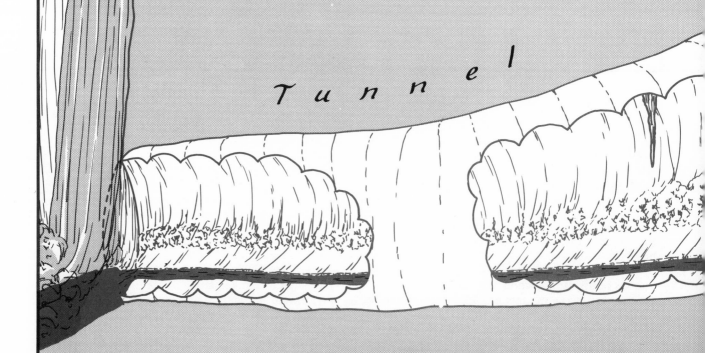

Chasm of Elena's Fall

Waterfall

Tunnel

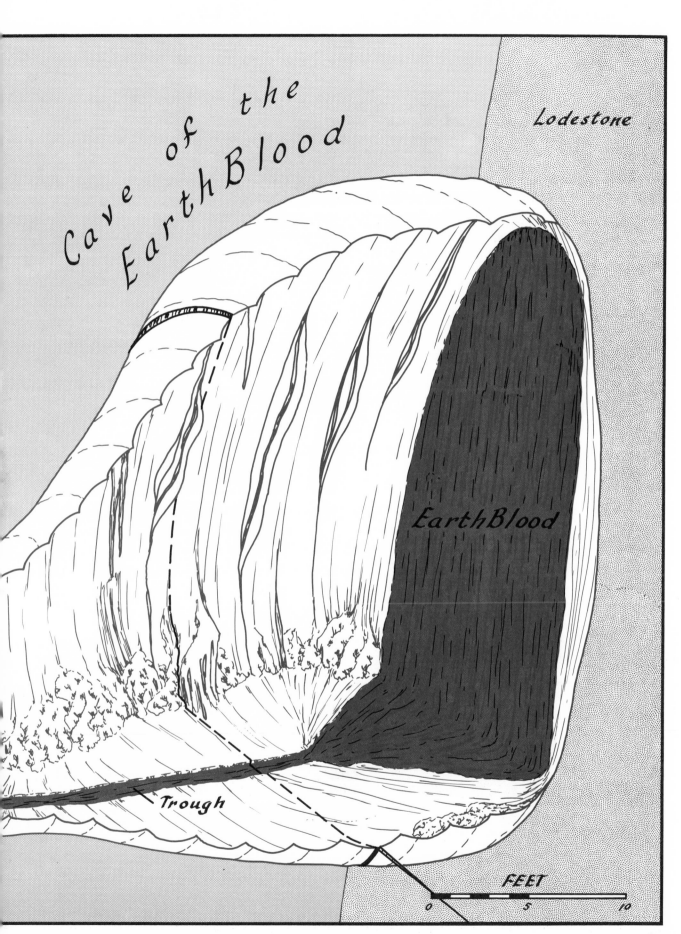

Cave of the EarthBlood

Lodestone

EarthBlood

Trough

FEET

0   5   10

GALLOWS HOWE

In the midst of Garroting Deep, near the south shore of the Black River stands Gallows Howe—the execution place of Caerroil Wildwood, the Forestal.[1] Howe means a hollow or dell,[2] but in the case of Gallows Howe, the hollow lies atop a hill. Millennia of death on the Forestal's gallows have made the hill itself lifeless, barren—nearly three hundred feet high at its crest—frowning over the tops of the surrounding trees.[3]

The gallows are the remains of a pair of trees which stand below the crown of the hill on the side away from the river.[4] Each has only a single branch remaining. Fifty feet above the ground the branches reach out and intertwine to form a crossbeam thirty feet in width.

It is to this hill that the Forestal brings the leaders from Revelstone: Mhoram, Callindrill, Troy, Quann, Amorine, and two Bloodguard. There they see that the body of Fleshharrower already hangs by the gibbet. It is also to this hill that Covenant is drawn after the escape from *Melenkurion* Skyweir. As Bannor beaches the boat nearby, the Unbeliever struggles over the slopes of the hill to the waiting people beyond.[5]

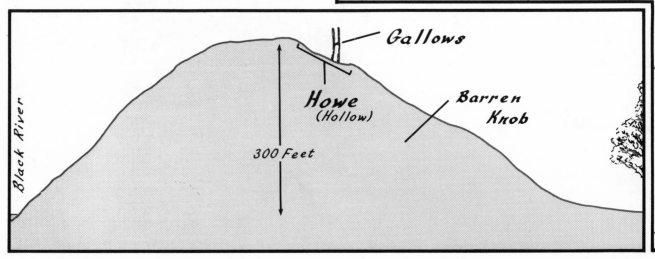

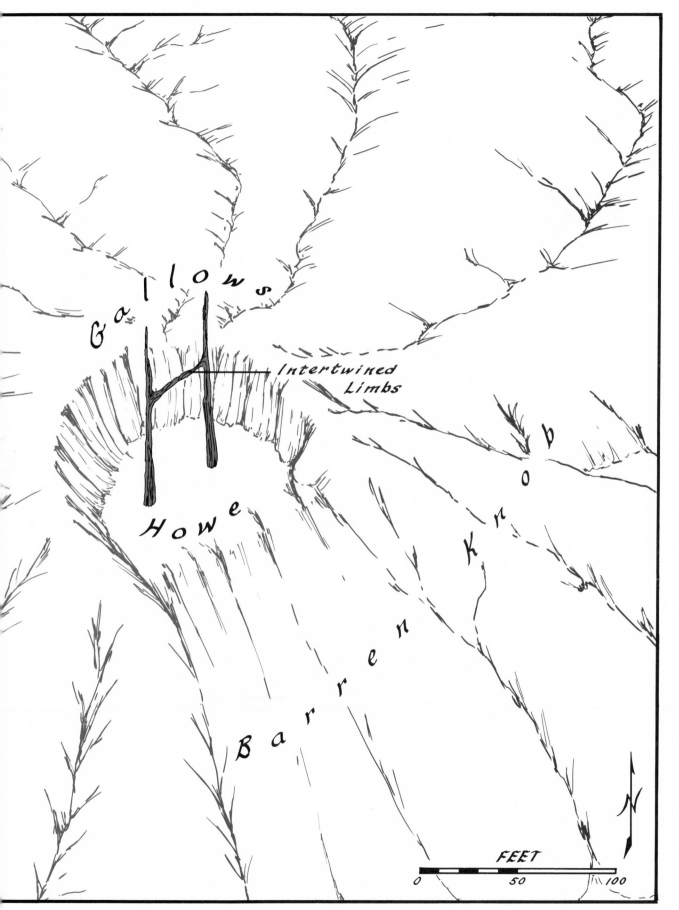

Gallows

Howe

Intertwined
Limbs

Barren Knob

FEET

0   50   100

THE
NORTHWEST

The northwest encompasses the lands from central Andelain through the Center Plains to the Westron Mountains, and north to Revelstone and Grimmerdhore toward the Northron Climbs. This is the most populous part of the Land during both Chronicles, excluding the areas holding Foul's servants. It contains Revelstone, with its thousands, and the villages clustered closely about in that fruitful area. Even in the time of the Clave, Sunder and Hollian find a series of villages along an arc between Landsdrop and Revelstone—although they have been recently decimated due to the Clave's increase in sacrifices.[1]

Southwest of Revelstone stands the second largest of the cities during the time of the Lords: Revelwood. The tree city holds only a fraction of the population of Revelstone, yet supports the Loresraat, the Warward training units, and more.[2] The two great cities are amply supplied by the fertile lands nearby.

Farther from the most fertile lands, the Center Plains "support life without encouraging it."[3] Many villages there house the Woodhelvennin and Stonedowners who care for the lands. Thanks to the frequent exposure to the march of Foul's armies, these villages also produce a product other than crops: warriors.[4]

Two areas in the northwest have inhabitants very different from the Woodhelvennin and Stonedowners: Grimmerdhore and Andelain. Grimmerdhore is a dark forest, often overrun with wolves and sometimes by ur-viles.[5] Originally, Andelain is home to the tiny Wraiths and to the Unfettered One who saves them,[6] but after the breaking of the Law of Death and the Sunbane-destruction of the forests, Andelain becomes the home to the spirits of the Land, and the last haven of Earthpower (supported by Caer-Caveral).[7]

The Andelainian Hills are bordered by the Soulsease and Mithil Rivers on the north, south, and east, and by the Center Plains on the west.

West of Andelain the hills disappear, but the Land is not entirely featureless. Ravines, old ridges, rock-strewn flats break the terrain. North is the ruin of During Stonedown, with the secret exit of the *rhysh* of the Waynhim.[8]

Trothgard and the Westron Mountains

Between the Maerl River and the Rill lies Trothgard. After the last battle prior to the Ritual of Desecration it became Kurash Plenethor, Stricken Stone—so broken and barren that the Maerl River is named for the heavy load of sediment it carried downstream from the erosion. During the First Chronicles, Trothgard becomes a verdant, hale woodland, with only occasional misshapen features serving as a reminder of its history. The Maerl flows in a gentle ravine, due to the centuries of erosion, but carries little silt.[9]

In the hilly area south of the ford of the Maerl is a unique point of interest: the Rock Gardens. During the reclamation of Trothgard, the craftsmasters of the Land shape some of the boulders in the *suru-pa-maerl* fashion. The boulders fill the face of one hill, but their pattern can only be discerned from the opposite ridge as an immensely smiling face.[10]

Near the southernmost portion of Trothgard lies the confluence of the Llurallin and Rill Rivers. They form a broad "V" which is bounded on all sides by hills, but encloses a relatively level area within its arms.[11] This is the site of Revelwood. From here, all of Trothgard rises three thousand feet in gently rolling curves to the foot of the Westron Mountains. In the southwest, Amok leads Elena and Covenant into the mountains by crossing the deep canyon of the swift-running Rill on an ancient bridge.[12] Farther north the high glacial spring of the Llurallin stands within Guards Gap—gateway to the Home of the *Haruchai*.[13]

Within the western reaches of the Westron Mountains the *Haruchai* clans inhabit "the caves and crags, the ice-grottoes and crevasses and eyries, [which] were snow-locked three seasons a year and in places perpetually clamped in blue glaciers."[14]

Revelstone and the North Plains

North of the Soulease, the hills also continue for a short distance, but gradually disappear into the North Plains.[15] Between the river and the Plains are more lands defined by Covenant's great run: Riversward, the flat bottomlands of the Soulsease; Graywightswath, a marshy area north of the river Bandsoil Bounds, a rocky stretch; rolling Riddenstretch, and the gentle hills of Consecear Redoin—where the hills end sixty leagues from Revelstone.[16]

At this location Covenant could be west of the former border of the forest of Grimmerdhore. The forest perished with the advent of the Sunbane; but when it is crossed by Korik's Mission to Seareach it stands on fairly rolling land, with an abandoned watercourse cutting through as a deeply eroded ravine.[17] East and north of Grimmerdhore lie the true Plains—flat grasslands which under the desert sun become like graveling.[18] As the Plains near the east-thrusting mountain spur which ends in the plateau of Revelstone, they become more rolling and gradually merge into the foothills surrounding the Keep.[19]

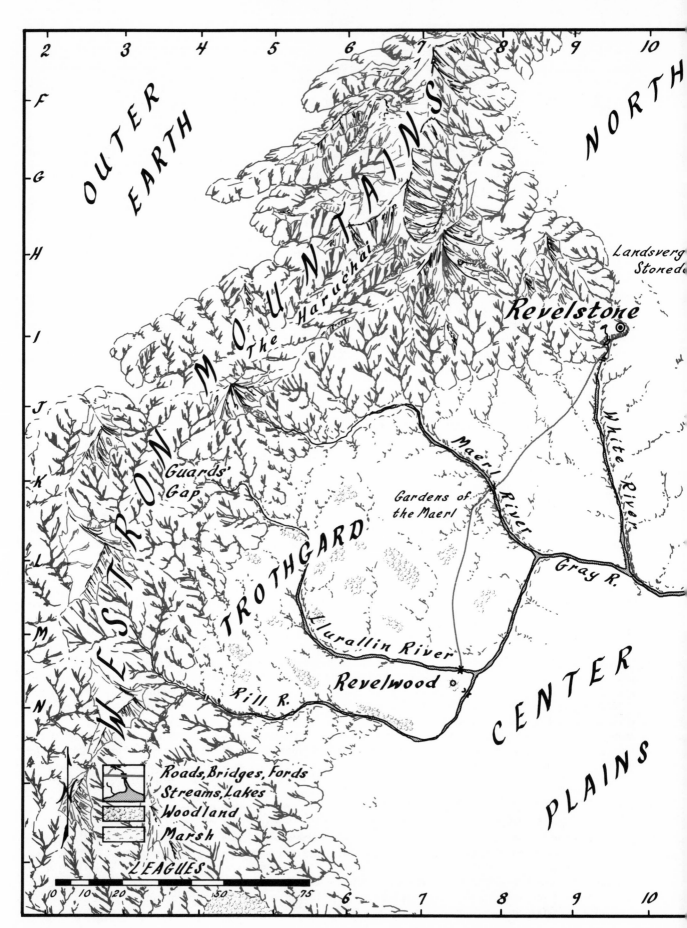

OUTER EARTH

NORTH

WESTRON MOUNTAINS

The Haruchai

Landsverg
Stoned

Revelstone

Guards'
Gap

TROTHGARD

Gardens of
the Maerl

Maerl River

White River

Gray R.

Llurallin River

Revelwood

Rill R.

CENTER

PLAINS

Roads, Bridges, Fords
Streams, Lakes
Woodland
Marsh

LEAGUES

10   10   20   50   75   6   7   8   9   10

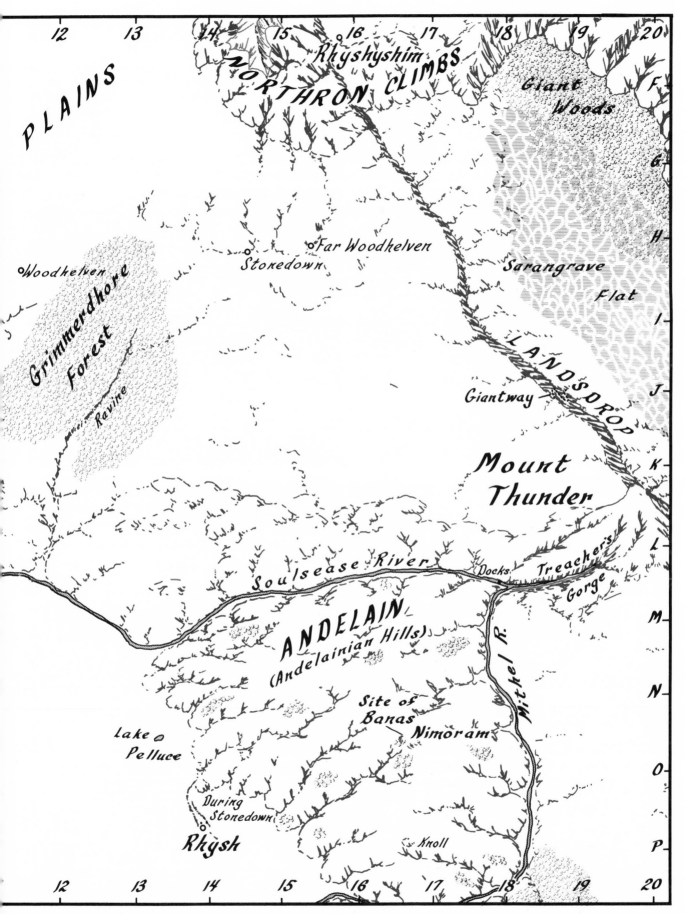

ANDELAIN
Banas Nimoram

In the heart of Andelain at the head of a broad valley stands a long, slow hill which is topped by a bowl-shaped hollow. A hundred yards above the valley head a pair of Gliden trees stand like sentinels, guiding Atiaran due east to the crest.[1] Within the hollow no trees or shrubs are present. The bowl is wide and perfectly smooth—"as regular as if the surface of the grass had been sanded and burnished."[2] Its perfection of line is in keeping with the awesome spectacle which only occurs there during the dark of the moon on the middle night of spring—*Banas Nimoram*, the Celebration of Spring.

The Celebration is the Dance of the Wraiths of Andelain. Thousands of the tiny flames join in the Dance. Initially, they seem to dance individually, but suddenly their private motions become unified—a "wheel-like pattern which filled half the bowl, and the wheel began to turn on its center . . . [with] a hub of stark blackness."[3] Within the large wheel are smaller wheels; and within the smaller wheels, each Wraith sways in its own tiny circle. As the whole wheel turns, the Wraiths move through the pattern, constantly changing places; yet the basic design remains the same—circles within circles within circles. Only the presence of the Unbeliever alters the design. In homage to Covenant's white gold ring the Wraiths stretch the rim of the wheel toward the west where Covenant sits, until they finally reach the rim of the bowl.[4]

In this pattern the Wraiths are bound until the Dance reaches its conclusion. As Atiaran and Covenant stand spellbound, the Dance is attacked. A wedge of ur-viles drives toward the heart of the Dance from the northeast. They reach the hub of the wheel and cannot be turned back. As the dancing Wraiths encounter the wedge, they are devoured. Thus, as the rotation of the design brings more Wraiths within reach of the ur-viles, a second darkness begins to appear on the far side of the ur-vile wedge—the void left by the destruction of the tiny Wraiths.[5]

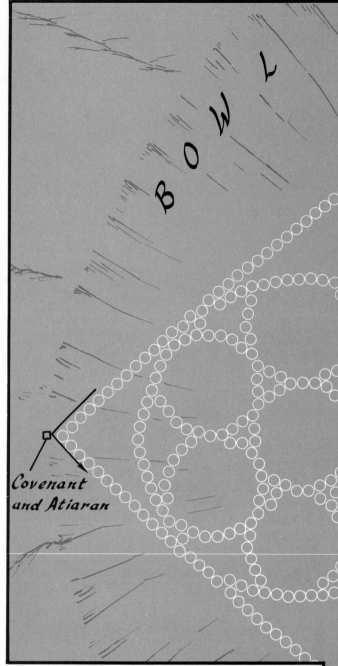

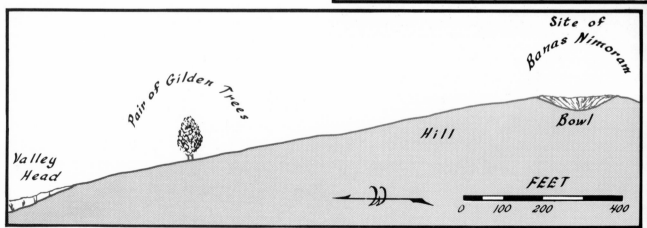

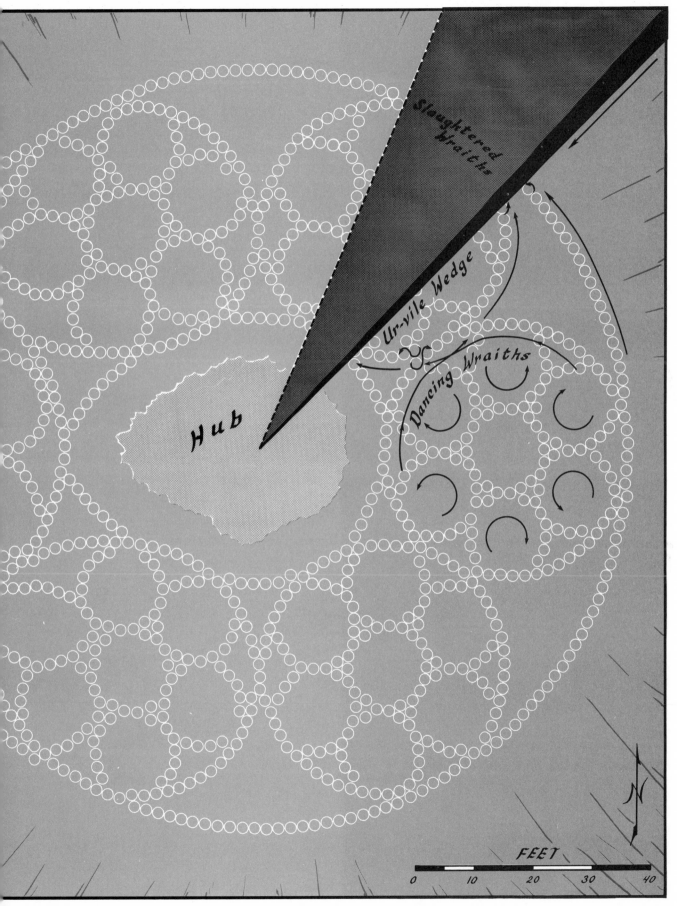

Slaughtered Wraiths

Ur-vile Wedge

Hub

Dancing Wraiths

FEET

0   10   20   30   40

53

THE <u>RHYSH</u> OF THE WAYNHIM

After falling into a Raver's trap, Covenant is rescued by Waynhim, and taken to their *rhysh* so he may recover. The *rhysh* is a community of Waynhim, normally containing a tiny population of only "one or two score."[1] This *rhysh* is larger than average by these standards. When Covenant is given blood-speed, eight Waynhim are involved in the sharing; another score are tending the plants; others walk in the complex of tunnels and tend the animals.[2]

While the *rhysh* is a "community," it is no ordinary village. It occupies a system of caverns, caves, and tunnels—not natural, but delved and shaped by the Waynhim.[3] Four locations within the *rhysh* are important: Covenant's room, the garden cavern, the animal cavern, and one of the exits.

Covenant is housed in a small cave. Its domed ceiling is not high, but is sufficient for Covenant's height. A raised platform in the center of the cave serves as a bed. Two low entrances stand on opposite walls of the room. As Hamako leads Covenant from the cave into the *rhysh*, they pass first through a long tunnel (barely high enough for Covenant to walk erect), then a network of tunnels, until the tunnel opens suddenly into an immense cavern.[4]

The cavern is more than a hundred feet high and three hundred feet broad. It is filled with trees, bushes, flowers, vines, grass—everything the Waynhim have managed to preserve from the Sunbane. Great vats of burning liquid light the cavern. A door at the far end leads into another series of corridors, angling steadily upward, that lead to "another large cave, not as high as the garden, but equally broad."[5] Tiny pens, designed to resemble natural habitat, contain numerous animal species—mostly small- to medium-sized mammals.

Beyond the zoo, the passages climb more steeply, finally ending in a spiral stair which leads to a small round chamber. Outside a lore-formed door of stone Covenant finds himself facing the sunrise among the ruins of During Stonedown—the abandoned home of Hamako's people.[6]

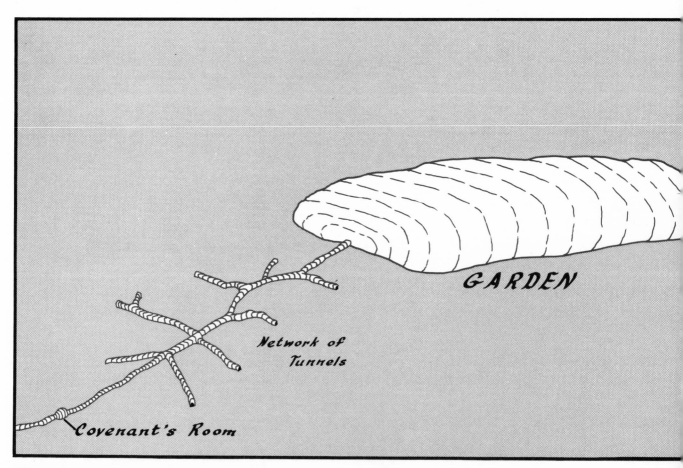

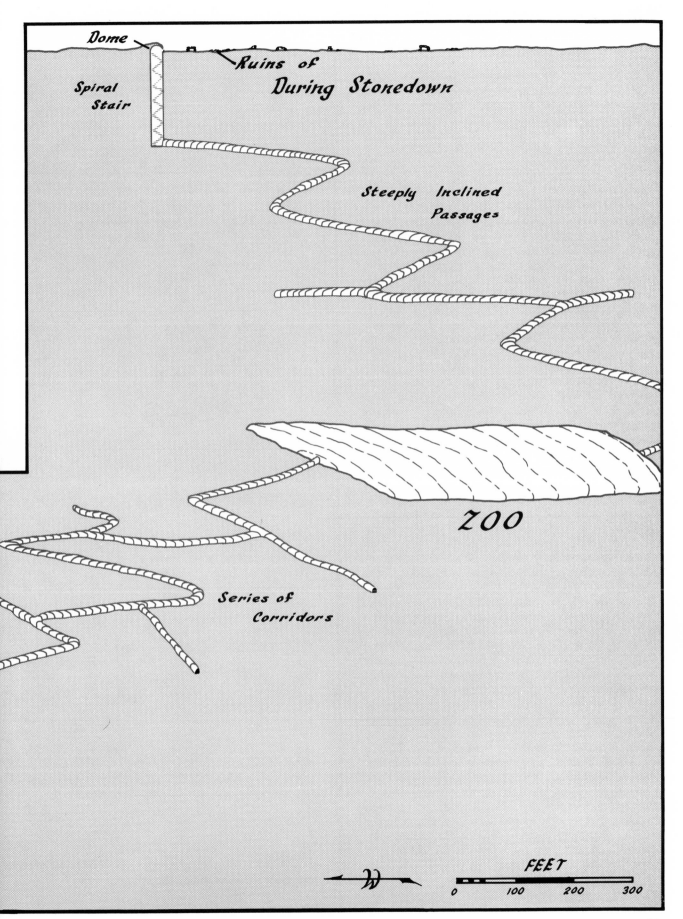

Dome

Spiral
Stair

Ruins of
During Stonedown

Steeply Inclined
Passages

ZOO

Series of
Corridors

FEET

0   100   200   300

REVELWOOD

The second most populous city of the Land, Revelwood,[1] is an immense banyan—lore-grown by the Lords using the Second Ward of Kevin following Covenant's first summoning to the Land, and destroyed by Satansfist prior to the siege of Revelstone.[2] Thus, it stands for fewer than fifty years.

A banyan is an extremely unusual tree. Although a member of the mulberry family, it is an "epiphyte"—originally it takes its nutrients and moisture from the air instead of the soil. It germinates on a host tree, sending down roots into the ground. Eventually the banyan surrounds the original host tree, which then disintegrates completely leaving only the banyan. A banyan grows more in breadth than in height—reaching over fifteen hundred feet in circumference.[3]

The lore-grown banyan of Revelwood is massive. It stands "the height of a mighty oak" (over one hundred sixty feet).[4] Beneath its boughs are gardens and practice fields for both Staff and Sword, covering several acres. Only seven trunks have been woven groundward—symmetrically placed for maximum support. Six trunks encircle the center one, with about three hundred feet between trunks.[5] The only access to the tree is via a ladder on the central trunk. The main boughs are wide enough to allow three abreast.[6] Other roots (which normally would extend to the ground) are interwoven with boughs to form the multitude of rooms necessary to contain the populace. Ladders provide access to higher levels.

The population of Revelwood is about two thousand, and the rooms of the great tree supply the full range of needs of such a large city—far more than can be shown on any diagram. There are hundreds of private quarters (such as the Sword-Elder's near the *viancome*), meeting and dining halls, teaching and study rooms, library, storage, a communal kitchen, and (high atop the crown) a watch platform.[7] Three of the six outer tree sections hold large halls—one in each of the alternate trunks.[8] One holds dining tables. Another is called the South Hall—possibly the main teaching hall of the Loresraat as it is given special mention during the tree's destruction by fire.[9]

None of the outer halls are as large as the gallery constructed around the central trunk in the upper reaches of the city—the *viancome*. This is the prime meeting place of Revelwood, and can contain half the city's population. The *viancome* is an immense net, draped on four massive boughs radiating from the central trunk, and anchored by roots from each of the six lesser trees. The bowl-shaped net is woven closely of lesser boughs, rarely with openings larger than a foot across. Unlike many of the smaller halls and living spaces, the *viancome* has no leaf-formed roof, but is open to the sky.[10]

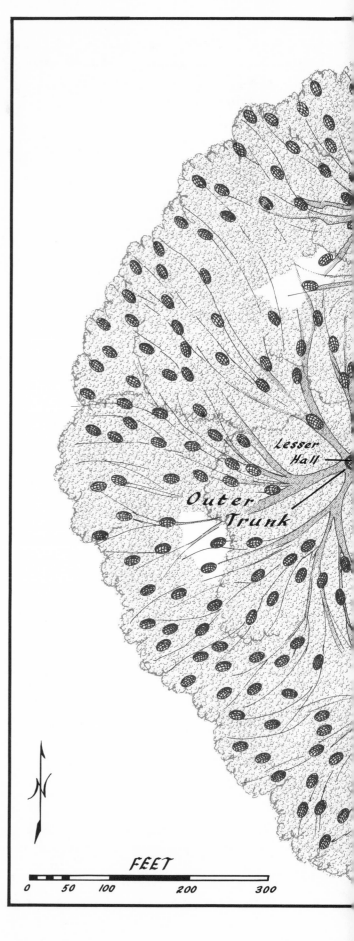

Lesser Hall

Outer Trunk

N

FEET

0   50   100   200   300

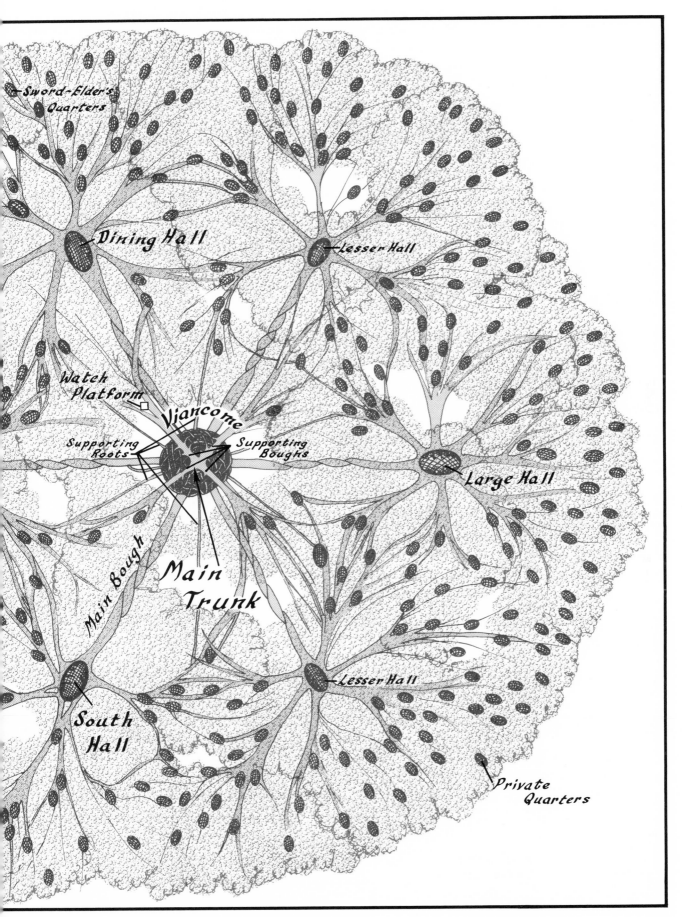

Sword-Elder's Quarters

Dining Hall

Lesser Hall

Watch Platform

Viancome

Supporting Roots

Supporting Boughs

Large Hall

Main Bough

Main Trunk

Lesser Hall

South Hall

Private Quarters

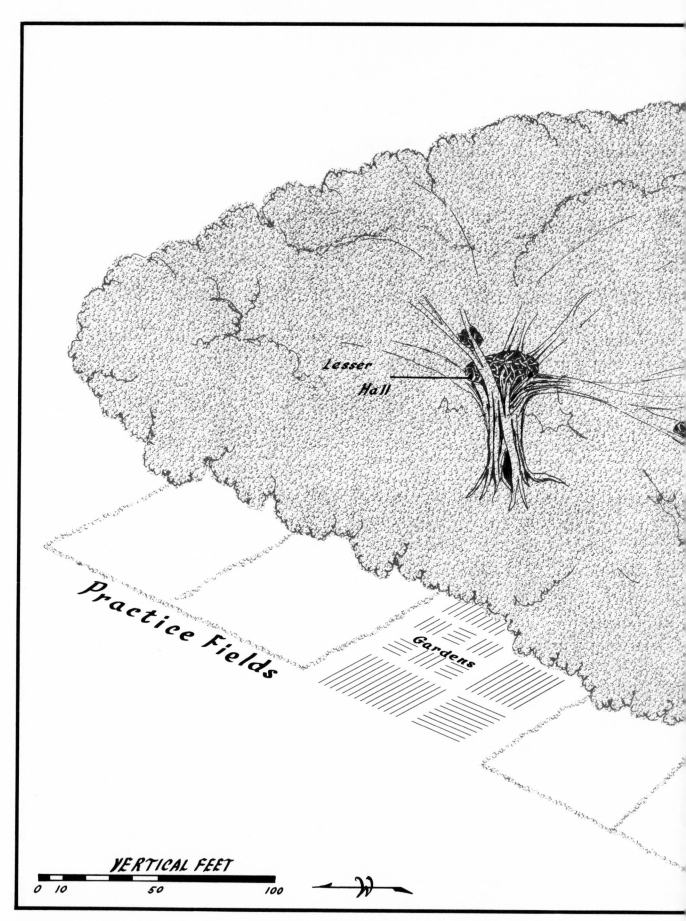

Lesser
Hall

Practice Fields

Gardens

VERTICAL FEET

0   10   50   100

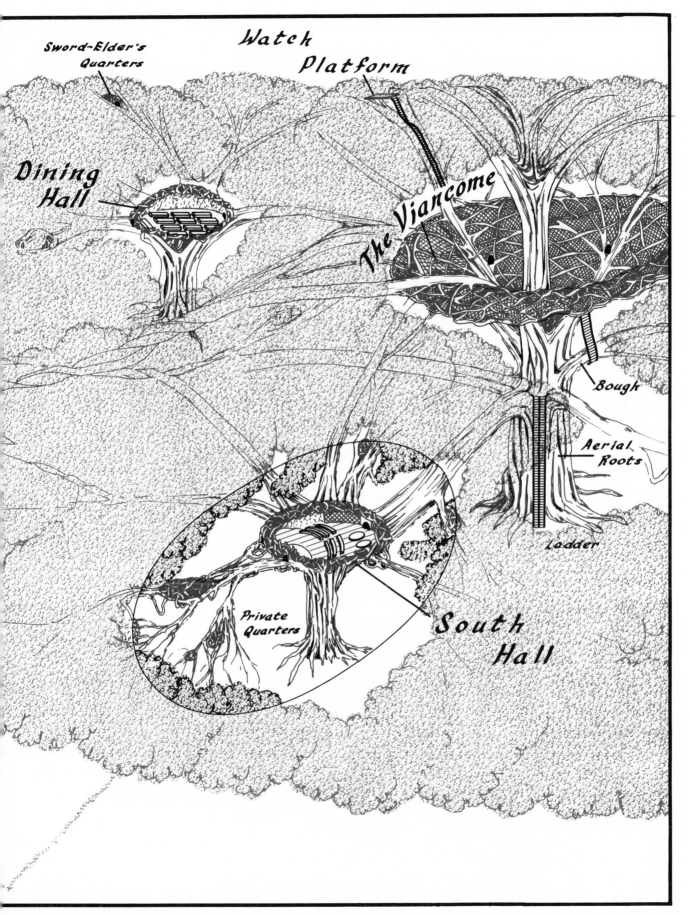

Sword-Elder's
Quarters

Watch
Platform

Dining
Hall

The Viancome

Bough

Aerial
Roots

Ladder

Private
Quarters

South
Hall

REVELWOOD

THE PLATEAU OF REVELSTONE

The largest city of the Land is housed on a plateau which juts from the Westron Mountains out into the lowlands between the North Plains and the rolling hills west of Grimmerdhore Forest. The plateau is situated in a shallow curve of the mountains, but most of its bulk extends east of the range, forming a wedge which narrows markedly at the tip. The southern cliffs of the plateau run almost due east to west, while the northern cliffs curve slightly, sweeping northwest to the mountains. Thus, the upland is protected on the west and north by almost impassable peaks. The tower at the eastern tip lies almost two leagues from the deepest portion of the upland.[1] The cliffs of the upland are sheer, rising two to three thousand feet above the foothills.[2]

The tongue of land which holds the Giant-wrought city displays only two visible features above the cliff: the open-air amphitheater, and the sole access between the upland and the populated halls.[3] During the time of the Clave a third manifestation is also visible: the light shaft of the Banefire. Its power allows it to pass from the chamber in the heart of the city out through the solid granite of the plateau at whatever angle is necessary for it to seek the sun.[4]

The cultivated fields lie in the southwest, beyond the stream that bisects the southern part of the plateau. The source of that stream is the clear mountain lake of Glimmermere. Although it draws its waters from the hills to the east and the mountains to the north and west, no incoming streams are visible, for its still waters are entirely spring-fed. Glimmermere is always strangely powerful, and even during the time of the Clave it defies the Sunbane.[5]

The stream flows slightly east of south through the upland until it reaches the midpoint of the southern cliff. There it plunges in majestic Furl Falls into a lake at the base. The western shores of the lake are filled with Gilden and pine trees, but the east shore holds two large piers and several small docks. On the south the White River rounds a hill and disappears on its way to the Soulsease.[6] The road from Revelwood follows the river's west bank until it crosses a bridge some distance south of the lake. A spur from the lake joins the main road just before it sweeps east, paralleling the cliff. At the eastern tip of the plateau the road turns sharply, and climbing directly up a last steep foothill, comes to the gates of the tower and the courtyard beyond.[7]

Lords' Keep—the city of Revelstone—occupies the eastern tip of the promontory. Except for the lowest fifty to one hundred feet, both cliff faces are "coigned and fortified, lined with abutments and balconies, punctuated by oriels, architraves, embrasures" until they fade into native rock half a league behind the tower entrance.[8] No diagram can give more than the merest hint of the intricacy of the Giants' grand design.

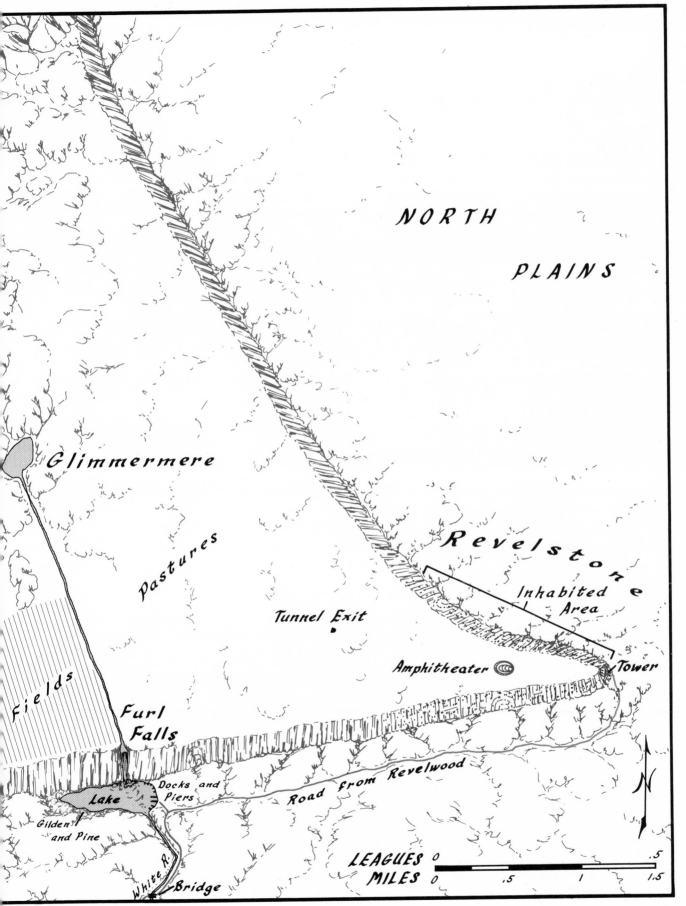

NORTH

PLAINS

Glimmermere

Pastures

Revelstone

Inhabited
Area

Tunnel Exit

Fields

Furl
Falls

Amphitheater

Tower

Docks and
Piers

Road from Revelwood

Lake

Gilden
and Pine

White R.

Bridge

LEAGUES 0 .5
MILES 0 .5 1 1.5

N

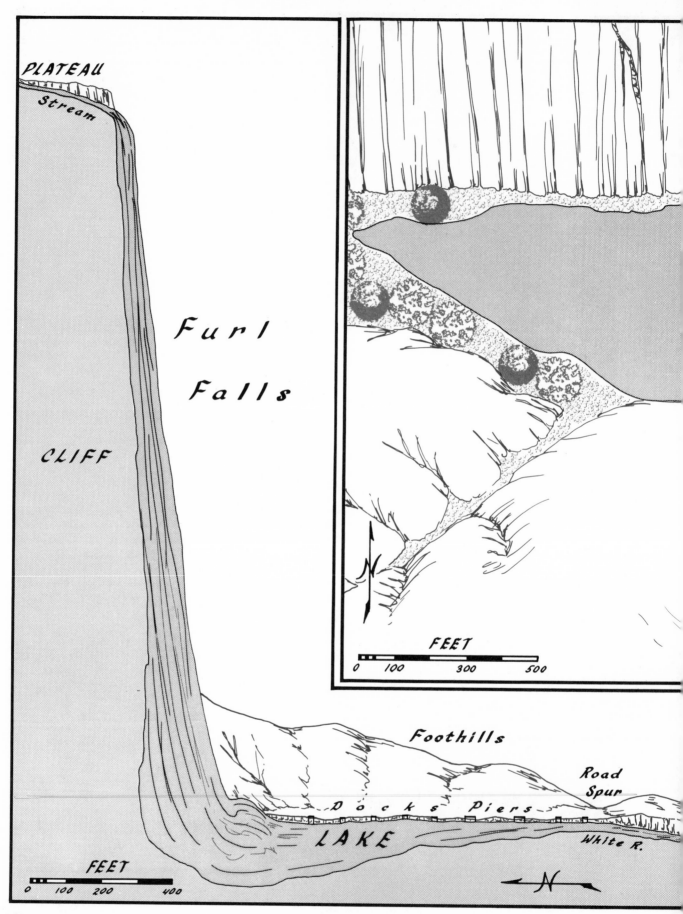

PLATEAU

Stream

Furl Falls

CLIFF

Foothills

Road Spur

Docks Piers

LAKE

White R.

FEET

0   100   200   400

FEET

0   100   300   500

N

N

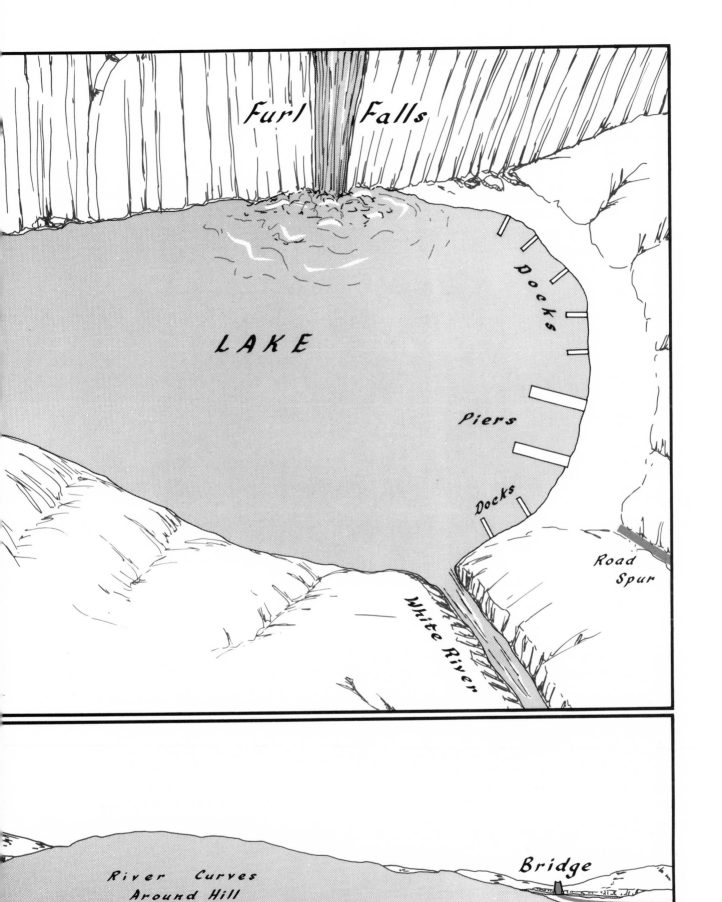

Furl Falls

LAKE

Docks

Piers

Docks

Road
Spur

White River

River Curves
Around Hill

Bridge

Road from Revelwood

FURL FALLS

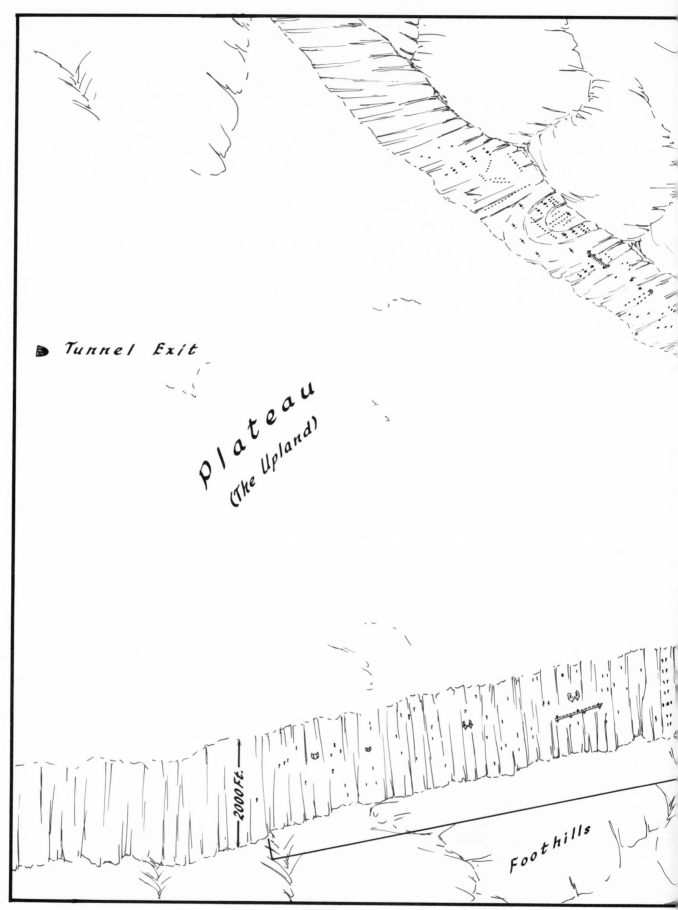

Tunnel Exit

Plateau
(The Upland)

2000 Ft.

Foothills

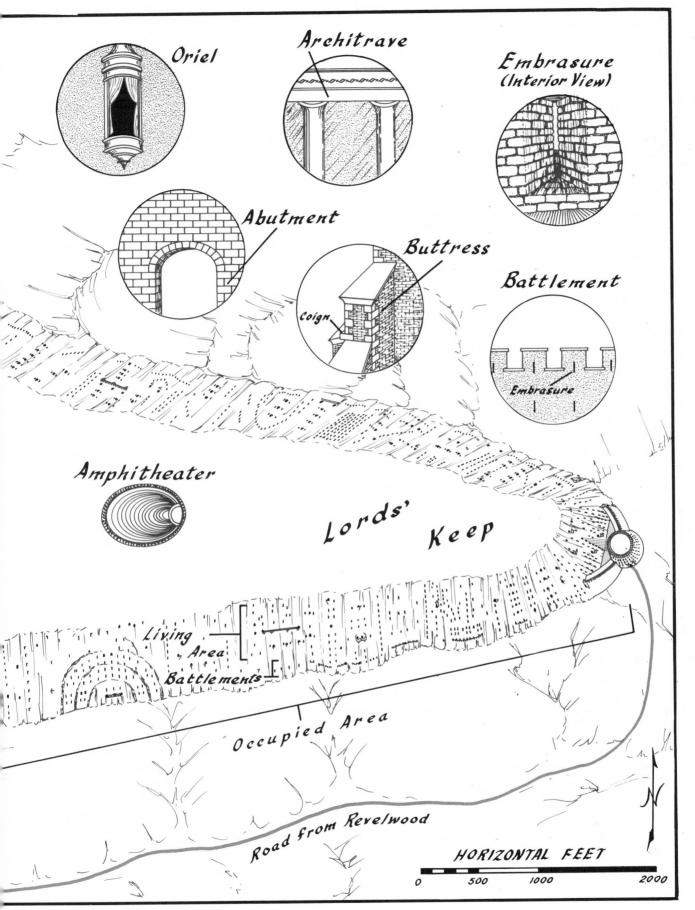

Oriel

Architrave

Embrasure
(Interior View)

Abutment

Buttress

Coign

Battlement

Embrasure

Amphitheater

Lords' Keep

Living Area

Battlements

Occupied Area

Road from Revelwood

HORIZONTAL FEET

0   500   1000   2000

N

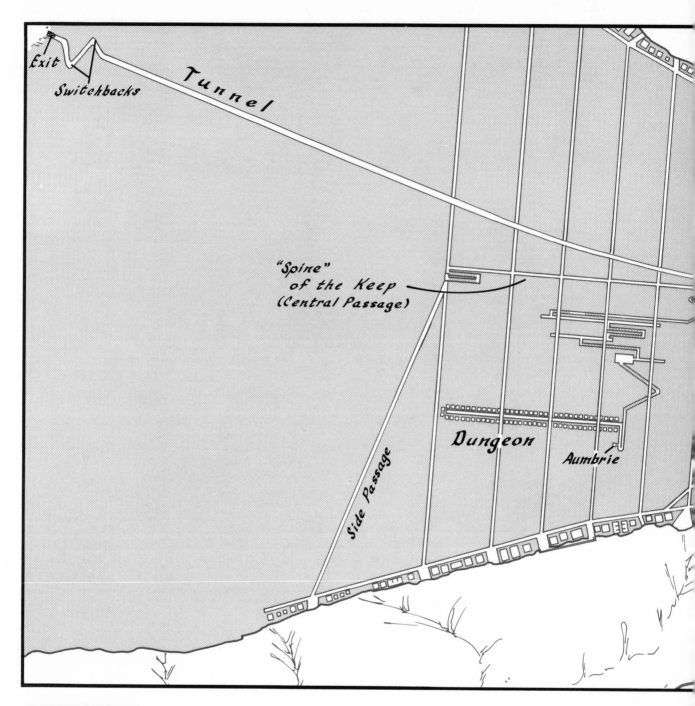

REVELSTONE

Within the eastern tongue of the plateau the Giants of Damelon's time had delved a massive city sufficient for almost ten thousand people—Revelstone.[1] Only the rooms directly related to Covenant's tales are included in the following pages: Covenant's assorted quarters during his various visits to Lords' Keep, the watchtower and courtyard, the amphitheater, the sacred enclosure (later the Hall of the Banefire), the Close, the Lords' quarters, the Hall of Gifts, the dungeon, the Bloodguards' cavern, and the main refectory.

The watchtower stands half as high as the plateau, and the courtyard walls are half the height of the tower. Within the tower are numerous rooms and mazing passages.[2] Walkways tie the tower to the main Keep.[3] The gate to the Keep opens onto a massive forehall, wide enough for six coursers to pass through abreast.[4] On each level a main central passage runs along the "spine" of the city. From the uppermost of these a slanting passage climbs toward the upland until (after two sharp switchbacks) its tunnel opens to the sky near the pastures.[5] The only other feature

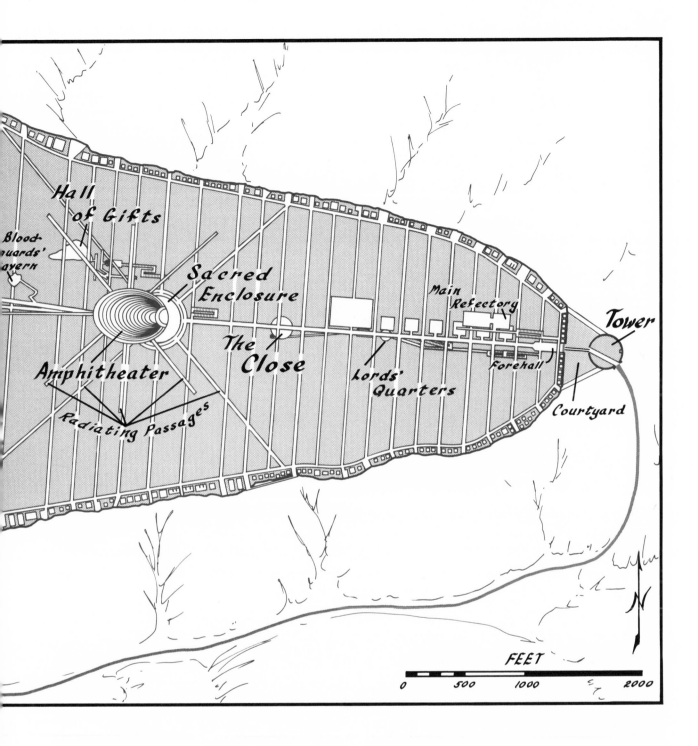

Hall
of Gifts

Blood-
guards'
Cavern

Sacred
Enclosure

Amphitheater

The
Close

Radiating Passages

Lords'
Quarters

Main
Refectory

Forehall

Tower

Courtyard

FEET

0   500   1000   2000

reported visible from above the Keep is the open-air amphitheater.

The largest cavern of the city is the sacred enclosure. From below the level of the foothills to half the height of the Keep it rises as a domed cylinder, occupying the physical heart of the city. At every level it is encircled with passages leading into its balconies.[6]

Another large domed room is the Close where the Lords hold council.[7] While the Close is deep in the levels of the Keep, the living quarters of the Lords are deeper still. The room around which the private

quarters are centered seems almost a small version of the sacred enclosure, but in place of the dais the very floor of the chamber is *the* Revelstone, the spiritual heart of the city.[8]

Two other important sites lie deeper still: the natural chamber of the Hall of Gifts, and the secret rooms (hewn after the coming of Gibbon) which contain the Aumbrie of the Clave and the dungeon.[9] Thus the beauty and the ugliness of the Land are both hidden in the deepest level during the Second Chronicles.

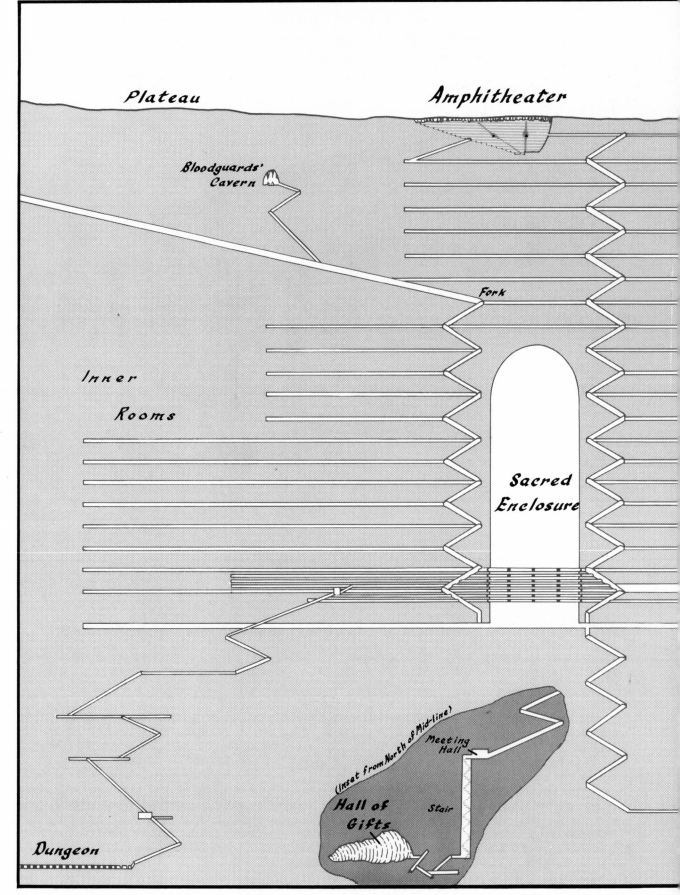

Plateau

Amphitheater

Bloodguards'
Cavern

Fork

Inner

Rooms

Sacred
Enclosure

(Inset from North of Mid-line)

Meeting
Hall

Hall of
Gifts

Stair

Dungeon

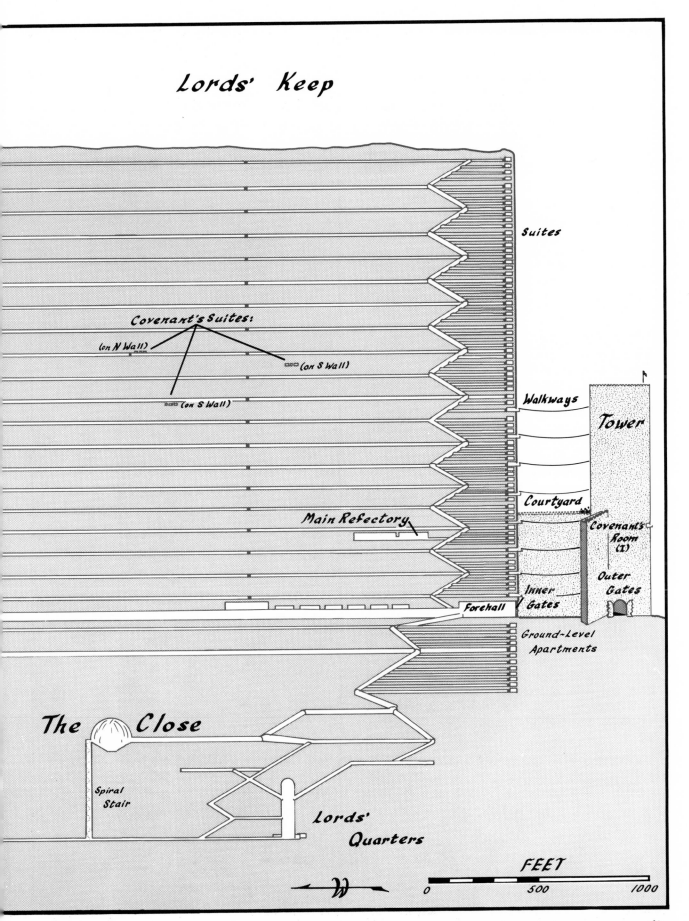

Lords' Keep

Suites

Covenant's Suites:

(on N Wall)

(on S Wall)

(on S Wall)

Walkways

Tower

Courtyard

Main Refectory

Covenant's Room (I)

Inner Gates

Outer Gates

Forehall

Ground-Level Apartments

The Close

Spiral Stair

Lords' Quarters

FEET

0   500   1000

The Watchtower and Courtyard

The watchtower is all that remains of the eastern tip of the plateau. The tower is the native granite of which the entire plateau is composed, as are the walls. The courtyard behind them was delved by completely removing tons of stone.[1] The tower stands a thousand feet—half the height of the cliff towering behind it; while the connecting wall is five hundred.[2] From a pole atop the tower the High Lord's Furl and other standards signal welcome or warning to the outer world.[3]

The courtyard is understandably shallow. In its midst the excavation has exposed a natural fountain, and a Gilden tree grows beside it.[4] They soften the otherwise martial—yet beautiful—appearance of the Keep. Eight walkways span the depth of the courtyard between the tower and the Keep. During the battle against Satansfist the walkways are destroyed one by one as the tower is evacuated.[5]

Beneath the tower is the only entrance to Revelstone, a massive tunnel cutting through the base of the tower. Its entrance faces southeast, so it enters the courtyard at an angle—a defensive mechanism against any frontal assault which might pass through the outer gates.[6] Above the gates a projecting abutment serves as a balcony for the Bloodguard currently on watch.[7]

The tower is round, with crenelated battlements on the peak. The outer gates which bar the tower entrance usually stand open, but when closed they show that they are rounded—conforming to the wall of the tower. Their shape, plus their interlocking edges combine to form a gate which is almost impossible to force inward.[8] In the tunnel which runs between the gates and the courtyard, windows in the ceiling allow defenders to attack from above.[9]

From the courtyard, small doors lead to the maze of the tower.[10] When Covenant is first brought to Revelstone, he is housed in the tower; and it is through one of these doors he gains access. Immediately inside the door a spiral staircase curves up "a hundred feet or more. Beyond . . . Covenant found himself in a jumbled maze of passageways, stairs, doors that soon confused his way . . . up and down unmeasured flights of steps, along broad and then narrow corridors."[11]

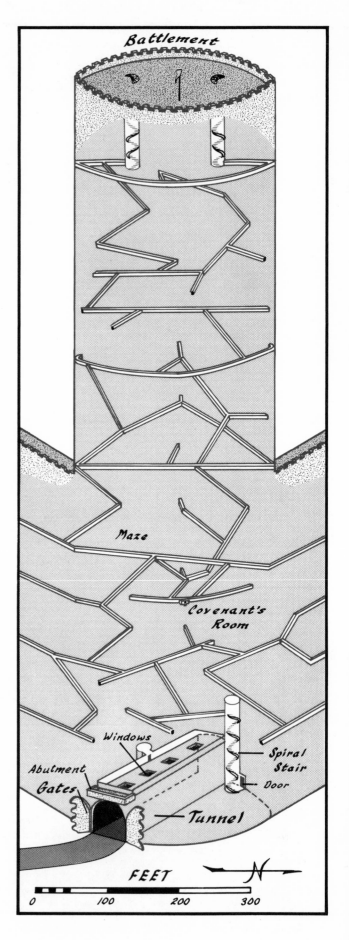

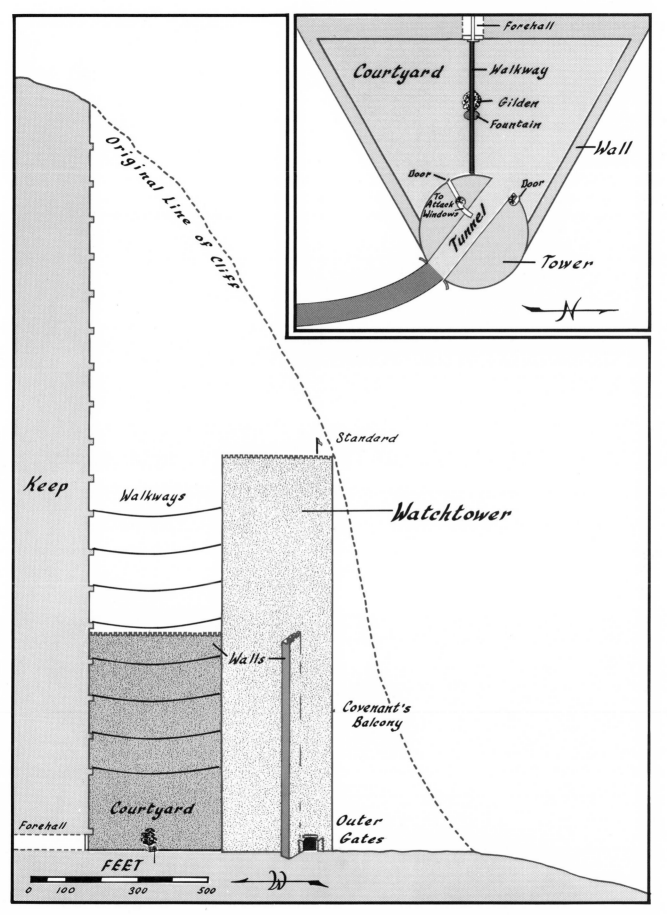

Forehall

Courtyard

Walkway

Gilden
Fountain

Wall

Door

Door

To Attack
Windows

Tunnel

Tower

N

Original Line of Cliff

Keep

Walkways

Standard

Watchtower

Walls

Covenant's
Balcony

Forehall

Courtyard

Outer Gates

FEET

0   100   300   500

71

Covenant's Suites

Covenant is given private suites each time he visits Revelstone. When he first arrives at Lords' Keep, his room is in the watchtower.[1] After he is declared ur-Lord, he is moved to the main Keep, in a suite halfway up the north cliff wall.[2]

Later, Elena gives him a suite on the south wall, as does Gibbon.

The tower room is the smallest of Covenant's residences. Its door is hidden from the outer passage, and cannot be opened from within.[3] The apartment is a single large room containing "a bed, a bath, a table arrayed with food, chairs . . . and an arras on one wall."[4] A balcony faces east, hanging three to four hundred feet above the level of the foothills.[5] *Lillianrill* torches and two pots of graveling light the room.[6]

The three suites in the Keep are basically similar, having a sitting room, bedroom, and small bath.[7] The suite on the north face has several windows, including an oriel complete with stone seat in the bedroom.[8] The suite selected by Elena on the south wall is so similar to the one on the north cliff that they have been combined in one diagram. The south-facing suite also has a large oriel beside the bed, but has a balcony off the sitting room in lieu of windows. The bathing room between the sitting room and bedroom contains a stone basin and tub with movable valves.[9]

The suite to which Gibbon guides Covenant contains the same three rooms, but the sitting room is in the center, and is flanked by the bedroom and bathing room. Although no windows are mentioned, they are probably present in the bath and bedroom, while the entrance to the balcony provides natural light to the sitting room.

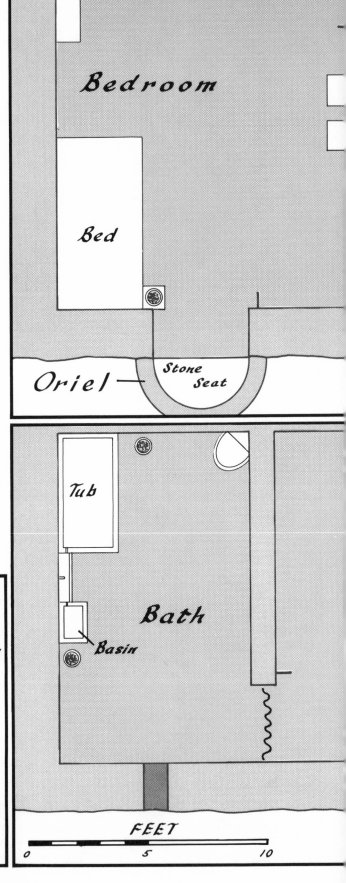

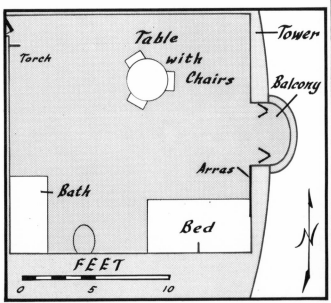

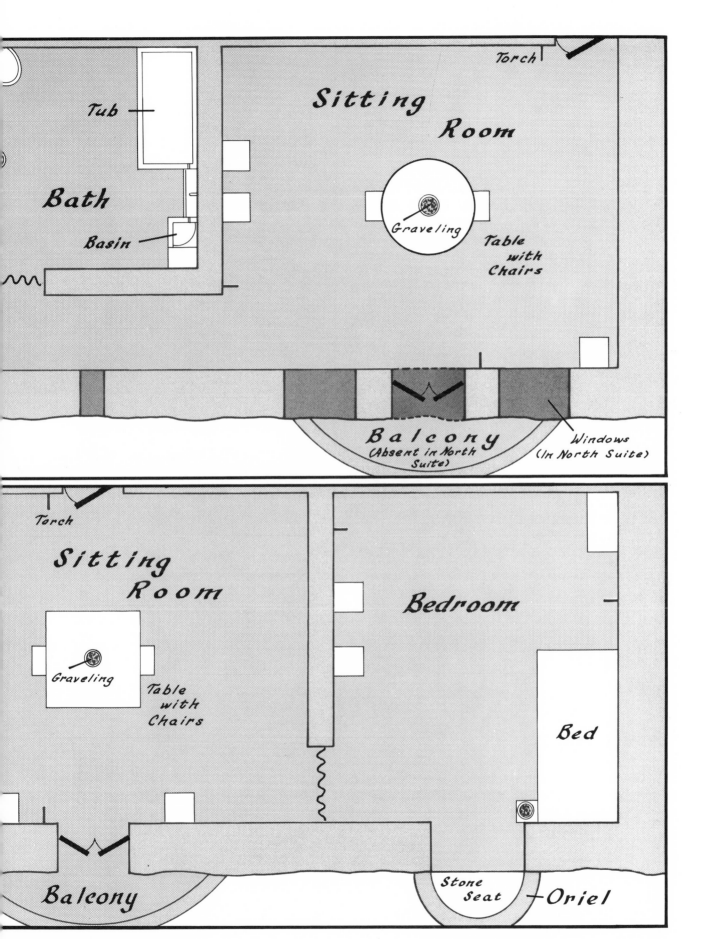

The Amphitheater

The highest feature within Lords' Keep is an amphitheater, open to the sky. Numerous passages from all parts of the city curve toward the theater, entering at several doors around the bowl.[1] Above the top row of benches walls rise twenty to thirty feet to the flat upland plateau.

Tiers of stone benches "curved downward to form a bowl around a flat center stage."[2] However, the bowl is not symmetrical, nor is the stage completely centered. A completely central stage results in a "theater-in-the-round" in which only half of the audience can see the presenter at any given time. Therefore, the amphitheater of Revelstone is an ellipse, with its stage projecting into the center of the lower benches, but with the eastern wall of the amphitheater rising unbroken, forming a backdrop behind the stage.[3]

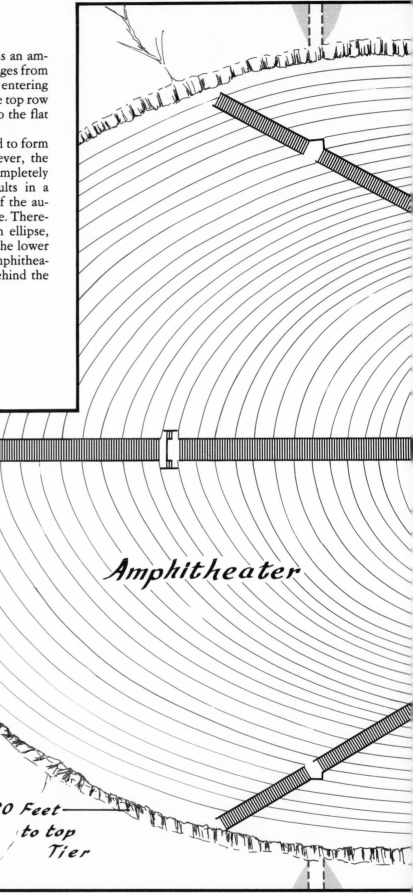

Amphitheater

Plateau

20 Feet to top Tier

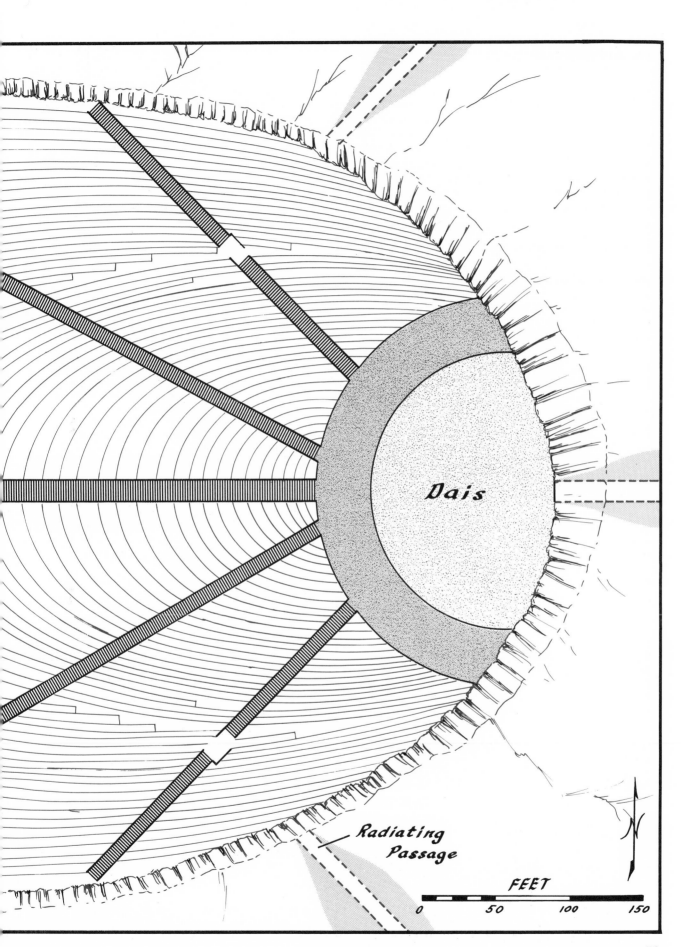

Dais

Radiating
Passage

FEET

0   50   100   150

N

The Sacred Enclosure—The Hall of the Banefire

In the "central depths of the Keep"[1] is an immense cavern, shaped like a domed cylinder. It rises from "below the level of the foothills more than halfway up the height of the Keep."[2] When Covenant first visits the cavern, it is the location of the Lords' nightly vespers—a focus for the populations' devotion to the Land and to Earthpower. As such, its purpose becomes holy, and it is known as the sacred enclosure.[3]

A dais stands to one side of the cavern floor. Seven balconies ring the lower walls of the cavern from which the people may stand looking down on the dais below. The lowest balcony is more than a hundred feet above the floor, yet the fourth is only two hundred feet high, so the vast expanse of the cavern towers up into blackness, hiding the Giant-carved figures in its domed ceiling.[4] Complementing the circular balconies within the cavern, passages ring the outer walls, fed by halls branching to all parts of the Keep.[5]

After the rise of the Clave, the cavern serves a far different purpose. It contains the Banefire and the *master-rukh*.[6] The massive triangle of the *master-rukh* rests its points on the fourth balcony. It is the focus of the fire which burns in the floor of the chamber. The fire is so great that even from two hundred feet above the floor the heat is intense, and for the first time the domed ceiling high above is illuminated. To allow for the fire the dais has been removed. In its place are troughs feeding into a central hollow. They supply the fuel—blood of the Land—for the Banefire.[7]

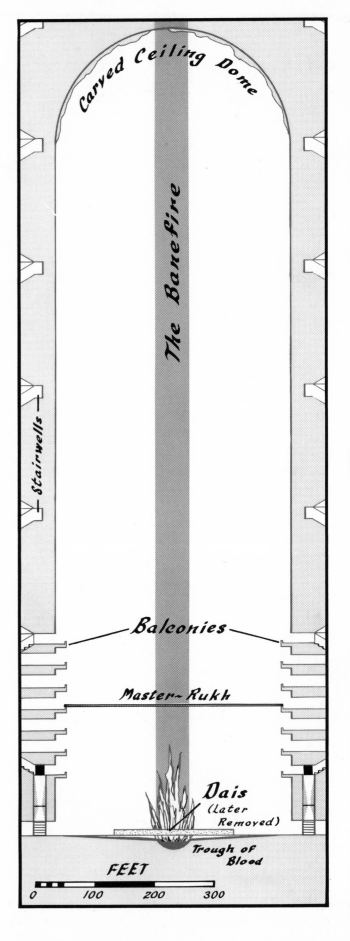

Carved Ceiling Dome

The Banefire

Stairwells

Balconies

Master-Rukh

Dais (Later Removed)

Trough of Blood

FEET

0   100   200   300

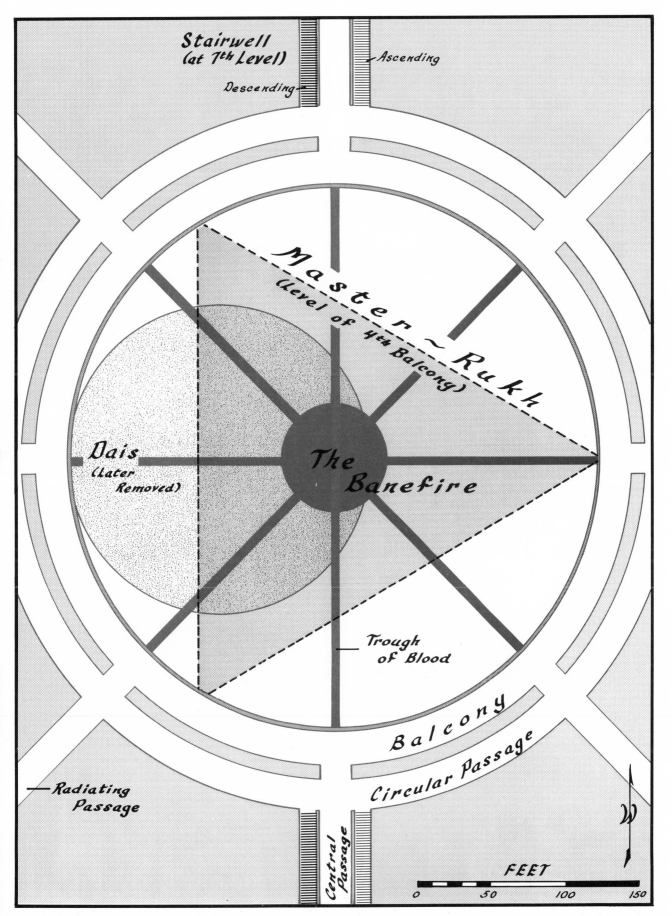

Stairwell
(at 7th Level)

Descending

Ascending

Master ~ Rukh
(level of 4th Balcony)

Dais
(Later
Removed)

The
Banefire

Trough
of Blood

Balcony

Circular Passage

Radiating
Passage

Central
Passage

FEET

0   50   100   150

The Close

The Council of Lords holds it meetings in a round, domed chamber—the Close. Within the chamber the circular pattern is followed by all the features. The lowest level of the chamber is a sunken pit of graveling, deep enough for the graveling, source of light and heat for the chamber, to lie below the level of the floor. The graveling is augmented by four huge *lillianrill* torches spaced around the upper walls.[1]

Around the graveling pit the table of the Lords forms a *C* enclosing three-quarters of a circle. The inner surface of the table descends to the second level of the floor—that on which Covenant's chair is placed during his various summonings.[2]

The Lords' chairs face inward on the third level—toward the table and the pit within. The *C* of the table is oriented so that the High Lord (at the center of the table) faces the main entrance of the Close.[3] So large is the table that during Covenant's first visit, Variol and Tamarantha are said to be seated "several feet" from the High Lord on either side[4]; and during his second summoning Covenant's lone chair in the lower level is twenty to thirty feet away from Elena.[5]

Rising in tiers above the table level are the galleries for the people who come to share the Lords' counsels—Bloodguard, warriors, Lorewardens, Hearthralls, and others.[6] Like the Lords' table the tiers are *C*-shaped, enclosing only three-quarters of the circle; but they face the opposite direction from the table, so that no seats occupy the quadrant immediately behind the High Lord.[7]

At the highest level of tiers wooden doors large enough for Giants form an arched entrance—the main access to the Close. Two smaller doors pierce the wall behind the Lords' table, one of which provides private access from the Lords' quarters via a spiral stair.[8] Stairs lead through the center of the tiers from the main entrance to the floor of the chamber, and on each side of the unoccupied quadrant from the small doors.

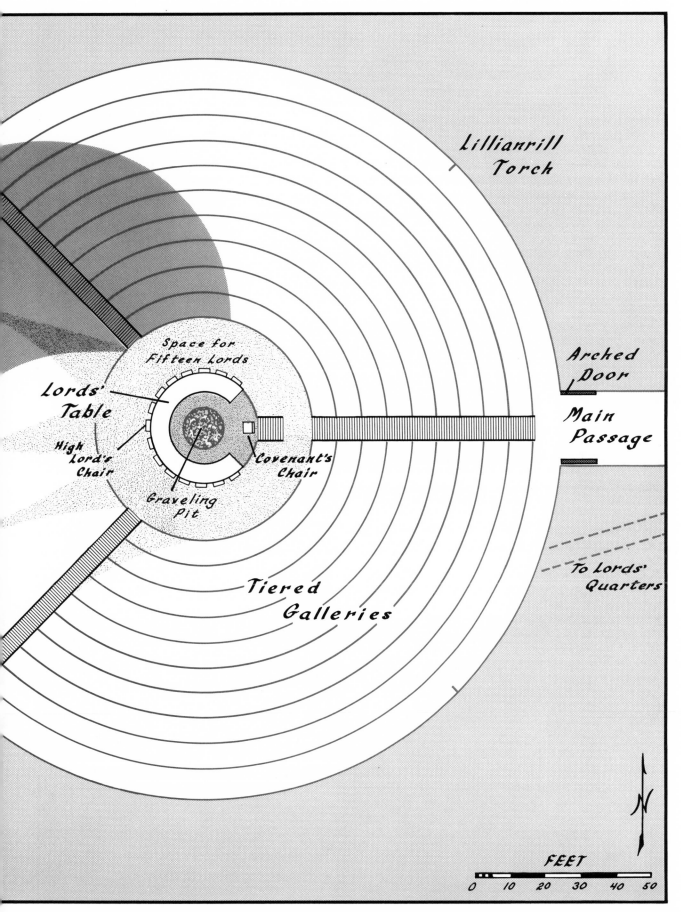

Lillianrill
Torch

Space for
Fifteen Lords

Lords'
Table

High
Lord's
Chair

Covenant's
Chair

Graveling
Pit

Arched
Door

Main
Passage

To Lords'
Quarters

Tiered
Galleries

N

FEET

0   10   20   30   40   50

The Lords' Quarters

Shaped like a minature version of the sacred enclosure, the central court of the Lords' quarters rises in a cylinder to its domed ceiling high above. Its walls are interrupted occasionally by projecting railed coigns forming balconylike structures from which messengers may call down to the Lords.[1]

In spite of the height of the cavern, the floor is the most striking feature. It is *the* Revelstone, the heart-rock of the Keep. Its granite was originally set afire by Kevin, and glows with such pure and penetrating light that no other is needed to brighten the entire cavity.[2] With the loss of Earthpower under the auspices of the Clave, however, the stone's inner radiance dies. Thus, torches are necessary until (during his release from the Soothtell) Covenant's white gold relights the stone, and sends a crack through the heart of the rock.[3]

Fifteen doors surround the courtyard of the cavern—the entrances to the private quarters of the Lords. At the time of Covenant's first visit there are only nine lords, and a sentry guards the door of each apartment currently occupied. Several feet into the floor from each respective door stands the wooden tripod designed to hold the Lord's staff when he or she is within the chambers.[4]

The living quarters vary in size—from those comfortable to a single Lord to ones large enough for an entire family. When both of a couple are Lords (such as Variol and Tamarantha or Verement and Shetra) they may share quarters, or utilize two adjoining apartments with a common door if more space is needed.[5]

Covenant has occasion to visit three of these private quarters: Elena's, Callindrill's, and Mhoram's.[6] No description is given of Callindrill's, but both Elena's and Mhoram's rooms are said to be bare. Elena's antechamber has a pot of graveling in each corner, a few stone chairs, and a central table with a marrowmeld carving of her Ranyhyn. Mhoram's room is similar, though at one time it contains the stone table with the impaled *krill* instead of its usual table.[7] Beyond the forechamber are two back rooms, one containing a bed, and the second with pantry shelves.[8]

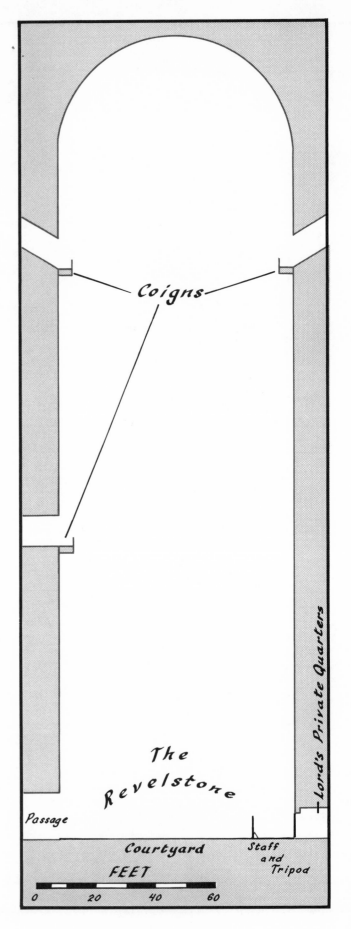

Coigns

The Revelstone

Lord's Private Quarters

Passage

Courtyard

Staff and Tripod

FEET

0   20   40   60

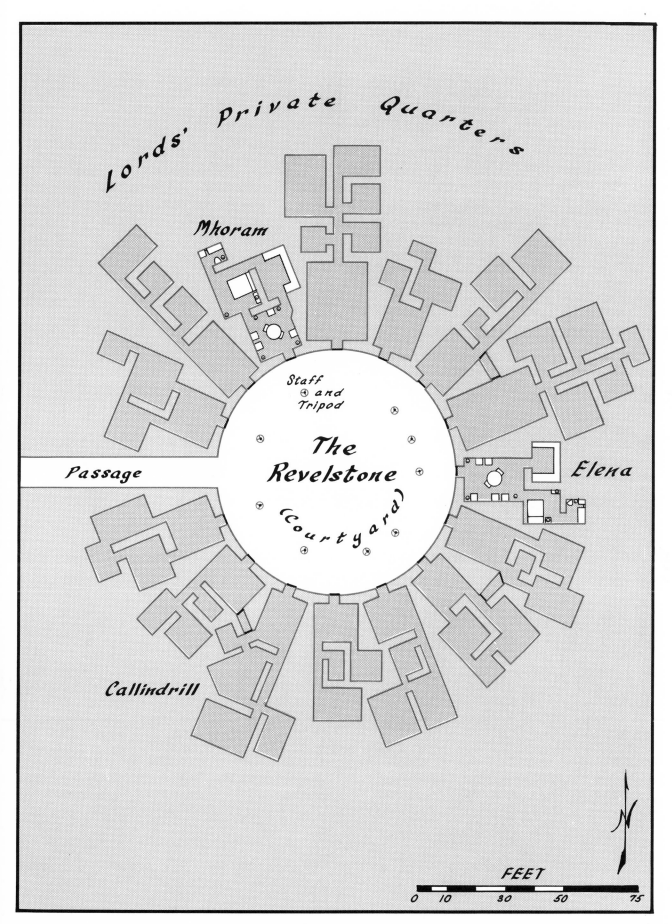

Lords' Private Quarters

Mhoram

Staff and Tripod

The Revelstone

(Courtyard)

Passage

Elena

Callindrill

FEET

0   10   30   50   75

The Hall of Gifts

Deep in the interior of Revelstone—both deep down and deep back—is the Hall of Gifts. It houses the cultural wealth of the Land during the time of the Lords. Although it seems difficult and "out of the way" to Covenant, its location is designed to protect the treasures within should Revelstone ever be over-run. Its entrance is hidden to the naked eye, appearing as "a blank wall of stone" until Bannor gives the three words of command.[1]

The hall is a spacious cavern. The floor is smoothed, but the walls, ceiling, and natural columns were left purposely in their original state to enhance the beauty of the gallery. Some of the "rude, rootlike pillars" are utilized as natural plinths for displaying sculpture—such as the one on which Elena's marrowmeld work of Covenant is eventually placed.[2]

During the time of the Clave the Hall of Gifts is still intact. Thus, Gibbon maliciously chooses the cavern as a fitting site to do battle with Covenant. A somewhat lurid mosaic of Kevin Landwaster has been added since the time of the Lords, and Honninscrave is imprisoned within it. To free the Giant, Nom must shatter the floor from wall to wall[3]—destroying the heart of the cavern and the works of art nearest the center as well. With them Nom builds a cairn for Honninscrave.[4]

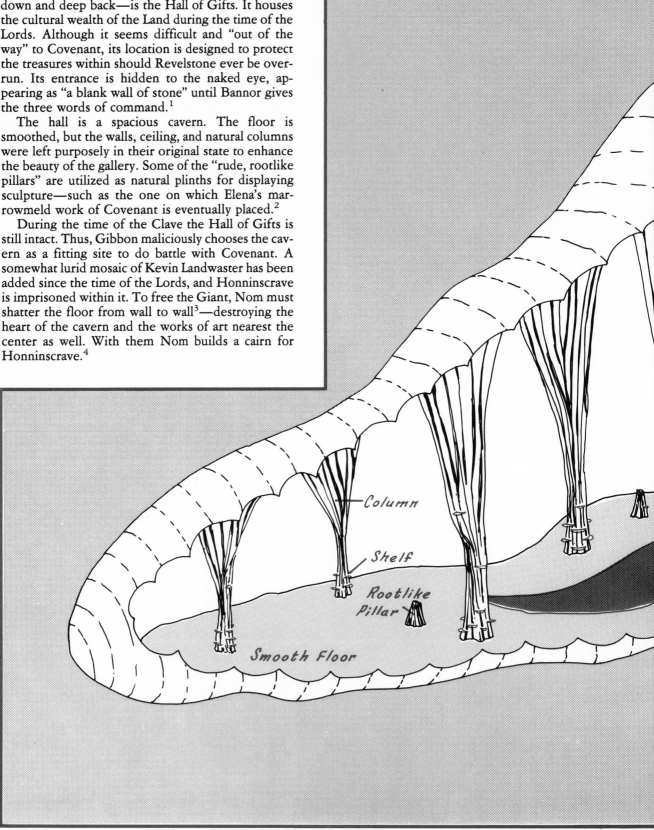

Column

Shelf

Rootlike Pillar

Smooth Floor

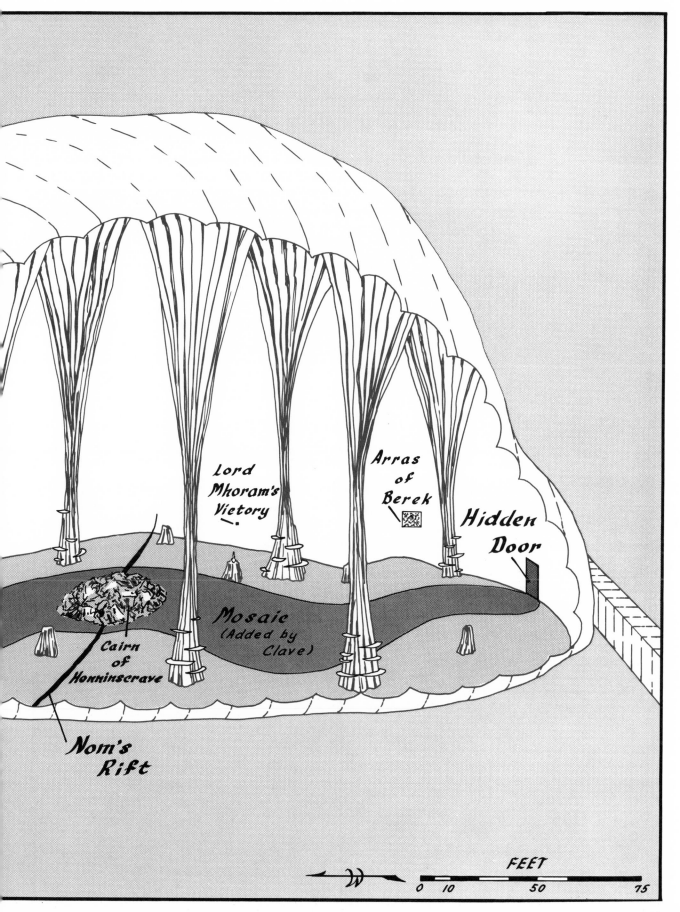

Lord
Mhoram's
Victory

Arras
of
Berek

Hidden
Door

Cairn
of
Honninscrave

Mosaic
(Added by
Clave)

Nom's
Rift

FEET

W

0   10   50   75

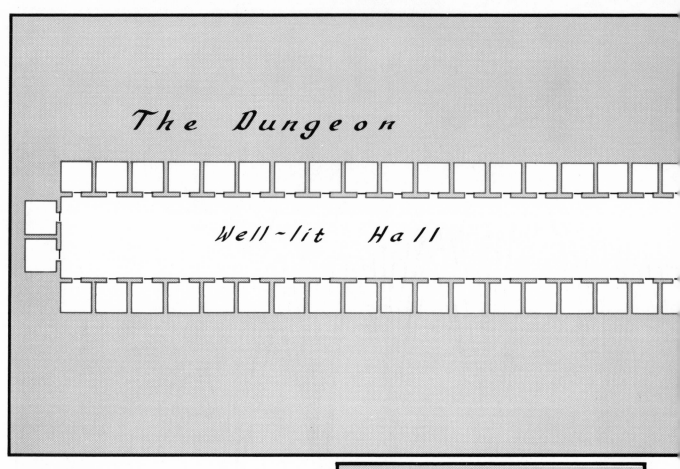

The Dungeon

Well-lit Hall

The Dungeon

Under the direction of the Clave an addition is made to Revelstone—one which would never have been allowed under the Lords: a dungeon. The first room to which Vain leads Covenant is a treasure-house, the Aumbrie (storeroom)[1] of the Clave. It does not contain treasures of art, such as those in the Hall of Gifts, but rather it holds treasures of weaponry and lore: the first three Wards of Kevin, staffs, scrolls, swords, periapts, talismans, and the heels of the Staff of Law.[2]

To reach the Aumbrie and the dungeon, Vain has led Covenant from the fourth balcony of the Hall of the Banefire through twisting passages deep into the Keep. They come at last into a tunnel which seems to end in a blank wall, but with a touch from Vain a door appears such as those Covenant had seen in Foul's Creche. Beyond it the passage curves back upon itself, so that the second hallway shares a common wall with the one they had just left. The new hall is roughly hewn, however, indicating it is not part of the original Giant-work.[3]

A short side-passage, only ten paces long, branches to the iron door of the Aumbrie. Beyond the side hall the main passage turns sharply, and opens out into a much wider hall. It is lined with small cells—enough to hold sixty-seven *Haruchai* plus other prisoners.[4]

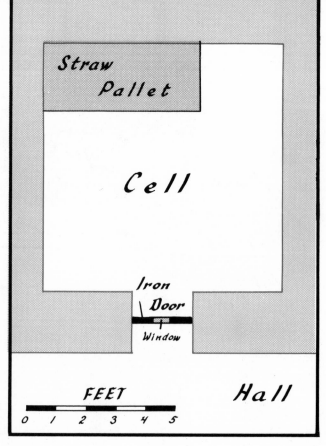

Straw Pallet

Cell

Iron
Door

Window

FEET

Hall

0   1   2   3   4   5

84

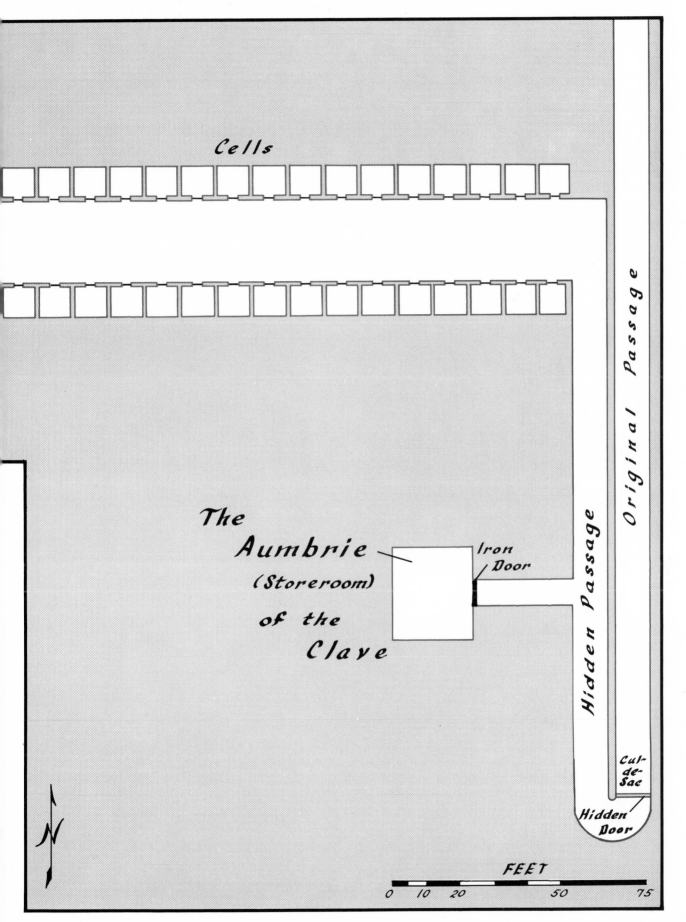

Cells

The
Aumbrie
(Storeroom)
of the
Clave

Iron
Door

Hidden Passage

Original Passage

Cul-
de-
Sac

Hidden
Door

N

FEET

0   10   20   50   75

85

THE
NORTHEAST

This portion of the Land includes all the lands northeast of Andelain; but in this quadrant, the Lower Land dominates, for Landsdrop cuts diagonally northwest to the southeast across only a corner of the area. On the Upper Land lie the battle-scarred plains and Mount Thunder.

The majestic Soulsease River, passing through the catacombs of Mount Thunder becomes (in a few short leagues) Defiles Course. Its fetid rivulets wander the spreading flats of the mighty Sarangrave and move sluggishly through the delta of the Great Swamp. Only in the north do the Boundary Hills of Seareach rise above the rancid lowlands, separating the land of the Giants from the northern reaches of Foul's domain.

The Battle Plain and Mount Thunder

Throughout the ages, when Foul seeks to assault the Old Lords, his forces are met above Landsdrop by the Warward, to give protection to the Ranyhyn and all the peoples of the Upper Land.[1] Thus, the Plains between the Roamsedge and Mount Thunder became broken wastelands and even in the time of the New Lords it remains "a stark, unfriendly flatland where no people lived and few willingly traveled."[2] At its northern edge rise the foothills of Mount Thunder.

The hills are "like a gnarled stone mantle" and make skirting the base of the peak extremely difficult.[3] The western slope of the mountain reaches out in ridges on either side of the Soulsease, forming Treacher's Gorge; while the eastern face descends Landsdrop, lending the mountain the appearance of a kneeling giant with arms on the Upper Land, and legs on the Lower.[4]

The Lower Land

Cutting through the heart of Mount Thunder is Landsdrop—that awesome east-facing escarpment which runs "half a thousand leagues" from the Southron Range into the Northron Climbs.[5] It stands the highest—four thousand feet—near Mount Thunder.[6] The fault is reported to have resulted from the Land's revulsion toward banes buried in Mount Thunder.

The division between the Upper Land and the Lower is sociological as well as physical. Although cavewights and ur-viles continue to inhabit Mount Thunder, malevolent creatures fill the Sarangrave and Lifeswallower, while further south Foul's armies and twisted creations occupy the Spoiled Plains, Shattered Hills, and Foul's Creche. Only the Giants, secure in their sanctuary by the Sunbirth Sea, manage to maintain not only their own lands, but also safe "Giantways" across the Sarangrave to Landsdrop until they meet their doom.[7]

At the base of Landsdrop lies a narrow band of rough foothills, keeping the encroachment of the Sarangrave from the base of the cliff.[8] It is through this narrow band that Korik's mission races from the Sarangrave to Defiles Course. Beyond the hills, both north and south of the river, lie the Sarangrave Flat: "a wet land, latticed with waterways like exposed veins," and filled with treacherous quagmires.[9] In the millennia between the two Chronicles the Sarangrave grows, taking over some lands lost by the Giant Woods north and east.[10] As Defiles Course passes through the Flat, it develops side currents which intertwine with the waters of the wetland, with islands becoming more frequent—such as the one on which Shetra spots the Warhaft.[11]

East of the Sarangrave, Defiles Course becomes a network of fluctuating channels, until finally the stream waters are carried almost entirely as groundwater in the oozing mud of the Lifeswallower's delta.[12] For a mere five leagues the land north of the delta is dry as it rises to the Boundary Hills of Seareach.[13]

Seareach

The Boundary Hills run from the Northron Climbs east-southeast to the Sunbirth Sea. From them the rolling lands dip to the sea "down fields like terraces cut for Giants."[14] When the Giants are alive, the whole area seems a garden: "crops of all kinds, vineyards, whole forests of redwood and teak."[15] Even millennia after their demise the area grows rich and natural with a variety of woodlands, out of reach of the Sunbane.[16]

On a last rise overlooking the Sea stands the Lighthouse which guides the Giantships to berth.[17] Nowhere else are any structures mentioned in all the expanse of Seareach, however, for the Giants did not live in their fields, but in that fantastic cliff-cut city along the Sea: *Coercri*, The Grieve.[18]

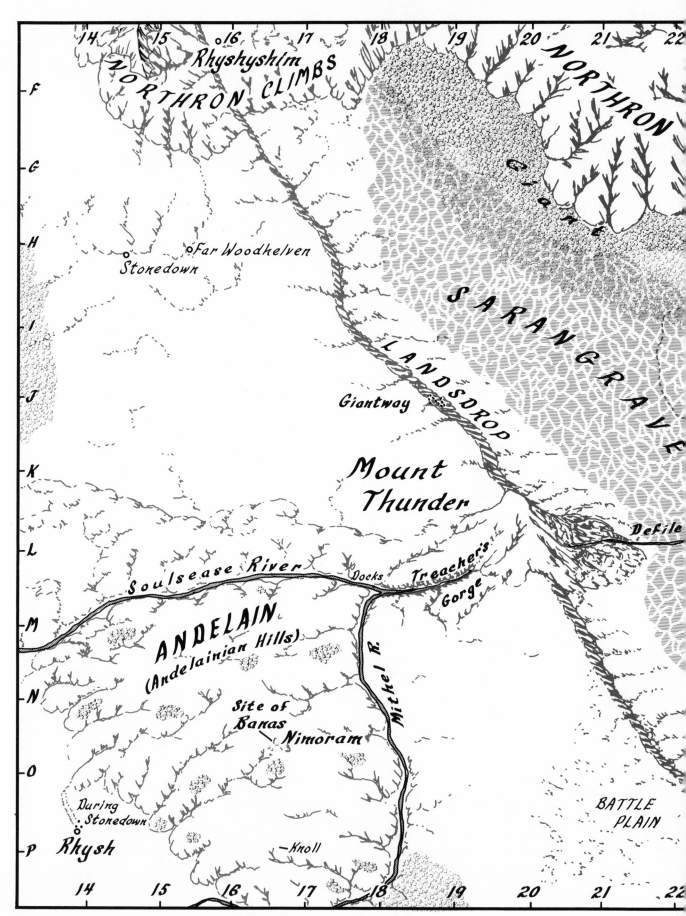

NORTHRON CLIMBS

Rhyshyshim

NORTHRON

SARANGRAVE

Giant

LANDSDROP

Far Woodhelven

Stonedown

Giantway

Mount
Thunder

Defile

Soulsease River

Docks

Treacher's
Gorge

ANDELAIN

(Andelainian Hills)

Mithel R.

Site of
Banas
Nimoram

BATTLE
PLAIN

During
Stonedown

Knoll

Rhysh

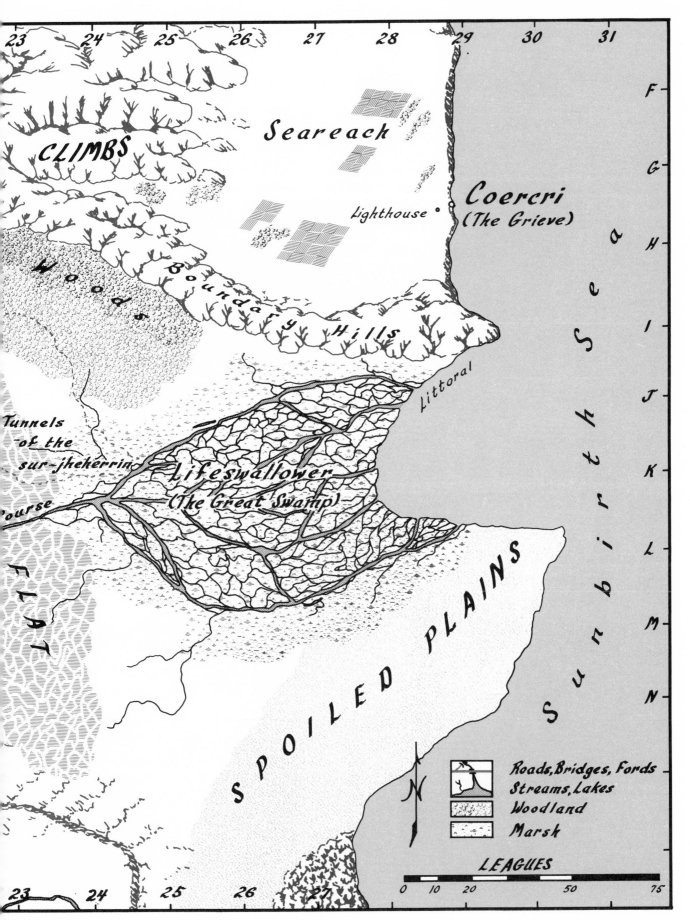

23　24　25　26　27　28　29　30　31

F

CLIMBS

Seareach

G

Coercri
(The Grieve)

Lighthouse °

H

Woods

Boundary

Hills

S u n b i r t h   S e a

I

Littoral

J

Tunnels
of the
sur-jheherrin

Lifeswallower
(The Great Swamp)

K

ourse

L

FLAT

M

SPOILED PLAINS

N

Roads, Bridges, Fords
Streams, Lakes
Woodland
Marsh

LEAGUES

0　10　20　　　50　　　75

23　24　25　26　27

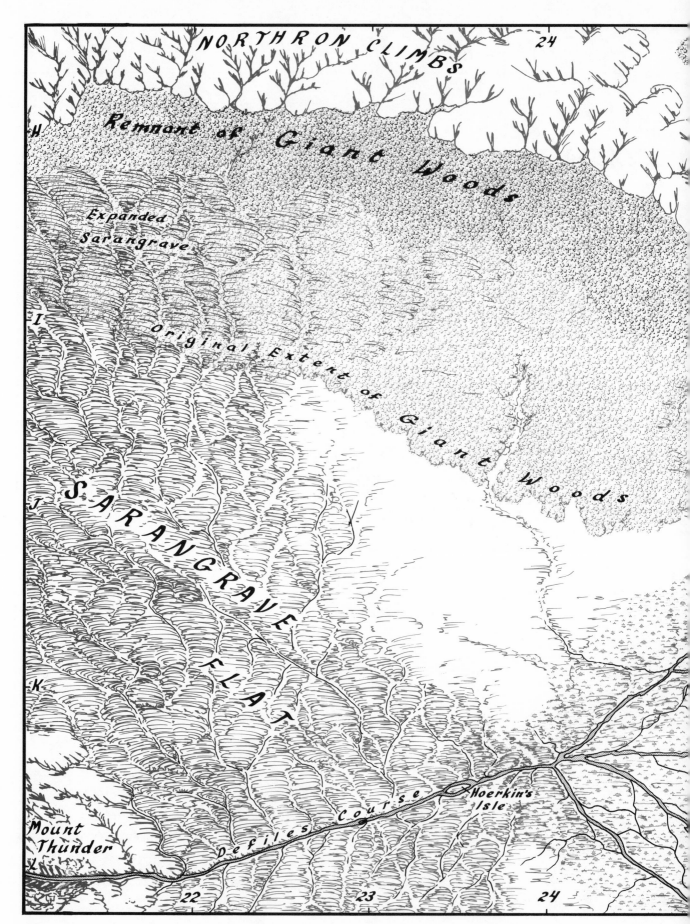

NORTHRON CLIMBS

24

Remnant of Giant Woods

Expanded
Sarangrave

Original Extent of Giant Woods

SARANGRAVE FLAT

Mount
Thunder

Defiles Course

Hoerkin's
Isle

22
23
24

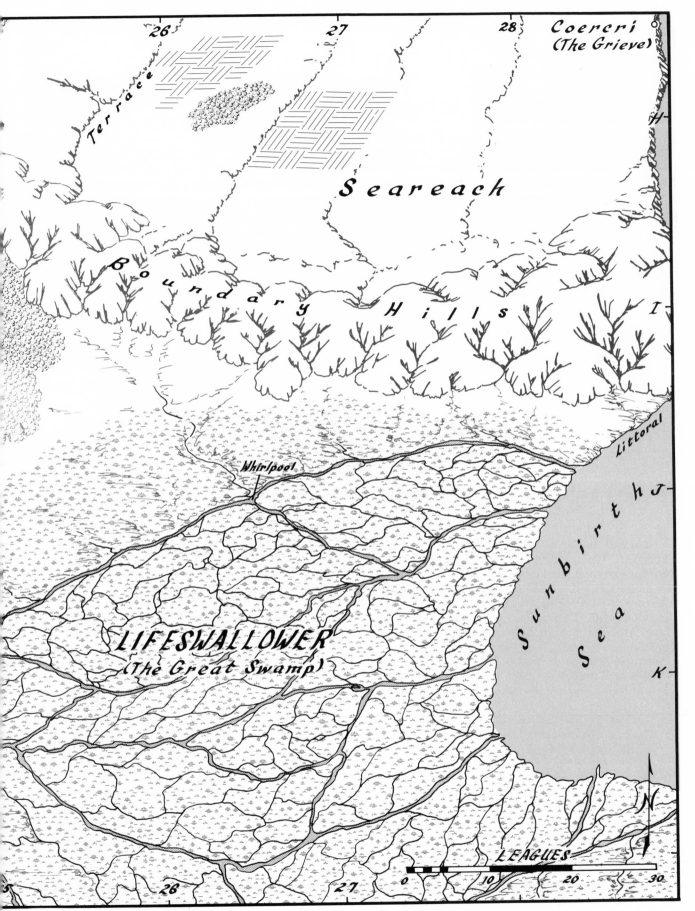

Coercri
(The Grieve)

Seareach

Boundary Hills

Whirlpool

LIFESWALLOWER
(The Great Swamp)

Littoral

Sunbirth Sea

LEAGUES

0   10   20   30

N

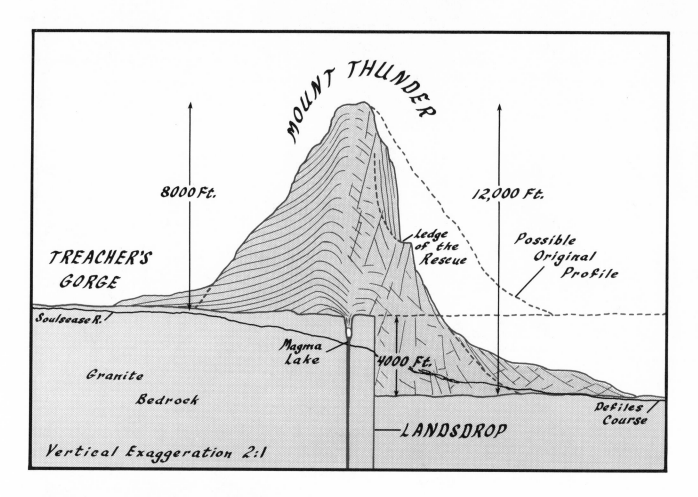

MOUNT THUNDER—EXTERIOR

East and slightly north of Andelain stands Gravin Threndor, Peak of the Fire-Lions: Mount Thunder.[1] For time beyond mind it has held in its bowels some of the worst evils—banes such as the Illearth Stone, warrens of the Cavewights, spawning grounds for the creations of the Demondim, and sometimes home to Lord Foul. Yet through the eons, Lord Kevin's power protects the Second Ward, and on the slopes Fire-Lions still respond to Prothall's summoning.[2]

Mount Thunder is an old peak. It existed even before Landsdrop as Lord Mhoram explains:

There is talk, unfounded even in the oldest legends, that the cleft of Landsdrop was caused by the sacrilege which buried immense banes under Mount Thunder's roots. In a cataclysm that shook its very heart, the Earth heaved with revulsion . . . And the force of that dismay broke the Upper Land from the Lower.[3]

The cliff of Landsdrop stands four thousand feet at Mount Thunder, elevating the peak of the mountain twelve thousand feet above Sarangrave Flat.[4] Thus, the height of the mountain above the Upper Land is eight thousand feet—high enough for snow, but not perpetually snowcapped.[5] The origin of the mountain is uncertain. Its isolation from the mountain ranges of the Land, and the presence of the rock-light lake within might indicate a volcanic origin. From a distance some of its cliffs appear "black as obsidian" although others are "gray as the ash of a granite fire."[6]

Treacher's Gorge is a granite channel, as is the tunnel immediately within the mountain,[7] but even that does not clarify the origin of the mountain. It is most likely that the ancient Soulsease River flowed in its current path before the mountain peak was ever formed. Possibly an upwelling of molten rock simply capped the river, building a peak over the preexisting channel. The sudden cataclysm which formed Landsdrop would have crumbled the eastern portion of the mountain, causing disruption of the river's course in that section, but the pent-up waters would have gradually cleared new paths among the rubble. The four thousand foot drop within the mountain would, over the millennia, account for a gradual deepening of the channels throughout the mountain, including west of the peak, in Treacher's Gorge.[8]

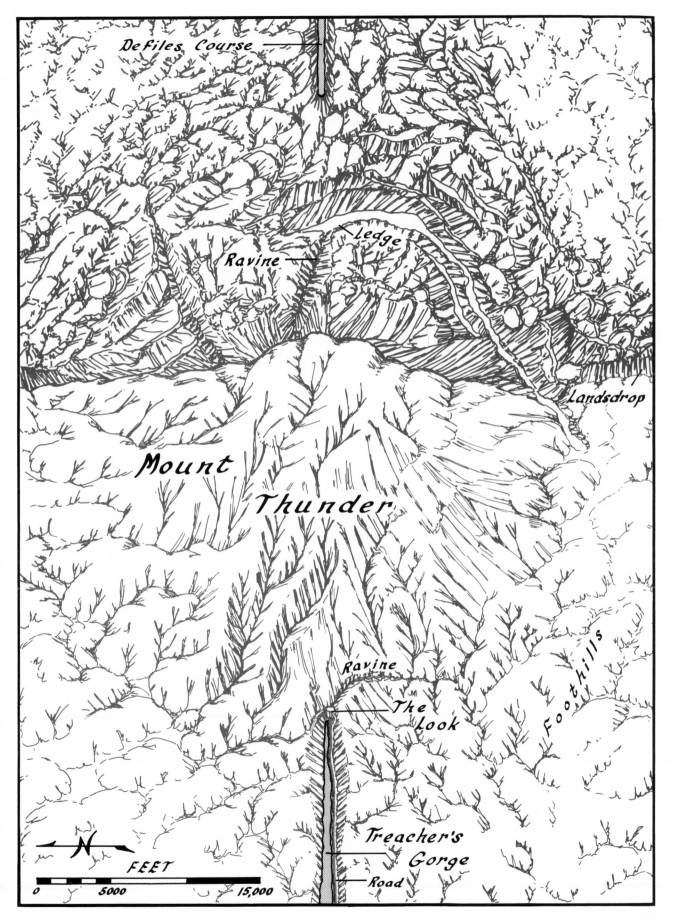

Defiles Course

Ledge

Ravine

Landsdrop

Mount

Thunder

Foothills

Ravine

The
Look

N

FEET

0   5000   15,000

Treacher's
Gorge

Road

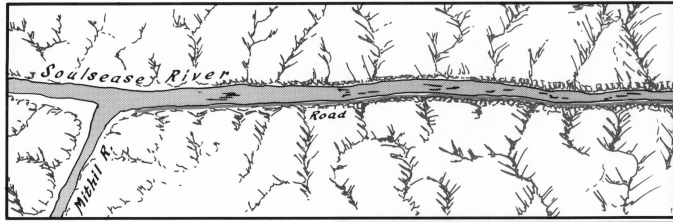

TREACHER'S GORGE

A league west of Mount Thunder the Soulsease River begins to narrow, and its turbulent waters surge through the canyon etched into the granite bedrock of the Upper Land: Treacher's Gorge.[1] The Soulsease is the mightiest river of the Land; its tributaries drain all the east slope of the Westron Mountains and the plains they border. The upper tributaries of the Soulsease drain the northern portion of the Upper Land, while the Black and Mithil Rivers gather all the waters of the south, joining the Soulsease just east of Andelain. Based on the total area of the drainage basin, the combined flow would almost be comparable to that of the Mississippi River, which averages 250,000 cubic feet per second.[2] To accommodate such volume, the river would have to alter from the broad, placid (yet strong) stream west of Andelain to a far deeper (yet still relatively wide) river roaring into the tunnel of Mount Thunder. There is little wonder Prothall's Quest finds the pathway treacherously wet and speech difficult—even one hundred feet above the water.[3]

Carved into the walls of Treacher's Gorge are two paths. The main path is a roadway on the south wall, only twenty feet above the crest of the river. It is along this road that armies march forth from the mountain.[4] During his return with Linden, Covenant also dares the open way, and walks along the road.[5]

The second path is the stairs giving access to the Look of Treacher's Gorge. The Look stands a hundred feet above the black maw through which the river enters the mountain. It was formed by Lord Foul prior to his first open treachery to High Lord Kevin.[6]

The stair is actually two irregularly cut sets of steps. A stair angles from the Look up the north wall of the gorge until it reaches the top of the cliff. The second stair descends along the south wall, spanning the eighty feet to the roadway below. Prothall's Quest reaches the Look by descending a ravine too narrow for horses which angles down from the south face of the mountain.[7]

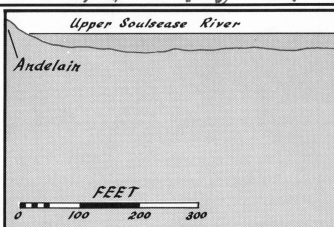

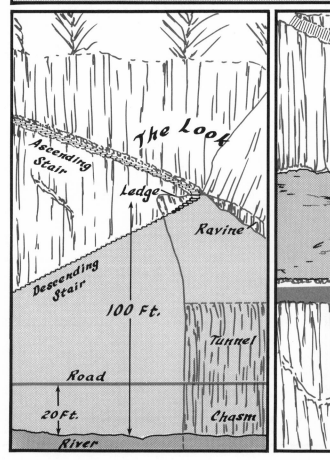

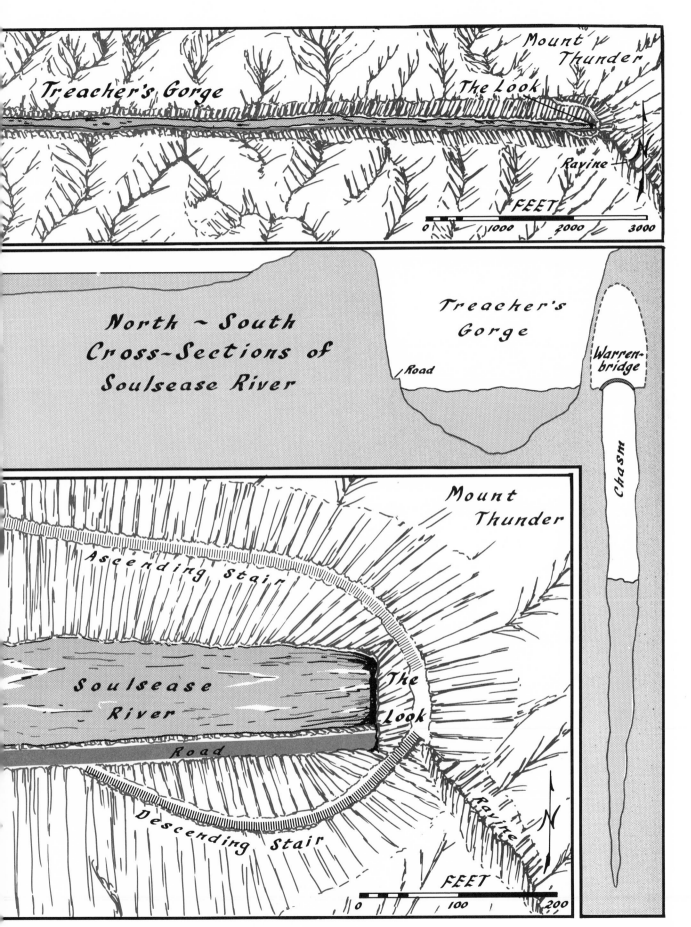

Treacher's Gorge

Mount Thunder

The Look

Ravine

FEET

0   1000   2000   3000

North ~ South
Cross-Sections of
Soulsease River

Treacher's Gorge

Road

Warren-
bridge

Chasm

Mount
Thunder

Ascending Stair

Soulsease
River

The
Look

Road

Ravine

Descending Stair

FEET

0   100   200

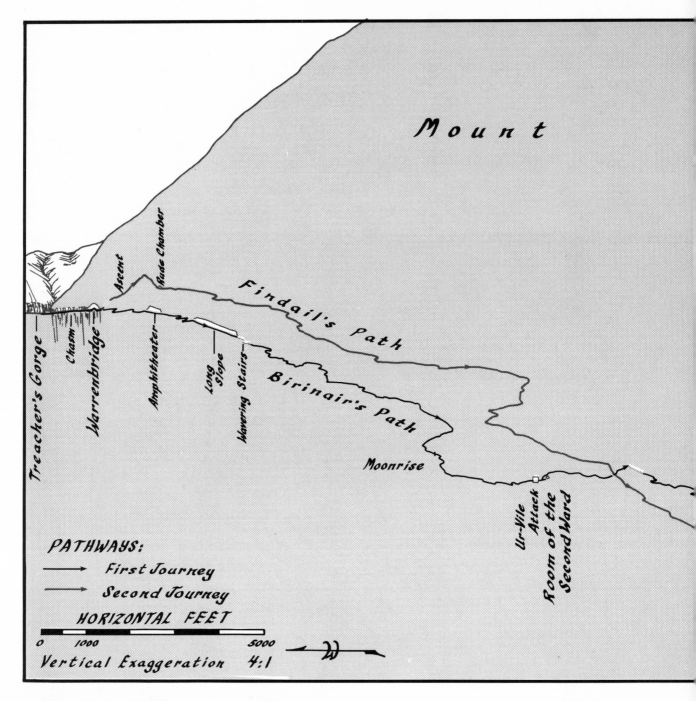

Mount

PATHWAYS:

→ First Journey

⟶ Second Journey

HORIZONTAL FEET

0   1000   5000

Vertical Exaggeration   4:1

Labels on map: Mount; Rude Chamber; Ascent; Findail's Path; Treacher's Gorge; Chasm; Warrenbridge; Amphitheater; Long Slope; Wavering Stairs; Birinair's Path; Moonrise; Ur-Vile Attack; Room of the Second Ward

MOUNT THUNDER—INTERIOR

The primary entrance to Mount Thunder is the roadway alongside the vast river-cut tunnel at the east end of Treacher's Gorge.[1]

The first major feature within the mountain is the domed cavern of Warrenbridge. Beyond the bridge a tunnel continues into the mountain.[2]

Both of Covenant's journeys initially lead to this point, but once within the tunnel Birinair and Findail choose different paths. As Birinair leads the Staff of Law Quest through the darkness Covenant senses in turn: an amphitheater; a low, narrow tunnel which requires a series of direction shifts; a long steep slope

zigzagging down to a wavering stair cut into the rock wall. Beyond lie more intricate paths "far from the main Wightwarrens."[3] There they find the Second Ward of Kevin's Lore.[4] Beyond, the company continues until they reach the rocklight cavern, with its pool of molten rock.[5]

Findail takes the first leftward way within the tunnel leaving the cavern of Warrenbridge. The passage leads to a "rude chamber,"[6] beyond which the abandoned tunnels descend at irregular intervals until they draw near the working heart of the Wightwarrens. There the tunnel ends abruptly at a noisome

98

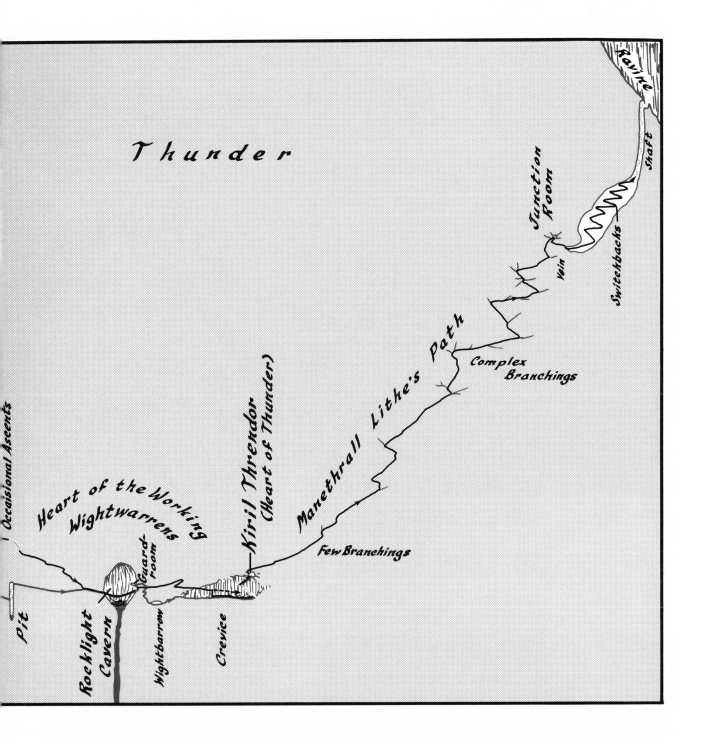

Thunder

Ravine

Junction Room

Shaft

Switchbacks

Vein

Complex Branchings

Manethrall Lithe's Path

Kiril Threndor (Heart of Thunder)

Heart of the Working

Wightwarrens

Occaisional Ascents

Guard-room

Few Branchings

Pit

Rocklight Cavern

Wightbarrow

Crevice

pit. From its top, Findail follows "a warren of corridors" to the rocklight cavern.[7]

Beyond the cavern, the paths taken by the travelers diverge once again. The left branch of a Y intersection leads to the guardroom where Linden and Covenant are captured.[8] From the guardroom two additional tunnels exit, one leading the prisoners to yet another cave: the cave of the Wightbarrow.[9] Beyond the Wightbarrow cave still another tunnel passes through a complex of passages until it reaches an opening at the base of a vast crevice.[10] The same crevice can be reached directly from the Y intersec-

tion near the rocklight cavern.

From the base of the crevice steps ascend the north wall to a tunnel leading directly inward to Kiril Threndor.[11]

The path beyond Kiril Threndor follows mazing paths which tend generally upward. After nearly a league the catacombs become more intricate, until they reach a room of many junctions.[12]

From there the Manethrall almost doubles back on the previous pathway. The new tunnel climbs a broad slope and ascends a chimney to the east face of the mountain.[13]

Warrenbridge

The roadway from Mount Thunder's entrance follows the river's chasm until a massive boulder covers the upper reaches of the chasm, forcing the road around the stone's outer edge. As the road turns around the face of the rock, the cavern of Warrenbridge—an immense, flat-floored chamber—becomes visible beyond. After passing around and under the far edge of the boulder, turning at right angles to its previous course, the river's chasm cuts directly across the cavern floor into the wall on the far side.[1]

At this point the river has narrowed to the confines of a fifty foot wide rift, yet flows deep in the chasm, continuing the descent it began immediately within the mountain's entrance. Across this fathomless depth the massive arched stone bridge gives the only access to the Wightwarrens' tunnels beyond.[2]

Warrenbridge provides an easy defense against intruders, evidenced by the unsuspecting Drool Rockworm posting only two sentries, trusting his lore to protect the Wightwarrens. Rocklight pillars "on either side of the bridge crest" anchor an invisible Word of Warning at the center of the bridge's arch.[3] Once aware of the Word, Prothall and Mhoram are able to move it enough to allow the company's passage over the bridge and into the tunnel beyond.[4]

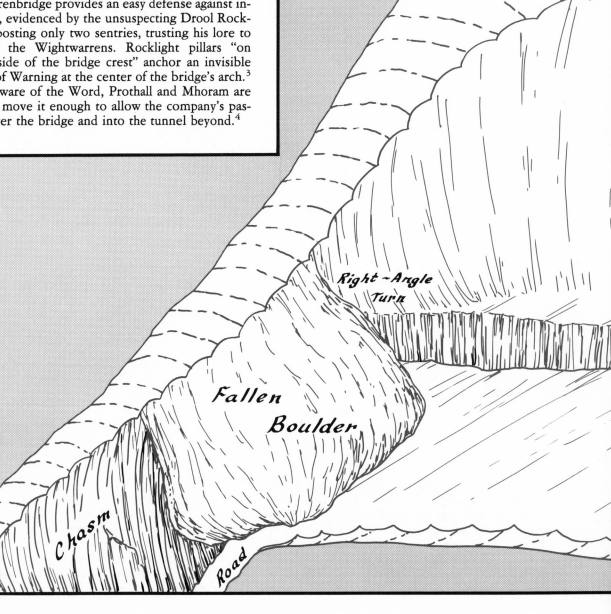

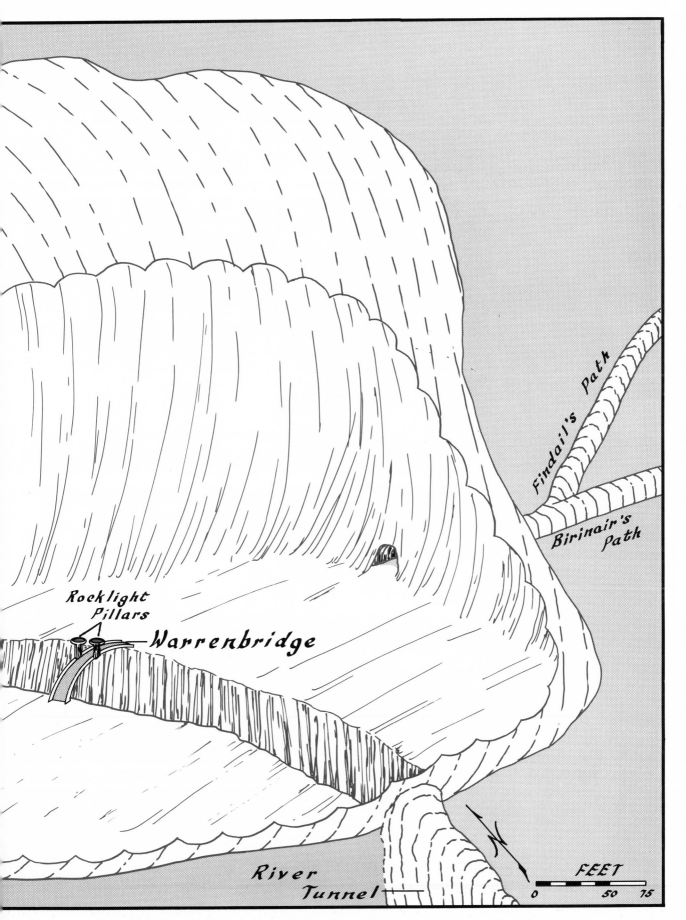

Findail's Path

Birinair's Path

Rocklight
Pillars

Warrenbridge

River
Tunnel

FEET

0   50   75

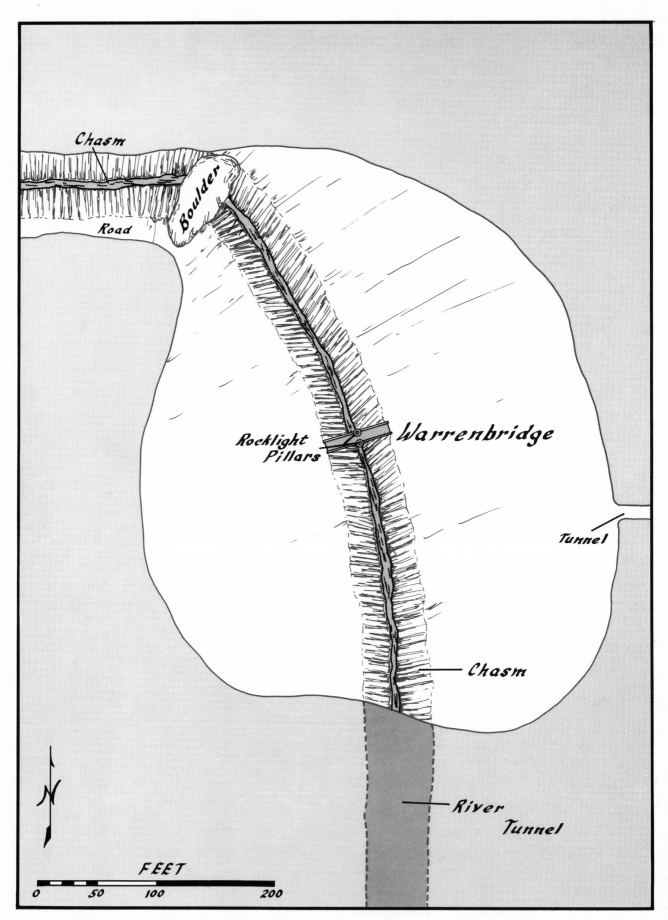

Chasm

Road

Boulder

Rocklight
Pillars

Warrenbridge

Tunnel

Chasm

N

River
Tunnel

FEET

0   50   100   200

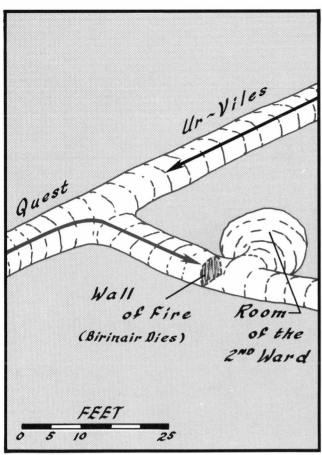

Room of the Second Ward

Far from the main Wightwarrens the Quest for the Staff of Law follows Birinair into a low tunnel to the right. Suddenly he is immolated in a wall of fire placed by High Lord Kevin to protect a chamber.[1]

Once the power barrier is destroyed, Lord Mhoram explores beyond, and locates the small chamber containing the Second Ward of High Lord kevin's Lore.[2]

The Pit

During Covenant's second journey through Mount Thunder, Findail's path leads to the heart of the Wightwarrens via a tunnel which ends at a deep charnal pit. The end of the wrought tunnel actually narrows into a rough crevice. The crevice intersects the pit in its midsection—higher than the fetid pit bottom, but so far below the top of the pit that a long spiraling stair ascends to the upper rim, stretching "beyond comprehension."[1]

The steps end at the top of the pit, opening into a more traveled tunnel. Rocklight reflects on its walls, even though "a warren of corridors" lie between it and the source of the light—the rocklight cavern.[2]

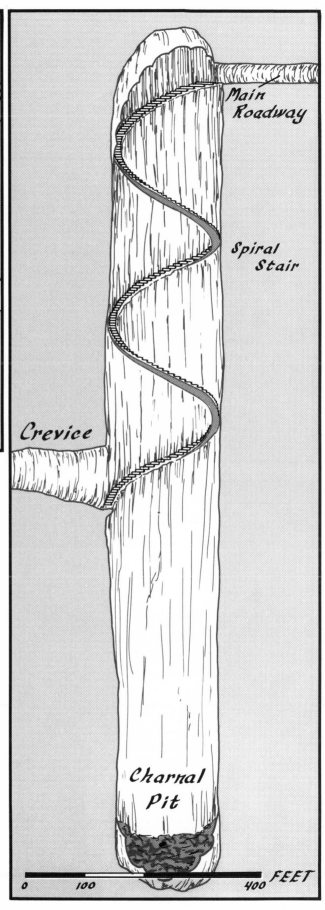

The Rocklight Cavern

Near the center of Mount Thunder is a magma lake. It is the incinerator for the Wightwarrens and, as the working heart of the warrens, is most concentrated near this natural furnace for easy access. Both Prothall (after Birinair's death) and Findail lead their respective companies to this chamber with great care.[1]

In spite of its importance the cavern has no direct inlets other than the tunnel (as large as a road) passing from the west, along a ledge on the right (south) wall, and out the east.[2] The ledge is so wide that the Cavewights attacking the second company cannot be contained by the First and Pitchwife.[3]

From the roadway edge the magma lies "far below," although spouts of lava constantly erupt from the boiling lake.[4] The cauldron's roar can be heard and its light seen long before reaching the actual cavern.[5] The size of the cavern is far more impressive in its vertical rather than horizontal scale. It is a capped magma pipe, so its diameter is probably only slightly wider in the open chamber than throughout the length of the immeasurably deep fissure extending from the depths of the earth.

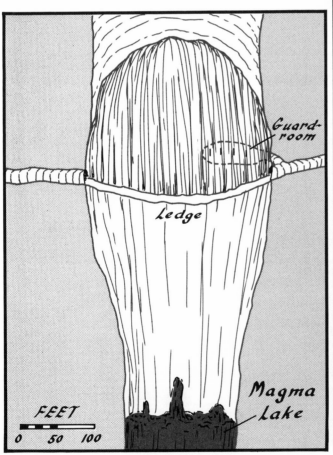

Guard-room

Ledge

FEET

0   50   100

Magma Lake

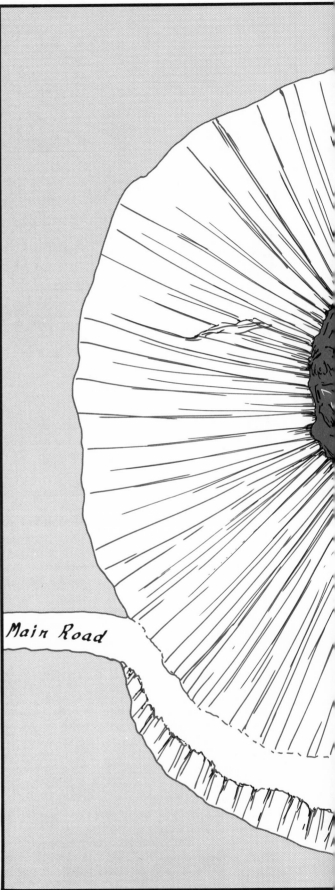

Main Road

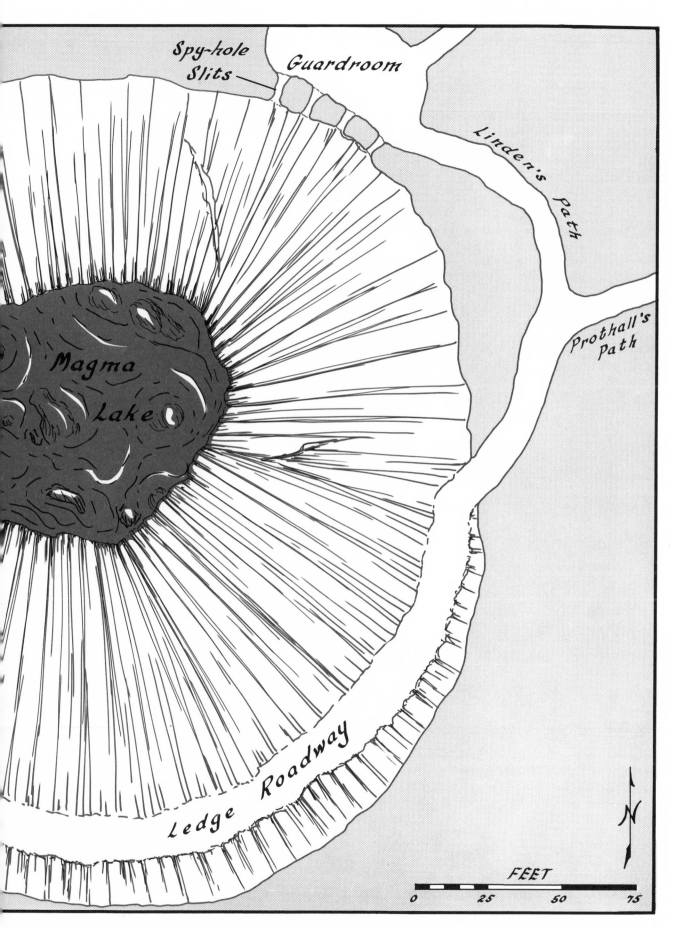

Spy-hole
Slits

Guardroom

Linden's Path

Prothall's Path

Magma Lake

Ledge Roadway

N

FEET

0   25   50   75

105

The Guardroom and the Wightbarrow

Immediately beyond the exit from the rocklight cavern the tunnel forks. The right fork continues into mazing passages, but the left tunnel leads directly into a hollow room behind the wall of the rocklight cavern. Slits along one side look out over the abyss of the cavern to the road ledge on the far wall. Unseen guards may observe any movement through the cavern. In addition to the tunnel leading from the fork, the guardroom has two other entrances, giving easy access to Cavewight troops.[1]

The Cavewights take Covenant by unknown passages to what must be a reasonably close cave. The cave is "crudely oval in shape," narrowing at both ends to tunnels.[2] In its center is an immense mound of Cavewight skeletons—the Wightbarrow.[3] At one side of the barrow a slight depression connects to a narrow trough leading under the mound—the intended catch basin to feed Covenant's blood to the mound.[4]

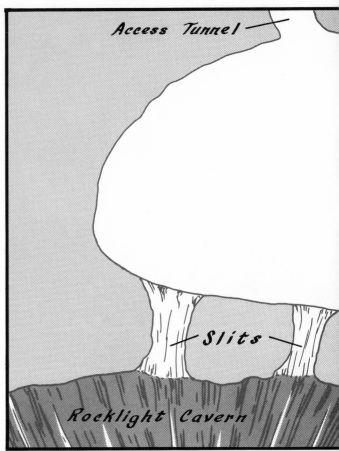

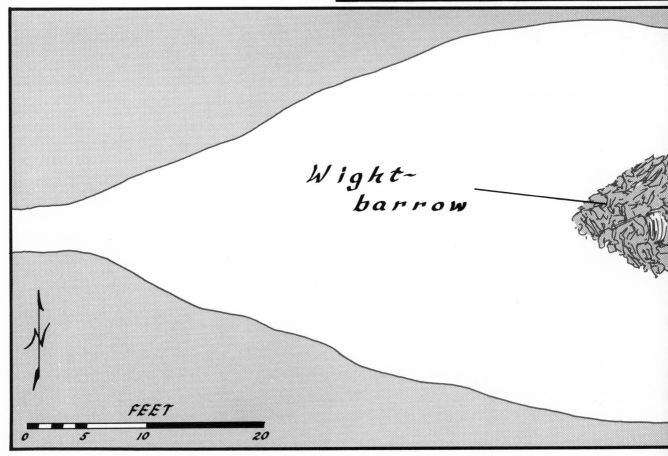

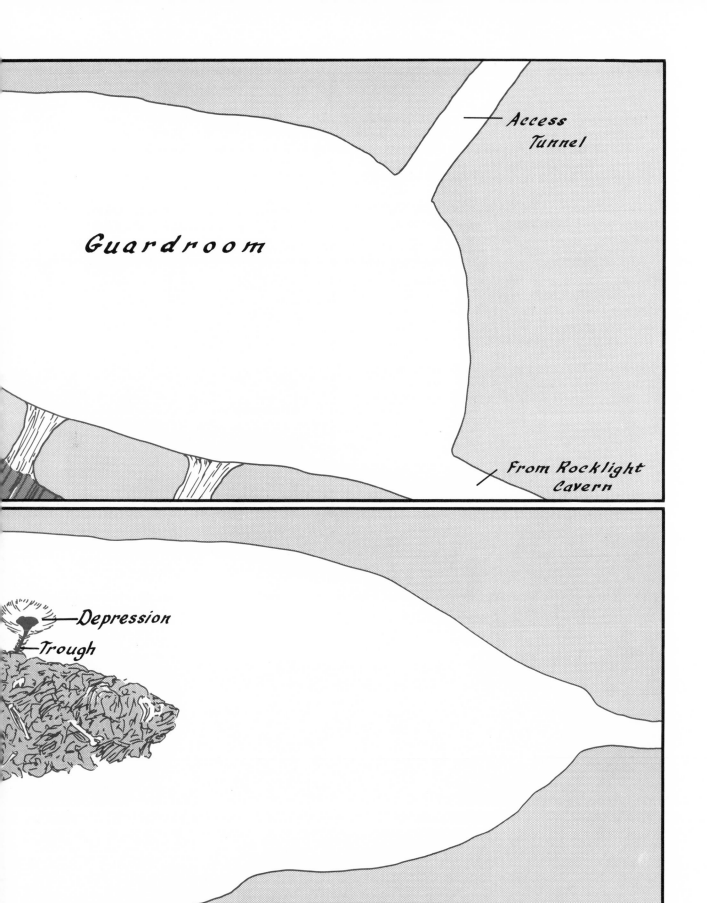

The Crevice

Beyond a maze of tunnels, both the path from the Wightbarrow and that from the right fork of the passage outside the rocklight cavern reach the same feature—a fault which has produced a deep narrow crevice. The two paths do not enter the crevice at the same location, however.

Prothall's path carries the company along a ledge with a steep vertical drop on their left (south face of the crevice).[1] Where the ledge eventually leads is not clear, for a lone ur-vile, hiding in a fissure next to the path attacks Covenant, and both fall into the crevice.[2] Covenant finds himself saved by the shattered rock scree in the floor of the crevice.[3]

When Linden leads Covenant to the same location, she arrives at the base of the crevice, rather than the upper ledge. The debris is too difficult to climb in the center, so they work along the left wall next to the cliff.[4] In the same wall is a rude stairway passing beyond sight—crudely hewn, but wide. Several hundred feet above the floor of the crevice is a tunnel entrance, leading directly into the cliffwall until it reaches Kiril Threndor.[5]

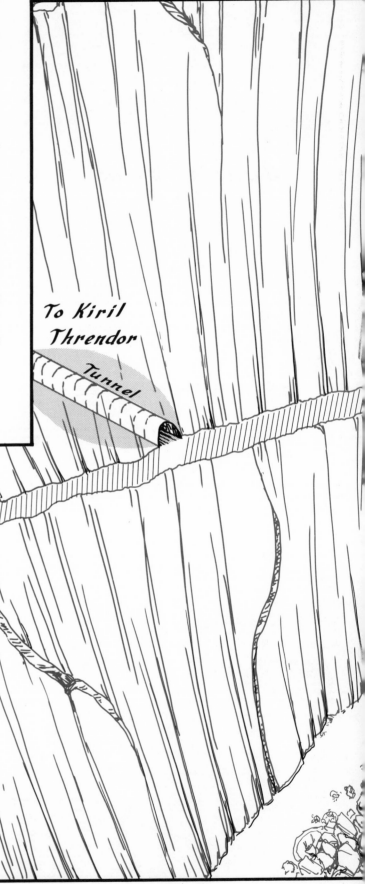

To Kiril Threndor

Tunnel

APPROXIMATE FEET

0   50   100

Stair

Rock-Strewn
Chasm Floor

Ledge

Fissure

Kiril Threndor

In the center of the mountain is a cavern—Kiril Threndor, the Heart of Thunder[1]—the thronehall for the ruler of the mountain domain: Drool Rockworm, during the first Quest, and Lord Foul, during the second.[2]

The cavern is high and domed, and from its ceiling hang a cluster of stalactites, which, like the faceted walls, are glowing with rocklight. The floor is smoothed from millennia of wear. A low dais, twisted and tortured from the proximity of Lord Foul and of banes such as the Illearth Stone, is the only addition.[3]

Several entrances surround the cavern, with tunnels radiating beyond, enabling the ruler to be supplied with a host of defenders in moments.[4] But access routes can also become escape routes. Once the Staff of Law has been recovered, the Lords seal one of the tunnels with a Forbidding, and follow Manethrall Lithe as she directs the first Quest out and away from Kiril Threndor.[5]

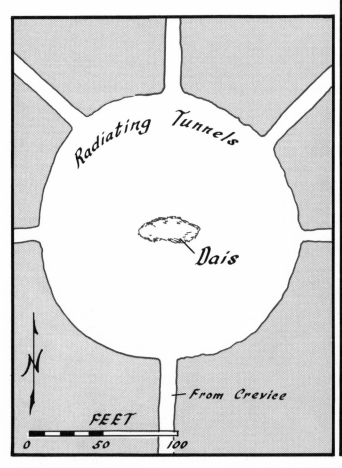

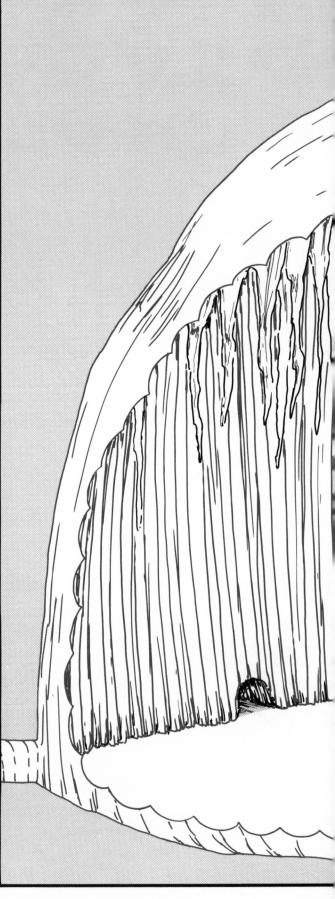

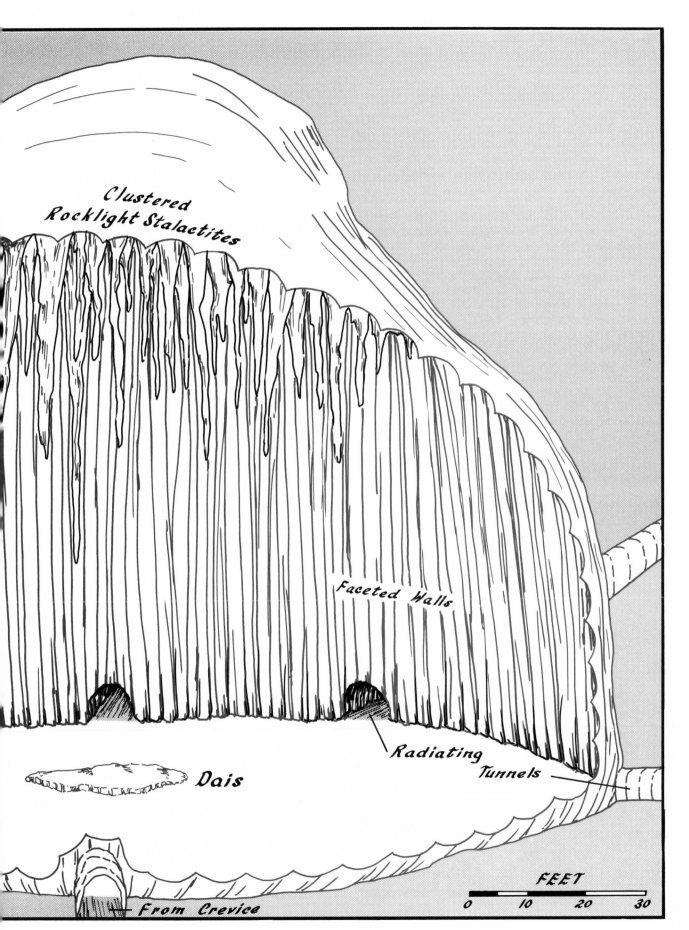

Clustered
Rocklight Stalactites

Faceted Walls

Radiating

Dais

Tunnels

From Crevice

FEET

0   10   20   30

The Manethrall's Path

As Manethrall Lithe follows her sure instinct through mazing passages which continuously ascend toward the east face of the mountain, there are two distinct locations worthy of note. After traveling a league through the twisted tunnels, the company arrives at a major junction room—a round chamber surrounded by entrances to tunnels radiating in all directions. Directly opposite from the tunnel from which the company entered the chamber is a matching tunnel, which continues the ascent. Next to the tunnel from which they entered is another which plunges back, and, instead of ascending, it descends slowly.[1]

Trusting her instincts, they take the latter passage. For some distance it continues as a wavering tunnel, but eventually it opens into "a vast impression of blank space" with such a steeply sloping floor that it must be climbed in a series of switchbacks.

At the top, the chasm narrows suddenly into a vertical chimney. A spiral stair ascends the chimney, with such narrow, rude steps that the company must climb single file.[2] As the shaft ascends, it continues to narrow. Finally, the top of the shaft reaches the outer edge of the mountain, opening partway down a ravine on the eastern face.[3]

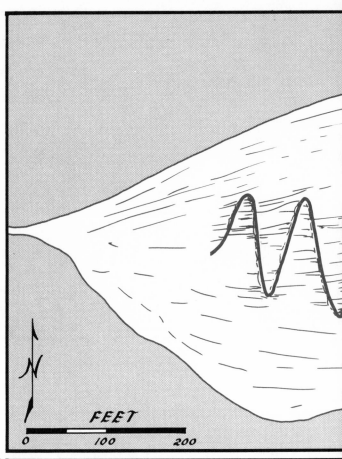

FEET

0   100   200

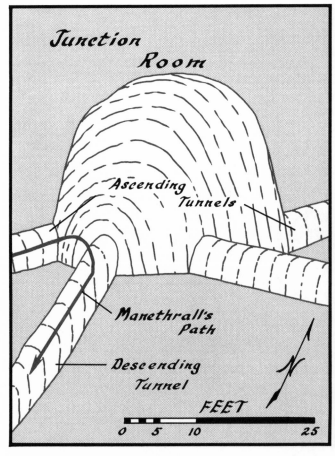

Junction Room

Ascending Tunnels

Manethrall's Path

Descending Tunnel

N

FEET

0   5   10   25

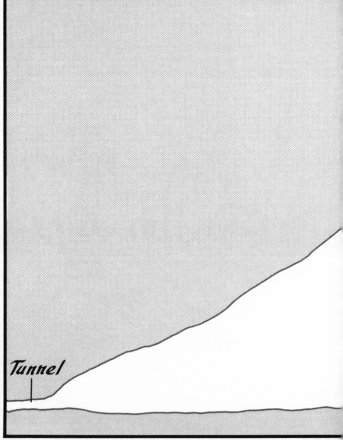

Tunnel

112

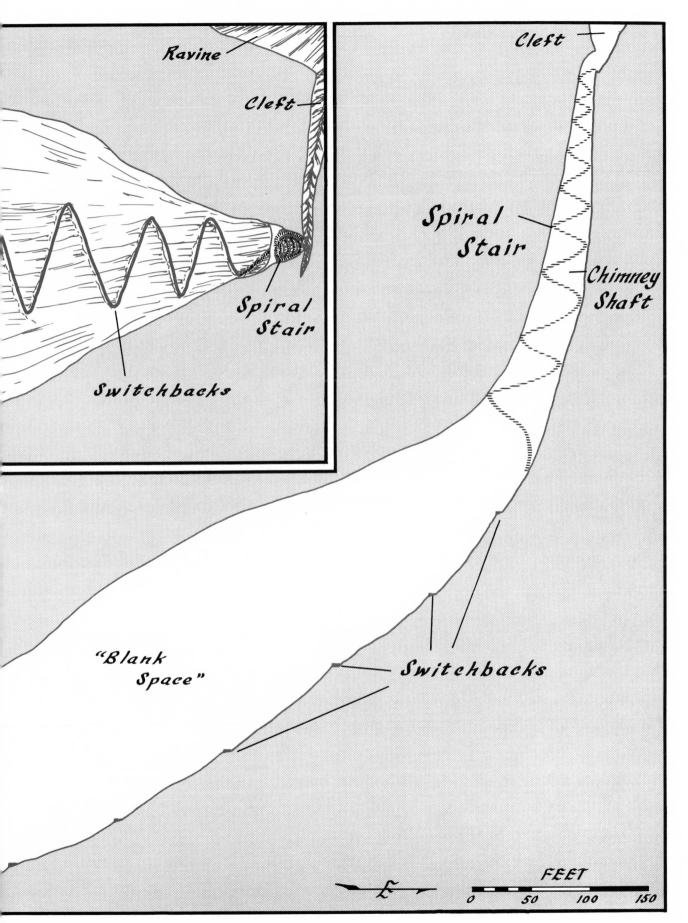

Ravine

Cleft

Cleft

Spiral
Stair

Switchbacks

Spiral
Stair

Chimney
Shaft

"Blank
Space"

Switchbacks

FEET

0   50   100   150

113

The Ravine of the Fire-Lions

On the eastern half of Mount Thunder are massive faults resulting from the mountain's collapse when Landsdrop was formed. It is near one such fault that the company finds itself after leaving the windblown shaft with its spiral stair. A lateral crevice of the fault contains the exit from the shaft. The crevice descends quickly to the base of the fault: a boulder-strewn ravine. Cutting like a knife-sharp fissure, the ravine descends to a cliff a half league below.[1]

Slightly over halfway down the ravine Mhoram selects a broad flat boulder which stands above the surrounding rubble, in hopes it will provide a base from which to defend against Drool's pursuing troops.[2] Drawing power from Covenant's ring and the Staff of Law, Prothall summons the Fire-Lions of Mount Thunder.[3] Racing from the Fire-Lions themselves, the company completes the descent of the ravine, yet they are still endangered.

The cliff at the foot of the ravine is probably a transverse fault. Its top forms a ledge a half league wide which curves south away from the ravine. The eastern face plunges sheerly down two thousand feet until it reaches still more of the jumbled mountain terrain.[4] The ledge is attainable by the Ranyhyn, and the company is saved.[5]

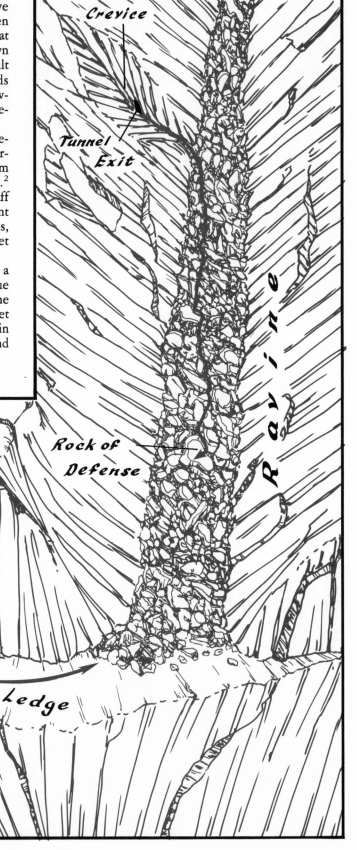

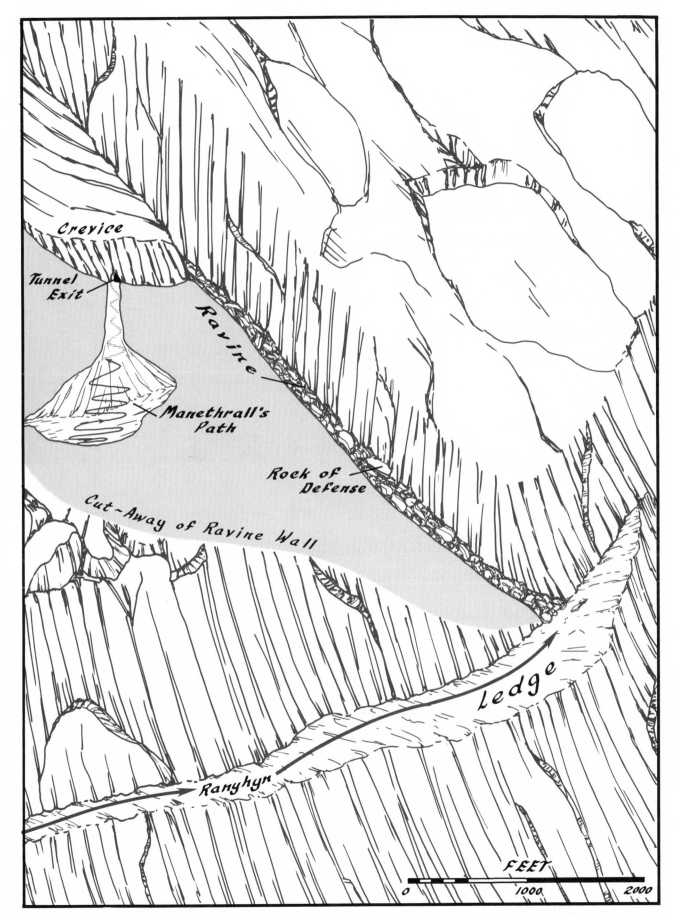

Crevice

Tunnel
Exit

Ravine

Manethrall's
Path

Rock of
Defense

Cut-Away of Ravine Wall

Ledge

Ranyhyn

FEET

0   1000   2000

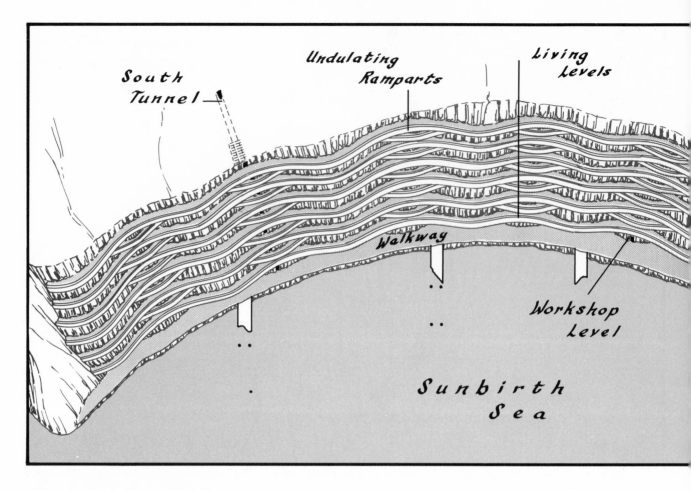

COERCRI—THE GRIEVE

On the most eastern coast of the Land, facing outward across the Sunbirth Sea, is the age old city of the Giants: *Coercri*, the Grieve.

Coercri is delved in a cliff face a thousand feet high, which rises almost vertically above the sea. The city is formed in a series of levels, each with its own rampartlike balcony undulating along the face of the cliff, alternating between levels. While one recesses into the cliff, the ramparts above and below jut out, giving the cliff face a knuckled appearance.[1]

The cliff projects out into the sea in a headland at the very heart of the city. Another promontory juts eastward at the south end of the city. Between the two projections the south half of the cliff face arcs. Beyond the central headland the northern half of the city is hidden from view, probably due to a similar configuration.[2]

There are three tunnel entrances to The Grieve from the upland terraces of Seareach which descend slowly to the upper ramparts. The main entrance is at the central headland, while the south tunnel descends near the southern promontory.[3]

Within the central promontory is a stairwell, with the flights alternately cutting seaward, then landward

within the cliff.[4] The tip of the promontory holds only the stairwell, but immediately on each side are apartments, kitchens, meeting halls (some large enough for five hundred Giants)—all the accoutrements of a city large enough for the thousand Giants who had originally lived there.[5]

The lowest levels are the workshops, each with a stone door, protecting it from the brine of the sea.[6] Several piers—large enough for the massive Giantships—originally lined the seawall along the cliff, but when Covenant comes to *Coercri*, millennia after the mass murder performed by Kinslaughterer, the only piers which have survived are the two at the very heart of the city.[7] They project just south of the central promontory, so that from the wide stone shelf at their head, the northern half of the city cannot be seen.[8] The piers are far enough apart to admit a Giantship, and long enough for the full length of one ship and half of another.[9] A small room which opens near the south end of the heardrock may have functioned as a harbormaster's quarters, for it is the only living area mentioned at the lowest level. It contains a single bed—and the remains of the last Giant murdered in The Grieve.[10]

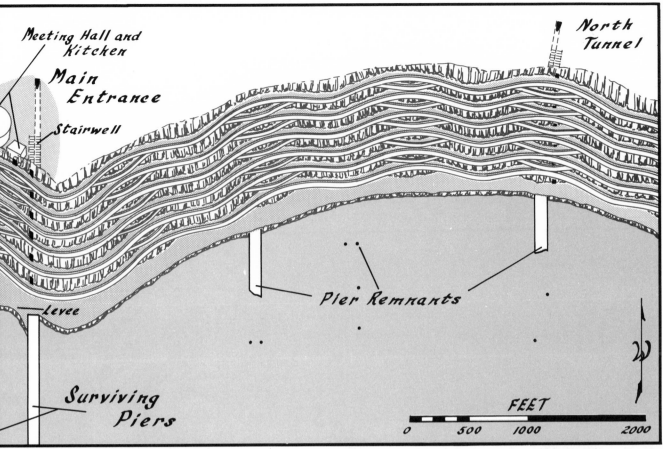

Meeting Hall and Kitchen

Main Entrance

Stairwell

North Tunnel

Pier Remnants

Levee

Surviving Piers

FEET

0   500   1000   2000

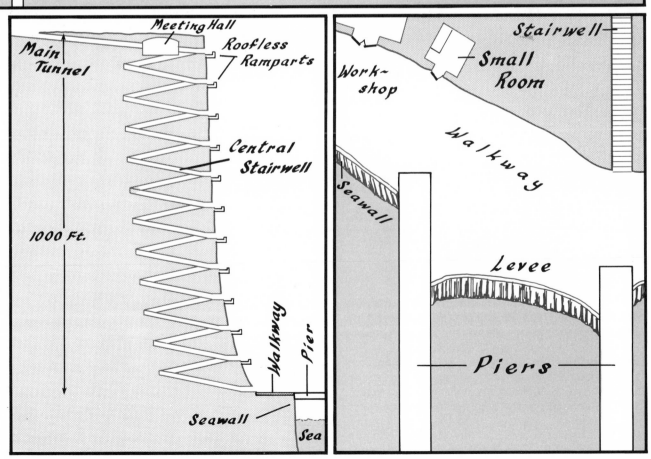

Main Tunnel

Meeting Hall

Roofless Ramparts

Central Stairwell

1000 Ft.

Walkway

Pier

Seawall

Sea

Stairwell

Small Room

Work-shop

Seawall

Walkway

Levee

Piers

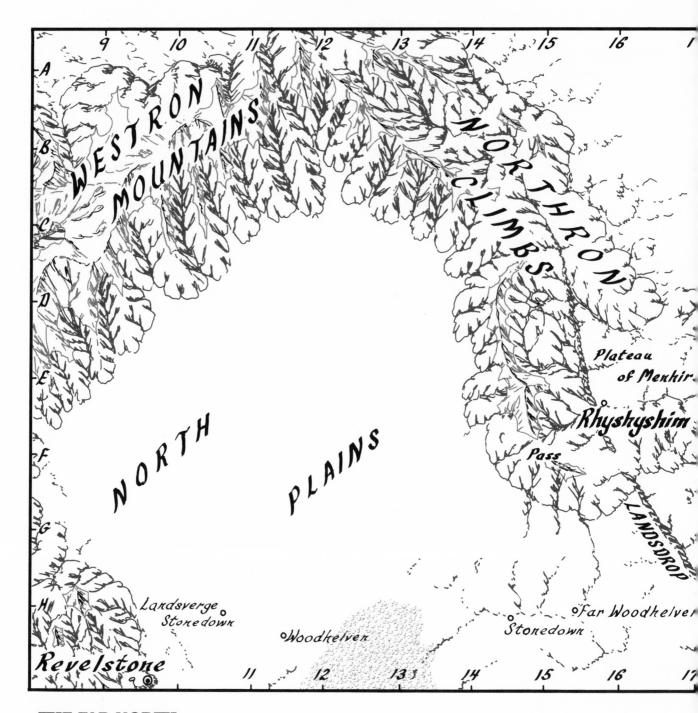

THE FAR NORTH

Upon the return to the Land after the voyage to the Isle of the One Tree, *Starfare's Gem* must be abandoned, locked in a sea of ice. The First judges them to be "four- or five-score leagues" (240 to 300 miles) north and east of Seareach, and "eighteenscore leagues from Revelstone."[1] Striking out across the frozen plain of Soulbiter, the company travels leagues upon leagues before reaching the freeflowing water along the shore.

The distances traveled by the company and the leagues remaining to Revelstone after Soulbiter is

crossed can be used to estimate the width of the Land north of Seareach. Along the coast is "an uneven line of hills," and beyond, "a long, low plain."[2] While the company journeys across the frozen plain, the Giants travel so quickly that Covenant mentally compares them with the Ranyhyn. As they reach the western end of the plain, mountains are visible both east and south of them, while foothills lie in their path. "This range was not especially tall or harsh. Its peaks were old . . ." and after ascending three thousand feet "they found themselves in a region that resembled

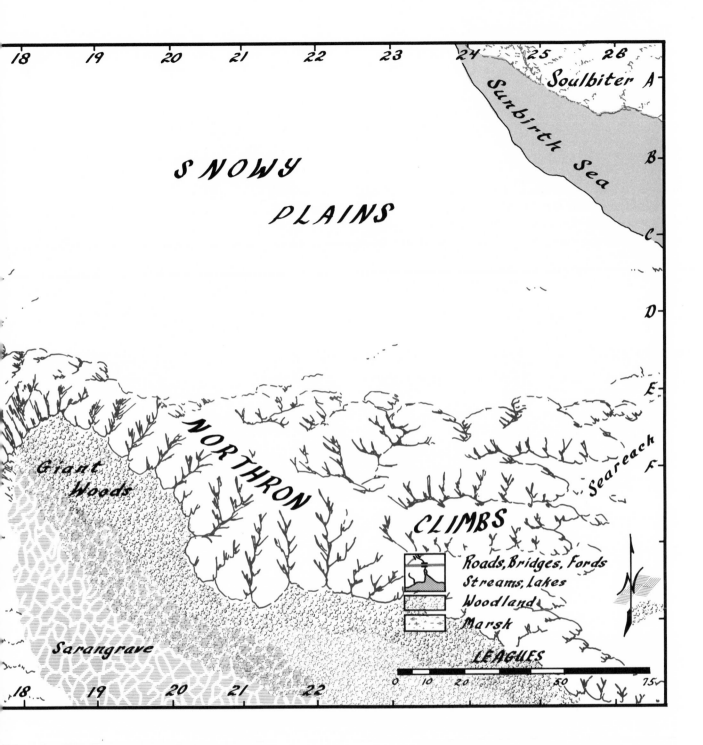

rolling hills rather than true mountains."[3]

Covenant surmises that this must be part of the Northron Climbs[4]—any of the rugged areas north of the inhabited Land. Though the Climbs are "mapless" they are certainly not pathless.[5] The plateaulike area is edged to the south with higher hills, and on the west by mountains, but it is relatively flat. Beyond the region of "jumbled monoliths" where the company battles the *arghuleh*, a plain extends half a league to the escarpment which contains the cave of the *rhyshyshim*.[6]

Just a short journey beyond the escarpment stands Landsdrop. Here it is a ragged cliff, standing a mere two hundred feet above the plateau[7]; but less than a league south "the precipice had collapsed, sending a wide scallop of earth down fanlike across its base."[8] West of Landsdrop the Climbs stand as a high ridge "tall and arduous as the Westron Mountains."[9] Among the jagged, snowcapped peaks, the Giants locate a pass, beyond which lies a long valley reaching into the foothills and beyond to the high North Plains.[10]

THE
SOUTHEAST

The southeast is the home of two major groups: the Ramen and Foul's creatures. In the hills just south of Andelain also stands Soaring Woodhelven, the tree village of Lord Prothall's time. Traditionally it has been more closely associated with the southwest than the southeast, but its eventual doom and the tale of its sole survivors links it forever with the Ramen and Lord Foul.

The Central Hills and Morinmoss

It is to Soaring Woodhelven that Atiaran leads Covenant on his first journey through the Land, and it is to there that he returns with the Lords, only to learn of its destruction. The hills south of the village reach to Kevin's Watch, and he passes through their heart on his first journey, and crosses them much farther south forty-seven years later with Foamfollower and Lena. The hills are noteworthy only because of their physical presence—neither unusually low or high, smooth or rugged. They act as a divide between the watershed of the Mithil River which eventually reaches the sea at Lifeswallower, and the Roamsedge, which empties south of the Shattered Hills.

Between the closest approach of the two rivers is Morinmoss—another remnant of the One Forest, but "wilder than Grimmerdhore."[1]

At the point where the Mithil turns north, the hills are slightly higher, and their southeastern slopes drop to the Roamsedge River through the width of the Morinmoss.[2] In a small cave near the heart of the forest lives the Unfettered Healer who saves Covenant at the cost of her own life.[3] Stumbling downhill from the cave Covenant comes upon a familiar site: Roamsedge Ford, the gateway to the Plains of Ra.

The Plains of Ra and the Southron Range

During the times of the Lords, the Plains of Ra are home for the great Ranyhyn and their nomadic tenders, the Ramen. The Plains, which extend for fifty leagues[4] southwest to northeast are so rolling in many parts that they are described as the "swift hills of Ra . . . short low slopes . . . shallow valleys . . . copses and small woods beside thin streams . . . broad flats."[5]

Other than when called by their chosen riders, the Ranyhyn usually remain on the Plains except during times of great emergency: the death of *Kelenbhrabanal*, the Ritual of Desecration, Foul's uprising during the First Chronicles, and the Sunbane.[6] Once a generation the Ranyhyn journey into the Southron Range (as Elena is privileged to see) for the horserite of *Kelenbhrabanal*. The rite is held in "a high valley, a grassy glen folded between sheer cliffs, with a rugged, spring-fed tarn near its center"—somewhere

south of Mithil Stonedown.[7] The range east of the peaks near Mithil Stonedown is not as high, but "rugged and raw as if high pinnacles had been shattered."[8]

Only at Manhome do the Ramen approach having a "normal" city. Manhome lies in the southeast; the dwellings are the hooped tents typical of the Ramen.[9] Elsewhere at several hidden locations throughout the Plains are Ramen coverts: "places of refuge where Manethralls tend injured Ranyhyn, and train Cords.[10] Only one is described in detail. It lies in a deep, overhung ravine in the hills immediately southwest of Roamsedge Ford. By the end of the First Chronicles Manhome is abandoned, and all the coverts have been treacherously revealed to the servants of Lord Foul; so with Covenant's release, the Ranyhyn flee their homeland into the mountains.[11]

The Lower Land

Where the Landrider tumbles over Landsdrop, the great escarpment runs almost due north-south and stands about two thousand feet above the lower Land. Its face is broken into a series of lesser faults giving it a tumbled appearance.[12] Back from the cliff somewhat, but near the fall of the Landrider River stands the Colossus.

Three to four leagues beyond the base of Landsdrop the Landrider begins to run through wastes, and becomes the Ruinwash.[13] The river has shrunk, leaving mud flats along its banks. From the Sarangrave, past the Ruinwash, and on to the Sunbirth Sea, once fertile plains have become eroded deadlands through millennia of misuse. Mass wasting has produced whole systems of gullies, with intervening ridges. Between two particularly steep north-south running ridges is a forest of thornbushes, interspersed with deep mud pits.[14]

Within the Spoiled Plains lie Kurash Qwellinir— the Shattered Hills. Bannor's recitation reveals that the origin of the Hills is uncertain: "Some say that these Hills were formed by the breaking of a mountain—others, that they were shaped from the slag and refuse of Corruption's war caverns, furnaces, breeding dens. However they were made, they are a maze."[15] The passages from Foul's Creche extend west under and beyond Hotash Slay, and his armies enter and exit from hidden places among the Hills;[16] so the possibility that the Hills are refuse from the massive excavation is not unfounded. Another possibility is that they are (at least in part) old lava flows—twisted and cooled and cracked—from upwellings of the source of Hotash Slay.[17] Thanks to the tunnels of the *jheherrin* Covenant and Foamfollower are spared all but a fraction of this rugged maze, so little is revealed of its nature. All that lies east of the Hills is the promontory of Foul's Creche, with its lava moat.

12   13   14   15   16   17   18   19   20

During
Stonedown

ANDELAIN
(Andelainian Hills)

P   Rhysh   Knoll

Mithil River

Q   Stonemight
                     Woodhelven   Soaring
         Crystal Gleam Hills   Woodhelven   Morinmoss
R   (later Crystal)   Forest
               Stonedown   Healer's
                                                     Cave
                                                         Roamsedge R.
S   SOUTH   PLAINS   Central
                                        Hills   Roamsedge
                                                  Arroyo   Ford

                  Windskorn   Covert
                  Stonedown   Ravine

T   Kevin's
                  Watch   PLAINS
                            Hidden   OF RA Manhome
U   Doom's   Valley
    Retreat
                       Mithil
V   Stonedown   Tarn of the
                                              Ranyhyn   S   O
W   The   U
      Wastes

X   Gray Desert
                    Roads, Bridges, Fords   Southron
              N   Streams, Lakes
                    Woodland   Wastes
                    Marsh
                                             16   17   18   19   20
         LEAGUES
    0   10   20   50   75

124

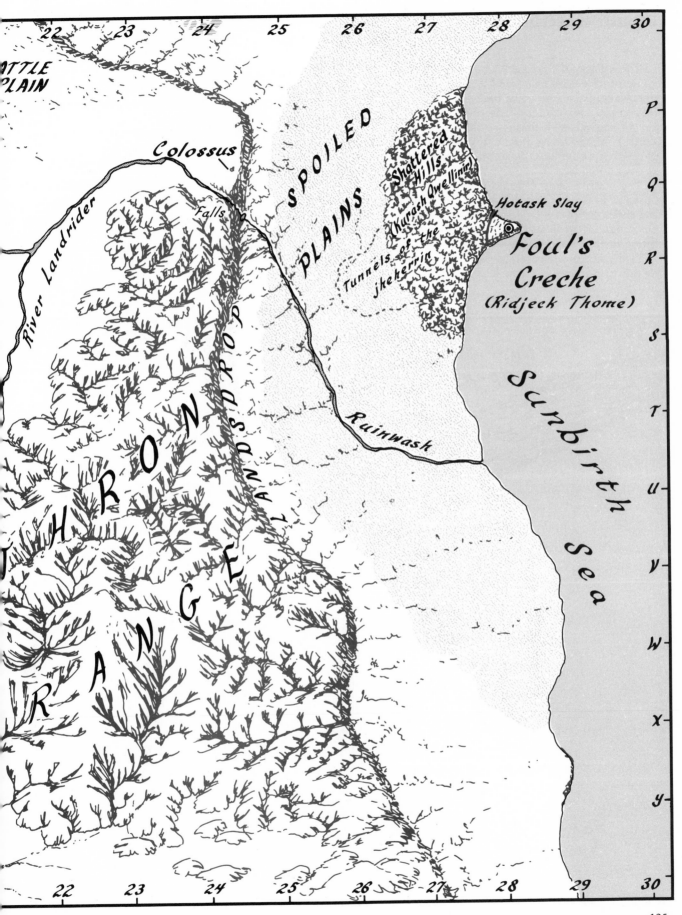

THE SOUTHEAST

SOARING WOODHELVEN

The village of Soaring Woodhelven occupies an immense tree—four hundred feet tall. The trunk is thirty feet in diameter at the base, and rises over forty feet to the lowest limbs. The crown is shaped like half of an oval, with foliage so thick that only occasional glimpses reveal that it is inhabited.[1] The size of the tree would be sufficient to house a population of over a hundred.

The massive central trunk, with its broad, gently upswept limbs are reminiscent of the sugar maple, and therefore of the Gilden which stands as the maple's counterpart in the Land.[2] Such a tree would be fitting for a Woodhelvennin village.

In the northwest curve of the trunk the entrance to the tree-village is formed by a natural opening.

Originally, no gate bars the entrance; but after the coming of the Raver, a wooden gate is quickly erected. The gate does not completely close the entrance. Beyond it Covenant can see a spiral stairway hewn into the inner cavity of the trunk. It ascends to an opening just above the lowest branch.[3]

The broad limbs form walkways radiating from the trunk, and numerous ladders span the gaps between successive levels—both on the trunk and from branch to branch.[4] The homes of the Woodhelvennin are woven of branches, twigs, and leaves, scattered throughout the tree.[5] The only home Covenant enters is that of Baradakas, the Hirebrand, two hundred feet above the ground—the closest home to the Heartwood Chamber in the center of the tree.[6]

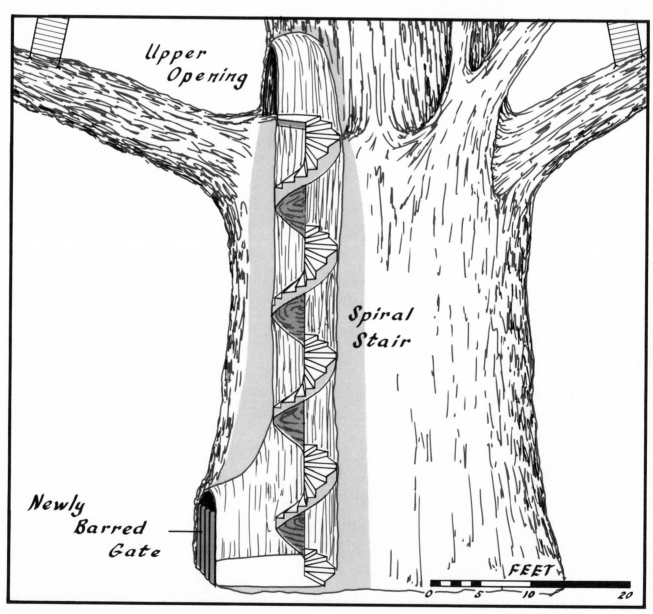

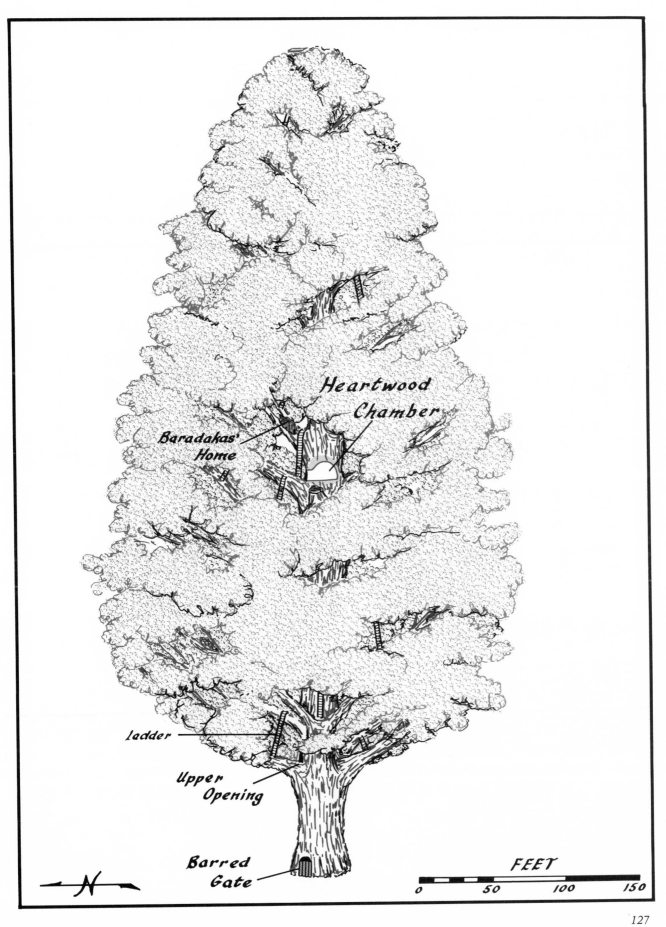

Heartwood
Chamber

Baradakas'
Home

ladder

Upper
Opening

Barred
Gate

N

FEET

0   50   100   150

127

The Heartwood Chamber

The center of Soaring Woodhelven—both spatially and socially—is the heartwood chamber, hewn from the core of the trunk. Even at some two hundred feet above the ground, the trunk is still sufficiently large to contain a chamber twenty feet in diameter.[1] Although to Covenant the chamber seems to fill the entire trunk, there is no danger of its damaging the tree—for the life of a tree is as always within a ring inside the outer bark.

The chamber entrance is cut into the trunk just above a massive limb. Like the village entrance far below, the heartwood chamber entrance must face roughly northwest, for when Covenant is hoisted from the ground, he ascends straight up to this level and is brought onto the limb near the chamber entrance.[2]

The heartwood chamber is unadorned, yet is magnificent in its natural state. Its polished floor reveals the concentric tree rings which convey the tree's history to anyone who knows how to read them. The walls, too, are polished, and must show the vertical grain of the wood; but high above, the ceiling is rough. No furnishings mar the perfection of the chamber, but *lillianrill* torches are set in the walls, brilliantly lighting the interior.[3]

Trunk

To Baradakas' Home

Entrance

FEET

0   5   10   NW

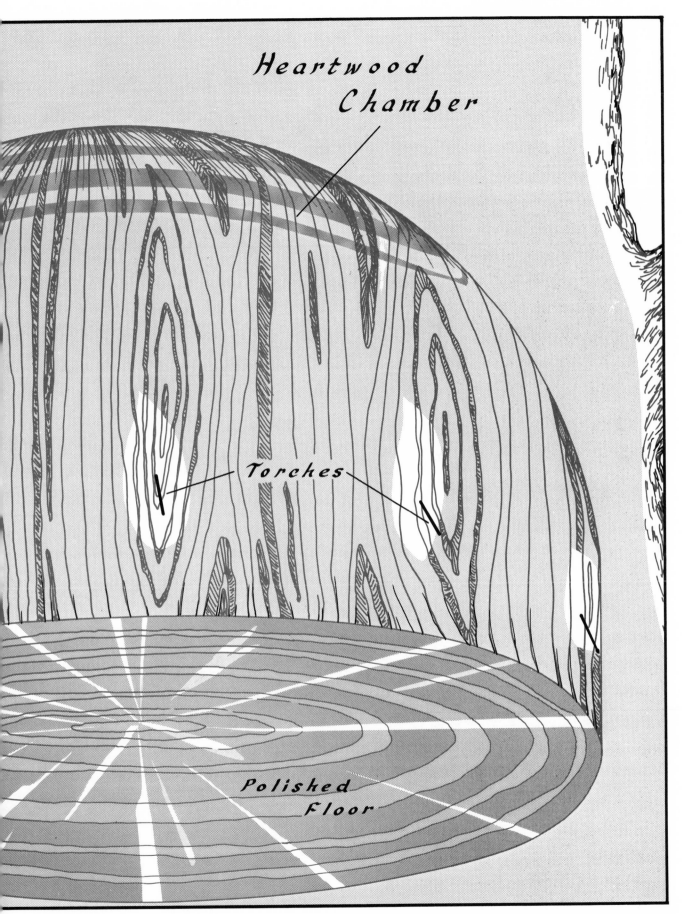

Heartwood
Chamber

Torches

Polished
Floor

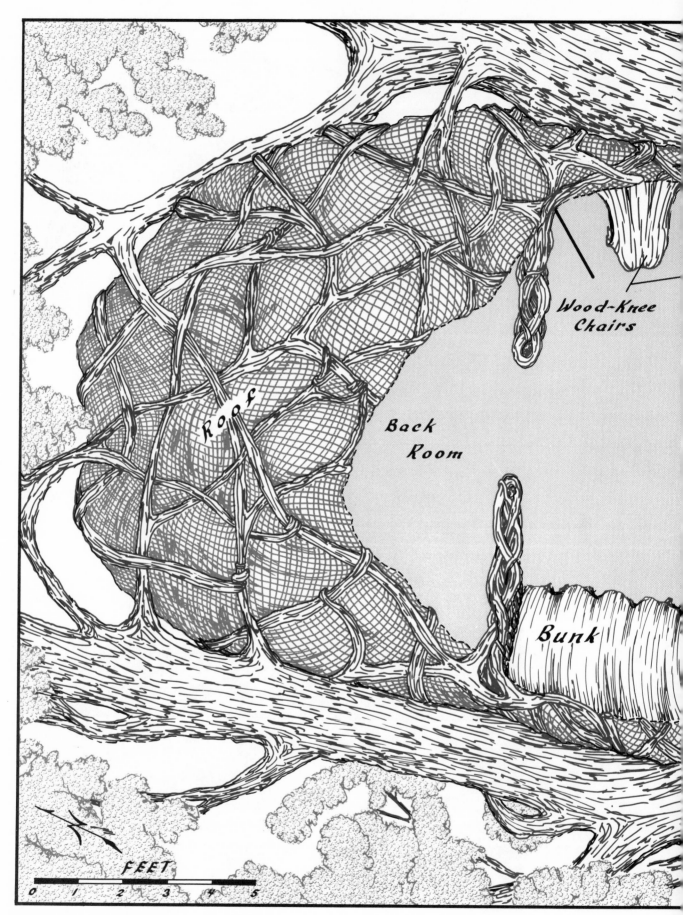

Wood-Knee
Chairs

Roof

Back
Room

Bunk

FEET

0   1   2   3   4   5

Three-Legged Table

Torch

Baradaka's Home

Nestled in the fork of the branch immediately above the level of the heartwood chamber is the home of the Hirebrand Baradakas. It can be reached from the heartwood chamber by climbing a ladder only a few steps away. The entrance to the home is only a few more short steps from the trunk.[1]

The dwelling contains two rooms. The front room serves as both living and sleeping chamber. The back room is doubtless also multipurpose, including food storage. The entire dwelling is formed entirely by the tree's branches—even the partition between the rooms. Only part of the floor is of branches, however, so firmer material is apparently superimposed on the woven mat. Even most of the furnishings are formed from the living tree: "broad knees of wood grew into the chamber like chairs."[2] The bunk on the opposite wall from the wood-knee chairs is laid on a similar configuration—just more densely grown.[3] The only movable furniture mentioned is a small three-legged table, which Baradakas sets near two of the chairs for eating. A torch in each side wall brightly lights the first room.

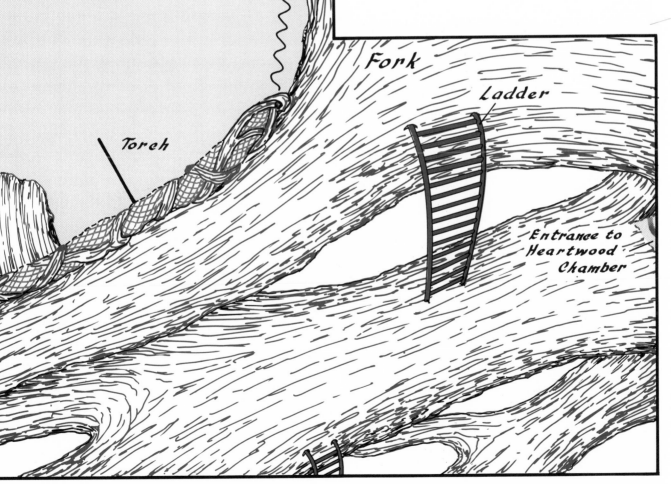

Fork

Ladder

Entrance to Heartwood Chamber

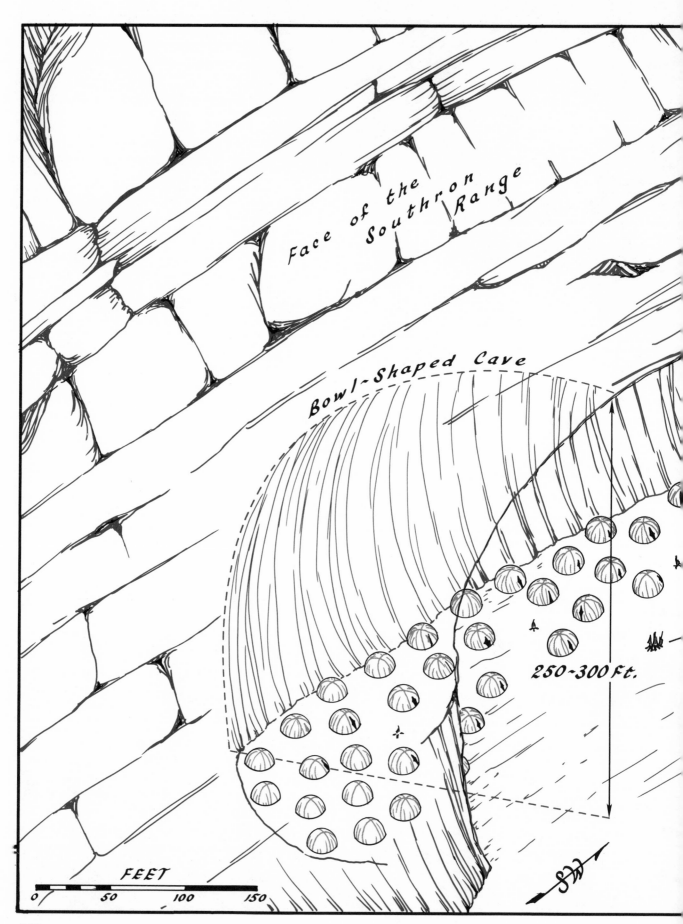

Face of the Southron Range

Bowl-Shaped Cave

250-300 Ft.

FEET

0   50   100   150

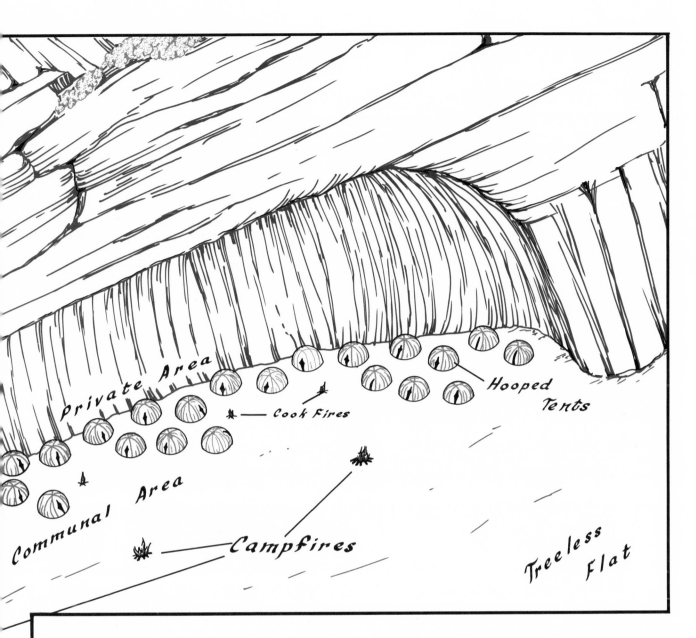

Private Area

Cook Fires

Hooped Tents

Communal Area

Campfires

Treeless Flat

MANHOME

On the south edge of the Plains of Ra, set into the mountain wall of the southron Range is the primary gathering place of the Ramen: Manhome. In spite of its importance, Manhome is no more than that—a gathering place. The Ramen are nomadic. They do not build homes or other structures, but live in the open or pitch their hooped tents at need.[1]

Coming over the last rise of the rolling Plains, the company can see a treeless flat at the foot of the mountains—large enough for a hundred Ranyhyn to circle Covenant when they are called.[2] The site of the village is no more than an undercut cliff on the northwest face of the mountains: "The bottom of the cliff face for the last two hundred fifty or three hundred feet inclined sharply inward along a broad, half-oval front, leaving a cave like a deep, vertical bowl in the rock."[3]

The Ramen tents are concentrated in the back of the cave. There they are protected from bad weather, but may still receive the morning sun.[4] Closer to the front, three campfires are surrounded by large open areas. The campfires, plus the cook fires further back into the cave, provide the only light during the hours of darkness. Around these fires the Ramen and the company eat and visit. The company of the Quest is split, with the Bloodguard at one fire, Covenant, Foamfollower and the Lords at the central one, and Quaan and his warriors at the third.[5]

Manhome is occupied by about a hundred Ramen during Covenant's visit—seventy of whom come forth when the company arrives.[6] During the attacks of Foul's long winter, Manhome's location is too well known, and the Ramen are forced to abandon it for the more hidden coverts.[7]

RAMEN COVERT

Among the hills at the northwest edge of the Plains of Ra is the last Ramen covert to elude the Despiser's searchers during the attacks of the long winter. It is approached through a hidden valley. The valley contains three copses—thickets of small trees—all killed by the preternatural winter. Behind the thickest of the copses is a narrow rift,[1] weathered so irregularly through the rock of the hills that the sky is invisible to Covenant as he passes through the narrow cut. After passing around numerous bends, the rift opens out into a chamber large enough to serve as an infirmary for several injured Ranyhyn.

Beyond the chamber the narrow rift continues for a short distance.[2] Suddenly the cleft widens into a long, sinuous valley. In keeping with the configuration of the cleft, the valley is so steep-walled that little sky is visible; but after the narrow cut of the entrance, the valley seems spacious. Weathered columns and fallen boulders provide shelter for the Ramen tents pitched along the valley walls.[3] Under the overhang of one massive rock at the far end of the vaguely S-shaped valley is the main cook fire.[4]

To produce a formation of this type, it is necessary for the bedrock of the valley to be layered, with a strong, massive rock overlying weaker strata. As the weak underlying rock is weathered more easily than the capstone, the cliffs are gradually undercut, leaving great overhanging rock masses. When weathering begins to occur in the vertical fissures as well, columns result. Eventually the undercutting leaves too little support for the gigantic overhangs, and the caprock breaks, falling aslant against the side walls of the valley.[5] It is these massive flat boulders which provide such excellent protection for the Ramen tents.[6]

Beyond the head of the valley, the walls draw close once again, and the cleft begins another winding cut through the hills. After some distance, the rift forks. Following Bannor's instructions, Covenant and Lena take the left branch of the fork—so narrow they must go single file, edging along it sideways. The cut must pass through a local drainage divide, for soon the cleft path begins to descend and, after becoming so steep it is difficult to traverse, roofs over into a tunnel. Within the tunnel the path levels and eventually ends in a thicket.[7] North and east a few leagues lies Roamsedge Ford.[8]

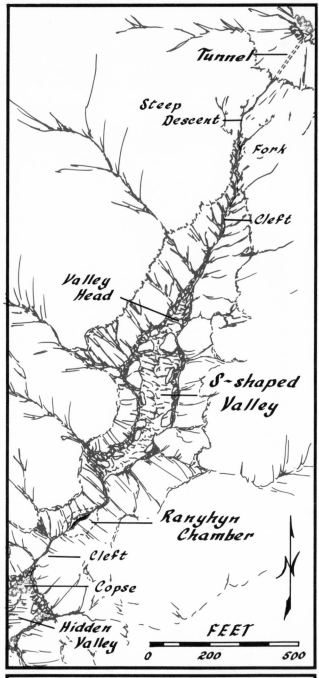

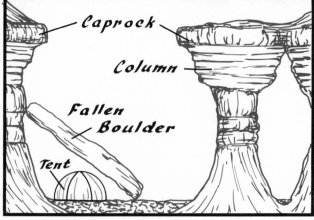

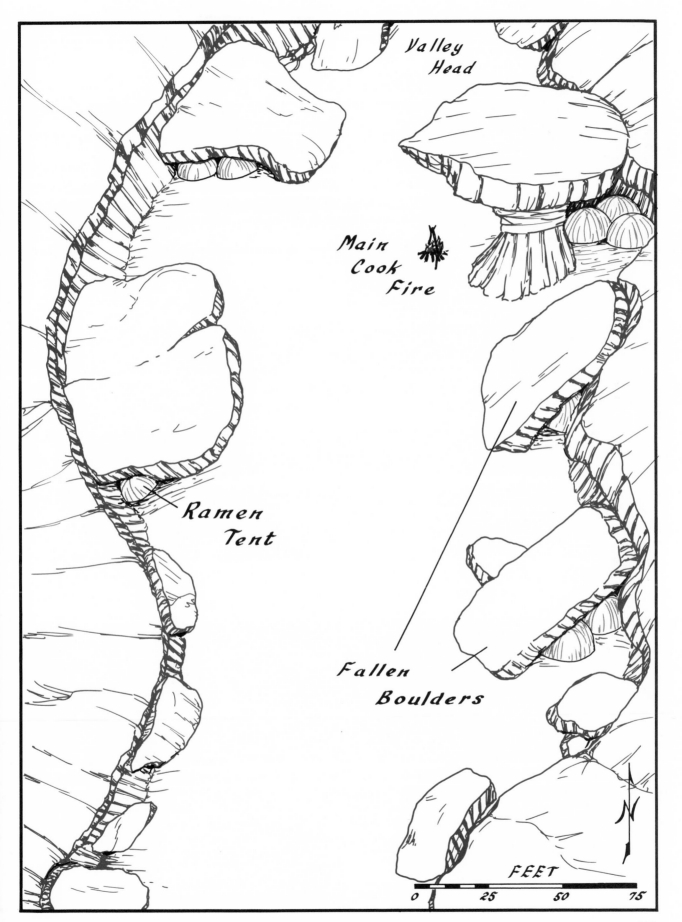

Valley
Head

Main
Cook
Fire

Ramen
Tent

Fallen
Boulders

N

FEET

0   25   50   75

135

MORINMOSS FOREST—
THE HEALER'S CAVE

In Morinmoss Forest an Unfettered Healer finds
Covenant and takes him to her dwelling. It is a small
low cave in the bank of a hill with a moss-curtained
entrance.[1] The Healer's needs are simple. A bed lies
along one wall, with a shelf above holding a pot of
graveling. At the far end of the cave is a cook fire
and a small supply of firewood.[2] Also, there reasonably should be a chair, possibly a small table, and
shelves to contain the Healer's herbs, cooking utensils and supplies.

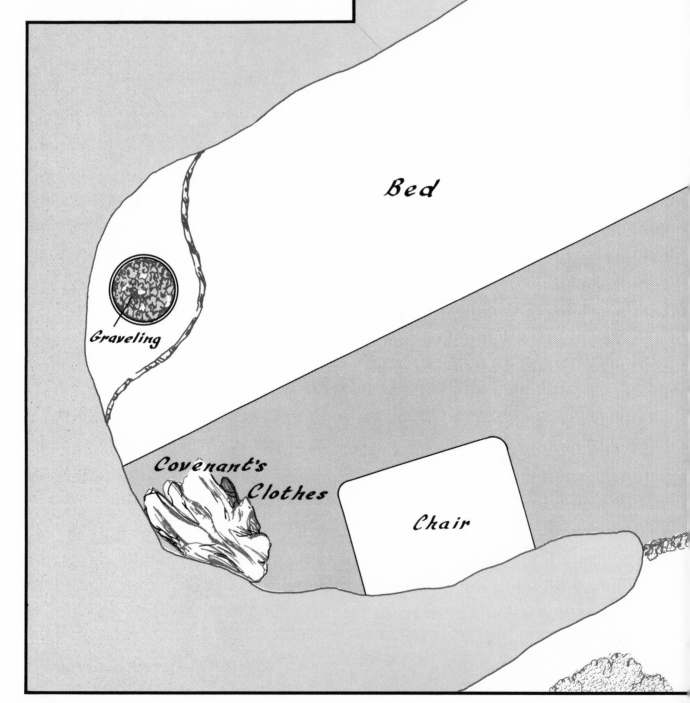

Low Hill

Bed

Graveling

Covenant's Clothes

Chair

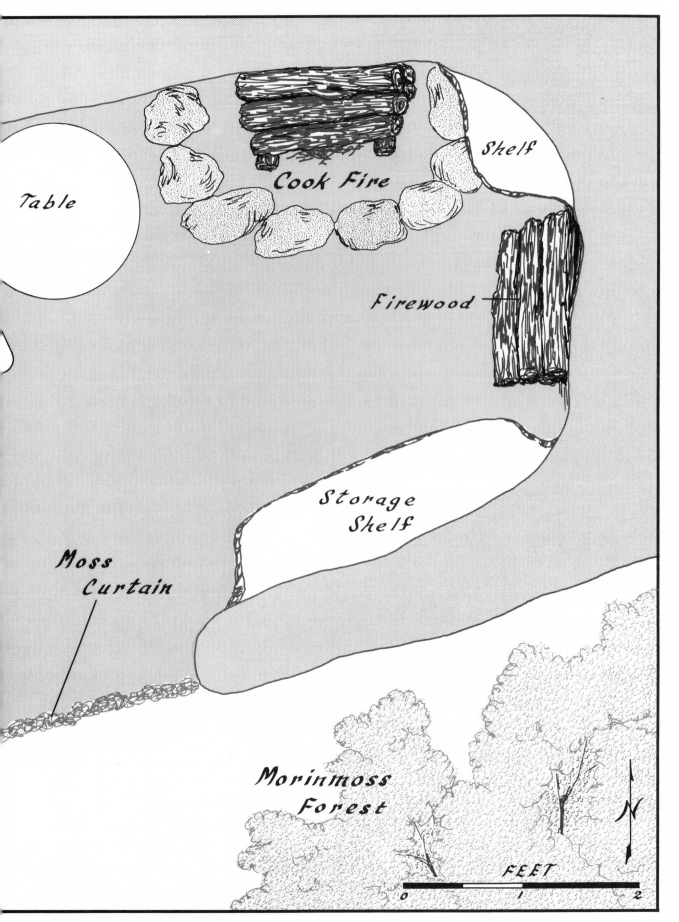

Table

Cook Fire

Shelf

Firewood

Moss
Curtain

Storage
Shelf

Morinmoss
Forest

FEET

0   1   2

N

COLOSSUS OF THE FALL

The Upper Land had been guarded from the Ravers by the spirit of an *Elohim*, embodied in an obsidian monolith forty feet tall, which overlooks the Lower Land from Landsdrop near the Fall of the River Landrider: the Colossus of the Fall.[1] It stands until the advent of the Sunbane destroys the forests, then it is unbound.[2] Millennia earlier, Elena—wielding the Staff of Law under Foul's control—attempts to destroy the Colossus, but is prevented by Covenant's destruction of the Staff.[3] This encounter reveals much of the terrain near the Colossus.

The Colossus stands near, but not immediately on the edge of Landsdrop.[4] Beyond a low line of hills, out of sight but within hearing, the Landrider River flows. It is close enough for Bannor and Foamfollower to conveniently use it to wash.[5] Afterward, Covenant is led "up the last of the hills" where he may see Landsdrop and the Spoiled Plains beyond.[6]

Landsdrop is highest at Mount Thunder, the center of the original cataclysm. Near the Colossus it is both less lofty and less sheer. For two thousand feet the waters of the Landrider fall to the Lower Land; but the cliff face is broken into "four or five ragged stairs," and the falls tumble in stages from step to step.[7] Foamfollower's and Covenant's descent of the cliff is long, but not particularly difficult.[8]

The steplike formation of the cliff could be due to the original pattern of faulting at the time of Landsdrop's appearance—producing several vertical faults, rather than the single massive one present at Mount Thunder. The formation could also have happened since the original time, with the sheer cliff buckling under its own weight, creeping down gradually over thousands of years.[9] Most reasonably, both processes could have occurred. Whatever the cause, the result is most often a rugged cliff face, with the tops of each shattered rock mass forming an almost zigzag trail from top to base. At the foot of the cliff, the water pools among the broken stones of the foothills, before sluggishly finding its way through the rubble and into the level Spoiled Plains to the east.[10]

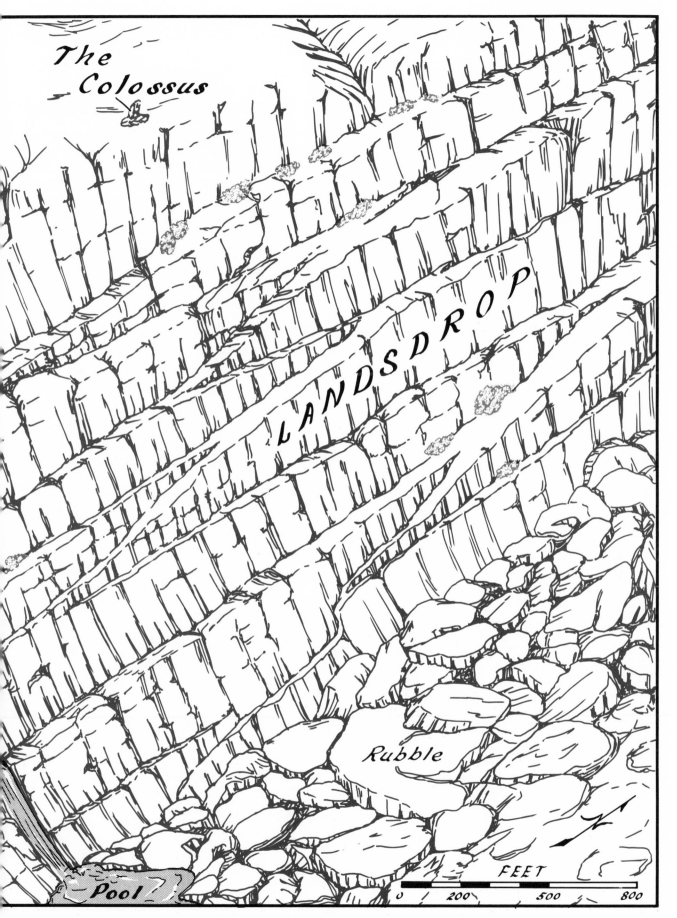

The Colossus

LANDSDROP

Rubble

Pool

FEET

0   200   500   800

THE TUNNELS OF THE JHEHERRIN

A few day's journey east of Landsdrop, as Foamfollower and Covenant are traversing a thornbush filled valley between ridges, they are forced to flee a fire. Taking refuge in one of the many mud pits in the valley, they are snatched down, then pulled sideways within the pit. Recovering from the shock, they find themselves at the blind end of one of the many tunnels of the *jheherrin*[1] which honeycomb the land from the thorn wastes of the Spoiled Plains, passing under the Shattered Hills to Foul's Creche where the passages lie adjacent to those of Foul. They reach all the way to the fiery quagmire from which the *jheherrin* creep after their injection by Foul as failed creations.[2]

As the *jheherrin* lead Covenant and Foamfollower from the mud pit, the interweavings of the tunnels become increasingly complex. At the other edges the tunnels are so low Covenant must crouch and Foamfollower crawl. Farther east, as the number of tunnels increases, the size does also, until Covenant (six feet tall) can stand, and Foamfollower (twelve feet) can crouch.[3] After several leagues the mud alters to stone. Leagues later, the tunnel enters directly into a rocklit cavern which is large enough to hold several hundred of the small *jheherrin*.[4]

Beyond the cavern one of the *jheherrin* guides them into a new tunnel. For a half league they climb upward through a complex chain of cold stone passages. After two sharp turns, the tunnel begins to ascend steeply, narrowing as it climbs. It ends abruptly, with no exit. Far higher than the earlier passages, this tunnel is so high that Foamfollower not only can stand, but even has room to reach his arms up full length. The only opening is a slit window in the blank end wall—almost out of even Foamfollower's reach. The window opens at the base of a "short, roofless corridor."[5] They are within Kurash Qwellinir—the Shattered Hills.[6]

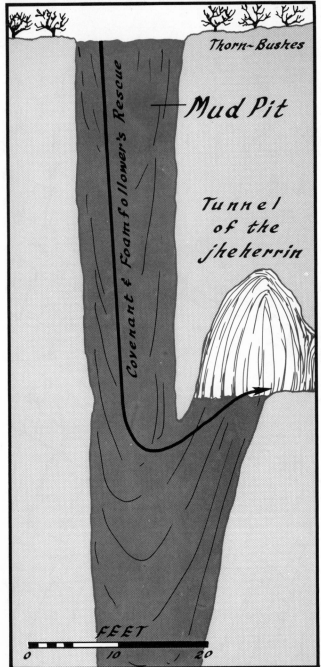

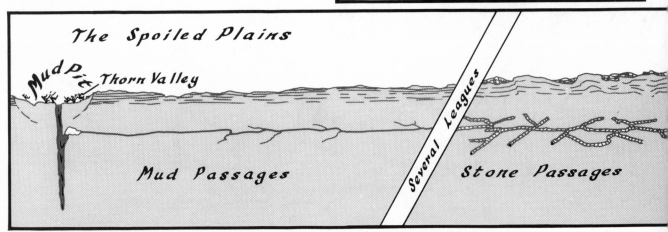

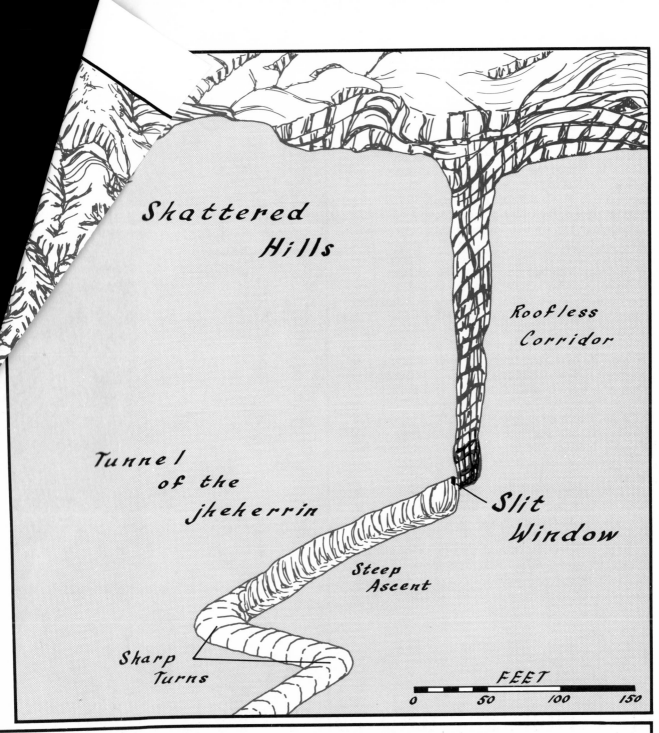

Shattered
Hills

Roofless
Corridor

Tunnel
of the
jheherrin

Slit
Window

Steep
Ascent

Sharp
Turns

FEET

0   50   100   150

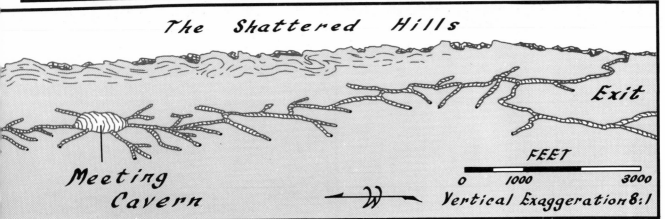

The Shattered Hills

Exit

Meeting
Cavern

FEET

0   1000   3000

Vertical Exaggeration 8:1

KURASH QWELLINIR— THE SHATTERED HILLS

The Shattered Hills are labyrinthian. As noted earlier, the origin of the Hills is not clear, but the walls of the corridor at which the jheherrin's tunnel ends are described as "sheer stone, scores of feet high" which look as if they are "rough-adzed out of raw, black, igneous rock."[1] This suggests yet another possible origin: flows of lava from Hotash Slay. The irregular flow of the lava, repeatedly oozing out across the surrounding lands, creeping around obstructions, then cracking and shattering as the molten rock cooled could also have produced the towering igneous rock with its tortuous maze of passages.[2]

In spite of the complexity of the maze, more than one route leads through the Hills. Bannor describes one which ends at the south end of Hotash Slay.[3] The journey through the tunnels of the *jheherrin* takes Covenant and Foamfollower much north of Bannor's route. The new route from the *jheherrin* tunnel exit to Hotash Slay is easily described: "'At every turn choose—the way toward the fire. You must pass a passage of the Maker. It will be guarded. Beyond it take each turn away from the fire.'"[4] The guarded passage is the exit door of a tunnel from Foul's Creche. It opens into an area which is wider than the surrounding stone passages, lit by two rocklight pillars.[5]

Although the route turns "away from the fire" at each intersection after the guarded passage, the general trend gradually brings Covenant and Foamfollower closer to the magma river, for the passages "reversed directions, twisted back on themselves."[6] Gradually Covenant and Foamfollower come closer to the magma river—until the convoluted passages end abruptly on the shores of Hotash Slay.[7]

The Shattered Hills

Hills

(Kurash Qwellinir)

N

⟶ jheherrin's Path
--⟶ Bannor's Path

FEET

0   1000   2500

Sunbirth
Sea

jheherrin
Tunnel
Exit

Wide
Area

Guarded
Passage

Hotash Slag

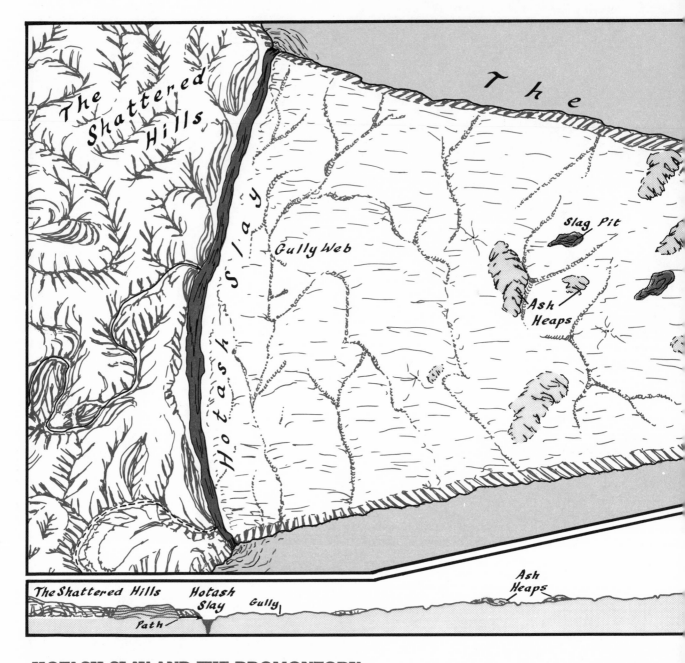

The Shattered Hills   Hotash   Ash

Slay   Gully   Heaps

Path

HOTASH SLAY AND THE PROMONTORY

Beyond the Shattered Hills a narrow peninsula juts into the Sunbirth Sea. For over a half league it rises to a promontory towering above the waves,[1] cut off from the mainland by a river of molten lava: Gorak Krembal, Hotash Slay.[2]

An ash beach, ten yards wide, lies between the Hills and the lava. The Slay is fifty yards wide where Covenant and Foamfollower make their crossing, but is more narrow at its southern end, where it cuts through the sea cliff.[3] The length may be almost a mile, for Covenant, from his vantage in one of the gullies closest to the Slay, notes the sheer sea cliffs lie "several hundred yards away from him on either side."[4]

Beyond Hotash Slay the promontory is pitted and

piled—"blasted and rough, scarred with slag pits, ash heaps, crevices . . . gullies . . . like a web of erosion scars."[5] Near the eastern tip, the promontory rises sharply. A "rugged, upraised rock," strewn with boulders, climbs to the entrance of Foul's Creche.[6]

Two slender towers, several hundred feet high, stand on each side of the entrance.[7] Windows top the towers, but the main warder stands at the mouth of Foul's Creche. In contrast to the pitted ugliness of the remainder of the promontory, the entrance "was smooth and symmetrical . . . perfectly made. The round opening stood in a massive abutment of wrought stone—a honed and polished fortification which cupped the entrance."[8]

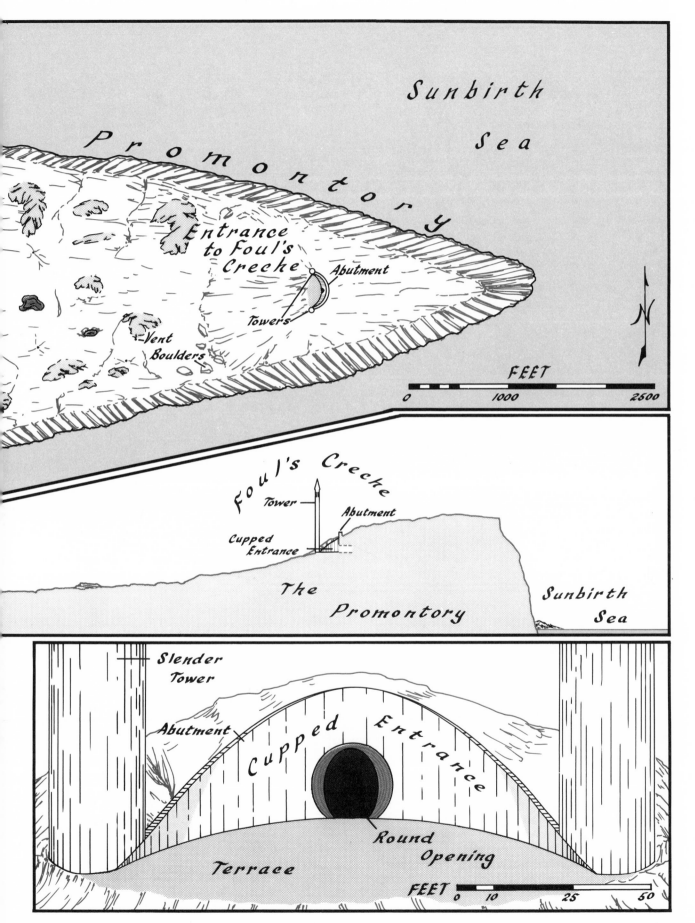

145

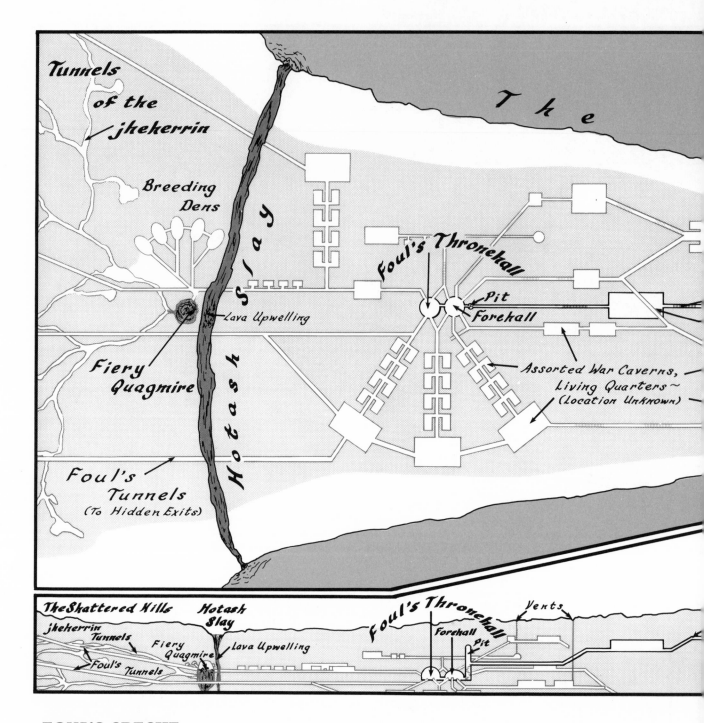

FOUL'S CRECHE

At the eastern edge of the Land, guarded by the Spoiled Plains and the Shattered Hills, lies the heart of Lord Foul's realm: Ridjeck Thome, Foul's Creche. Although the Creche is a city large enough to house Foul's thousands of servants, and muster his armies, little is known of its layout. Among its passages lie "war caverns, furnaces, breeding dens."[1] There, too, is the fiery quagmire into which his failed creations are discarded.[2] The extensive network of tunnels and caverns is not contained entirely within the promon-

tory.[3] The tunnels reach under Hotash Slay—far out into the Shattered Hills, where secret openings give the only access other than the visible entrance at the tip of the promontory.[4]

Within the promontory's entrance, the egg-shaped entry hall is the most seaward chamber of the entire complex.[5] From the widest point of the entry hall a pair of passages lead to the two watchtowers. The far end sinks faultlessly down into a massive spiral stair which arcs landward as it descends, cutting back to-

146

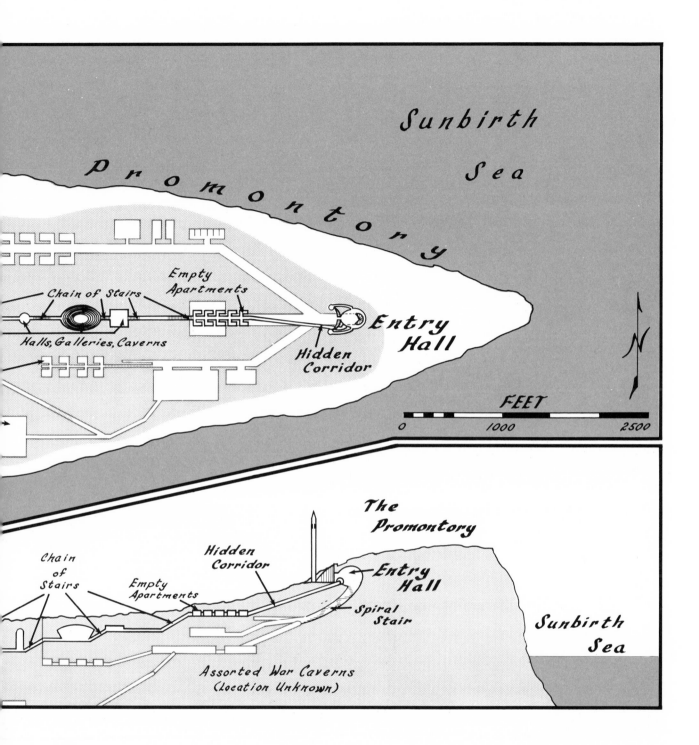

ward the heart of the tunnel system.[6]

Behind a hidden door is a small chamber, followed by a long, steeply descending corridor leading to "a series of unadorned, unfurnished apartments—starkly exact and symmetrical."[7]

Beyond the apartments, the pathway to the thronehall follows a chain of stairs which descend through numerous levels. Along the way are huge caverns, and galleries large enough to hold thousands. The path eventually descends an empty pit, and stops. In

the wall of the pit is another hidden door: an entrance to the forehall of Foul's thronehall.[8]

The forehall is a round, high chamber, symmetrically ringed by eight stone doors. One of the eight leads into Foul's thronehall.[9] The thronehall is similar to the forehall, but far higher, and with fewer doors. In contrast to the perfection of the Creche, Foul's throne and dais are warped by the centuries of his presence. The jaw-shaped throne looks out toward the forehall entrance across the Illearth Stone.[10]

147

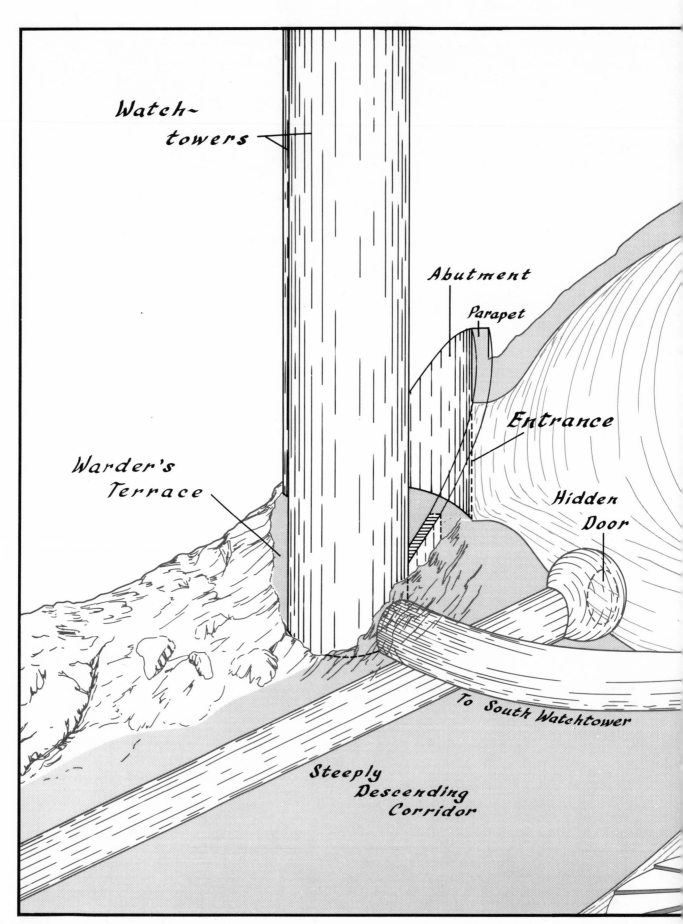

Watch-
towers

Abutment

Parapet

Entrance

Warder's
Terrace

Hidden
Door

To South Watchtower

Steeply
Descending
Corridor

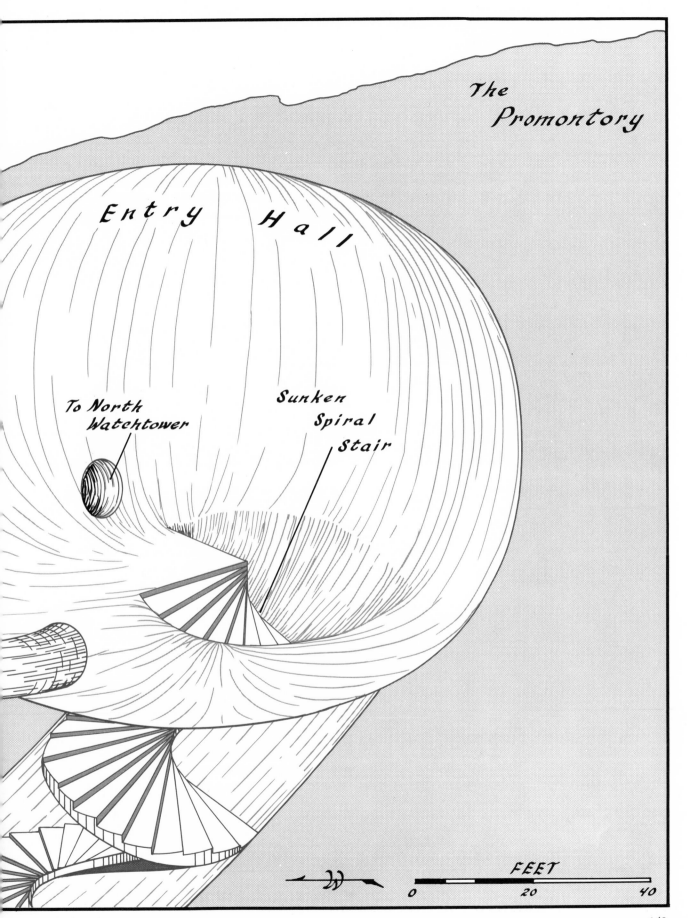

The Promontory

Entry Hall

To North
Watchtower

Sunken
Spiral
Stair

FEET

0   20   40

ENTRY HALL

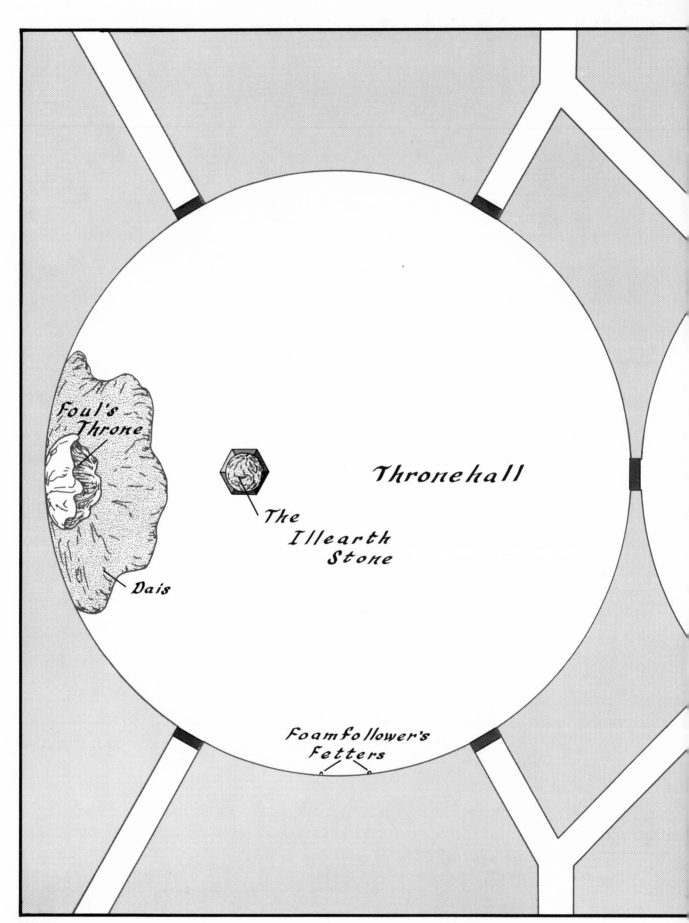

Foul's Throne

Dais

The Illearth Stone

Thronehall

Foamfollower's Fetters

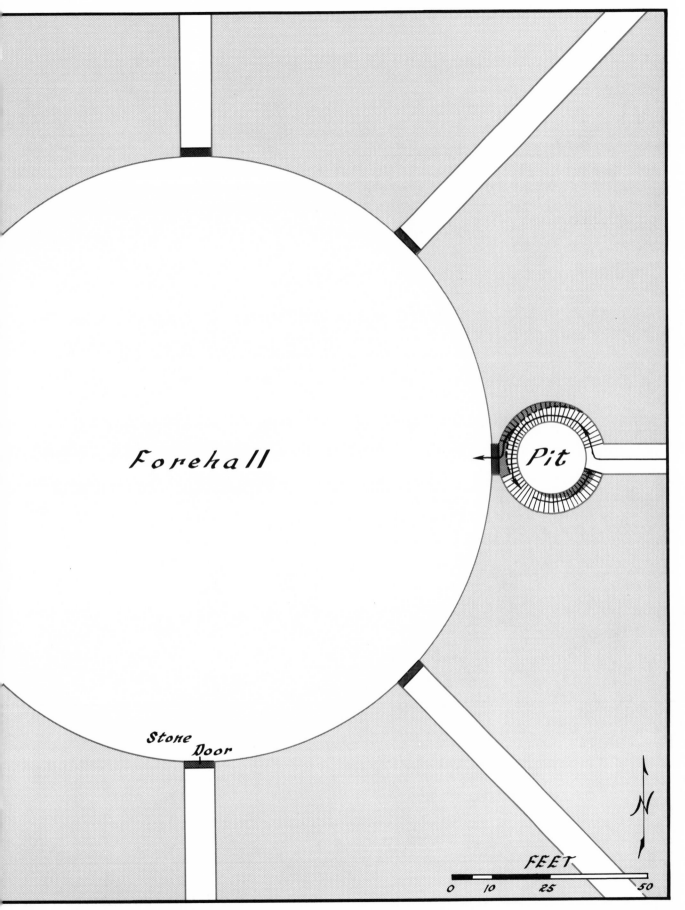

Forehall

Pit

Stone
Door

FEET

0   10   25   50

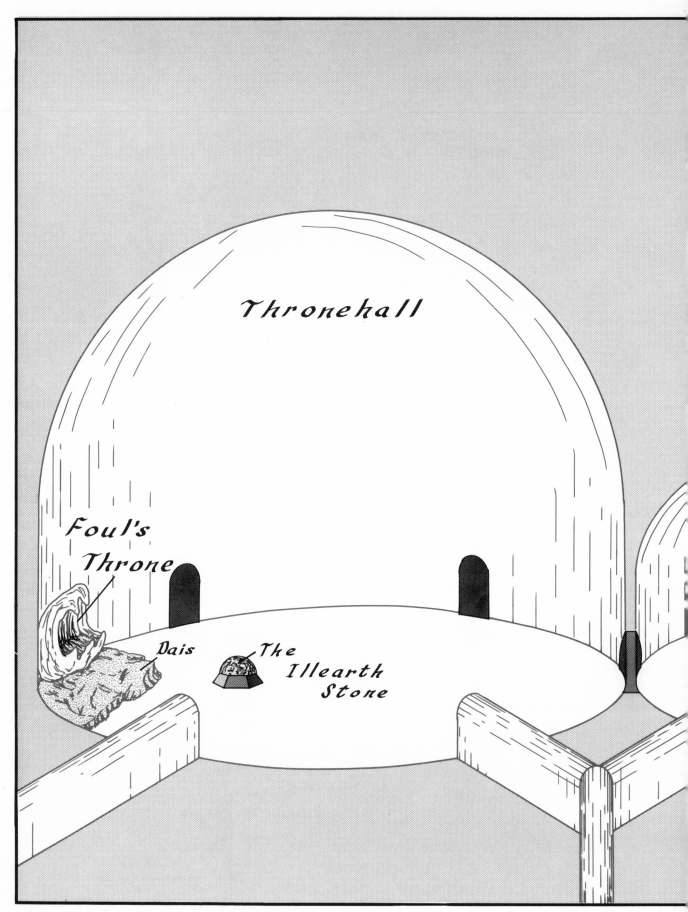

Thronehall

Foul's
Throne

Dais

The
Illearth
Stone

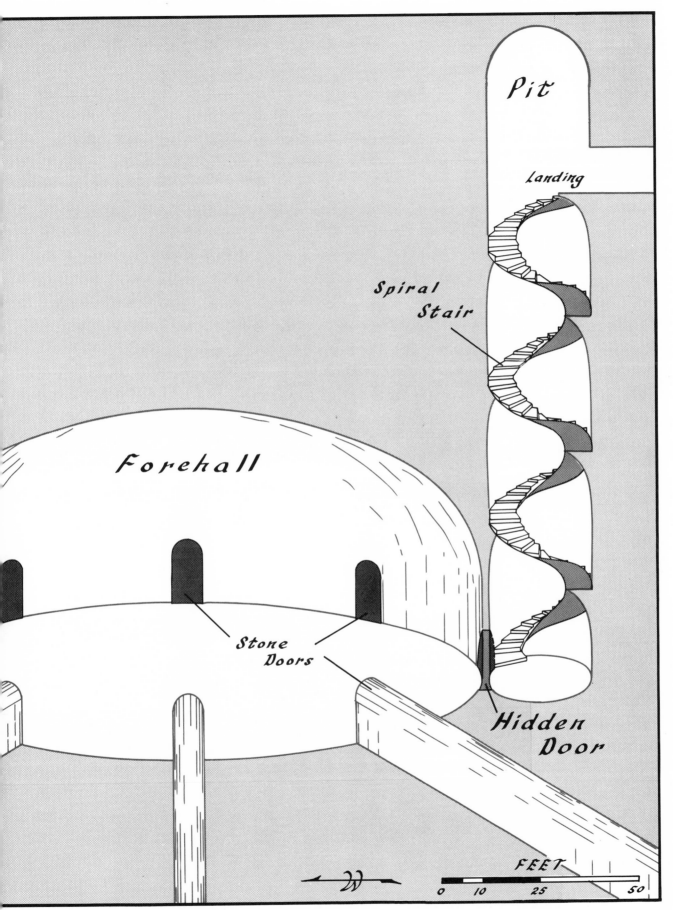

Pit

Landing

Spiral
Stair

Forehall

Stone
Doors

Hidden
Door

FEET

0   10   25   50

LANDS
OF THE
VOYAGE

The voyage in search of the One Tree takes Covenant, Linden and the Giants of the Search away from the Land. They embark from the pier at *Coercri*, and return sixty-five days later to the coast north of Seareach. During the intervening time all but scant days are spent on the Sea.

It is appropriate, therefore, that a diagram of Starfare's Gem be foremost in this section. Aboard the Giantship the company sails hundreds of leagues on the path of their untraceable voyage. They visit, in turn, the land of the *Elohim, Brathairealm,* and the Isle of the One Tree. Between landings they are beset by Ravers, doldrums, a hurricane, *merewives, Nicor,* and the Soulbiter.

The locations visited by the company are almost as inhospitable as the danger of the voyage—and as the jealous and dangerous inhabitants of those places. The first land sighted is Bareisle, whose name embodies its description. The entrance to the land of the *Elohim* is equally unwelcoming, and suits its name: The Raw. The *maidan*, the entrance to *Elemesnedene*, is the only gentle land seen during the entire journey. Even *Elemesnedene* is barren and plain once the wonders of the *Elohim* are removed.

Brathairain Town, with its Harbor and high Sandhold, is dry. The only green is in the few fields wrested from the edge of the desert with irrigation. The city stands precariously in an uneasy truce between the ocean and the desert—a shipping port.

The One Tree is the goal of the voyage, and its location is learned from the *Elohim*. Following the directions revealed to them, the company eventually reaches the isle in which the One Tree is hidden, and find it as barren and forbidding as the other lands they have visited.

STARFARE'S GEM

The ship commissioned for the Giants of the Search is one of the proudest *dromonds* of the fleet of Home.[1] It rises from the sea like a stone castle as it approaches the pier at *Coercri*.[2] This comparison refers to both size and materials, for the Giantship is formed of granite from mast to keel (as are its longboats). Both the *dromond* and the longboats are moiremarked.[3]

Like the *dromonds* of Earth's Middle Ages, Starfare's Gem is more similar to a Spanish galleon than to the fast, low clipper ships of later times.[4] It has a towering stern, with a wheeldeck which rises high above the level of the main deck reachable only by two steep stairways. Atop the wheeldeck, unprotected from the weather, is the great stone wheel: *Shipsheartthew*.[5] The longboats are moored below the rail of the wheeldeck, while the wheelbox contains the massive machinery which transmits the wheel's motions to the rudder far below.[6]

Three masts, each with three sails, tower above the main deck. As with the entire ship, "the crew has Giantish names for every line and sheet," but the only one mentioned is Dawngreeter, the highest sail on the foremast.[7] The midmast is slightly taller than the other two masts, and the lookout (Horizonscan) peers out from its top.[8] The masts pass completely through the ship, rooted in the hull directly above the massive stone keel.

In the center of the main deck, spanning the ship from port to starboard is the flat-roofed structure of Foodfendhall: the galley and eating-hall. The galley is on the starboard side, and contains stoves and tables.[9] Storage lockers fill the portside, and the eating-hall lies aft. Seadoors, with high stormsills, open at each end of the structure, and those walking between fore and aft must pass through the hall from end to end.[10] After the damage to Foodfendhall during the hurricane—including the ripping removal of the midmast (which passes through the center of the eating-hall)—the port side of the hall is destroyed. The starboard remains are rebuilt into a housing, and the fore- and afterdecks are directly joined on the portside.[11]

Below the wheeldeck are the private sleeping quarters of the ship. Immediately within the steep stairways to the wheeldeck are two seadoors—one portside and one starboard. These lead to stone ladders which descend to the private cabins.[12] There are at least eight cabins. Covenant, Brinn, and Hergrom are housed on the portside.[13] Linden's cabin is on the starboard side, as are those of Cail and Ceer.[14] The Giants considerately substitute furnishings in keeping with the passengers' smaller size: chairs and a table, and a ladder with which to reach the Giant-sized hammock.[15]

Pitchwife and the First share a cabin; while Honninscrave, as captain, has a private one which contains the bare necessities. The remaining forty Giants occupy the communal quarters of Saltroamrest—a cavernous bunkhold, with hammocks slung between the supporting pillars. A longtable extends through the center of the floor.[16] Unlike the private cabins, Saltroamrest has no portholes, but is lit by the lanterns hung from every pillar.[17]

The bunkhold lies under the foredeck, and can be reached by ladders which descend from the deck hatches, but it does not reach all the way back to the private cabins.[18] Between the two sleeping areas lie such things as storage lockers, possibly the square hold used for carpentry, and access to the grainholds, wood storage, and other holds of the levels below.[19]

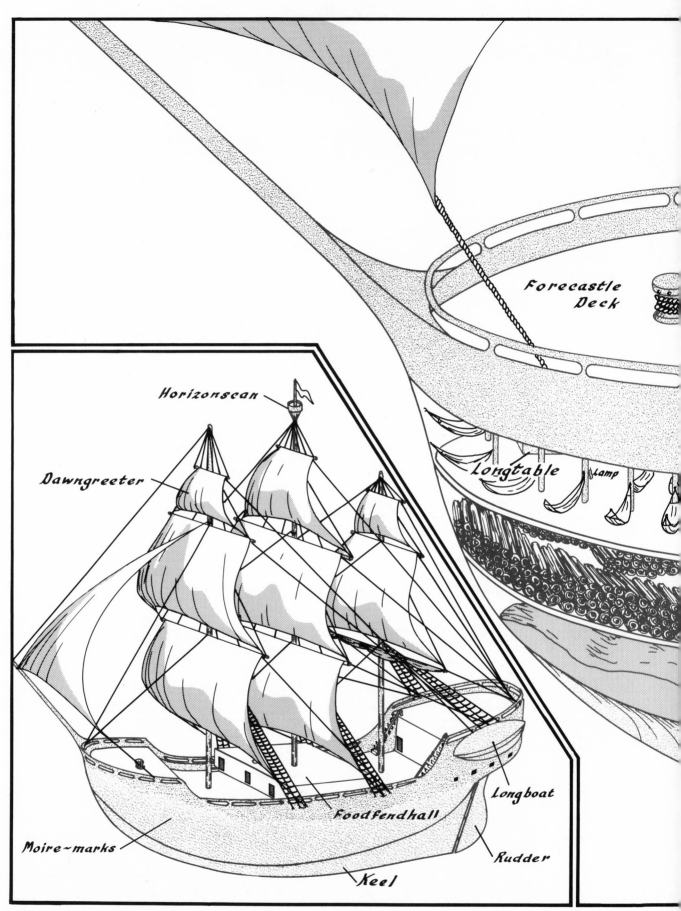

Horizonscan

Dawngreeter

Forecastle
Deck

Longtable

Lamp

Moire~marks

Foodfendhall

Longboat

Rudder

Keel

158

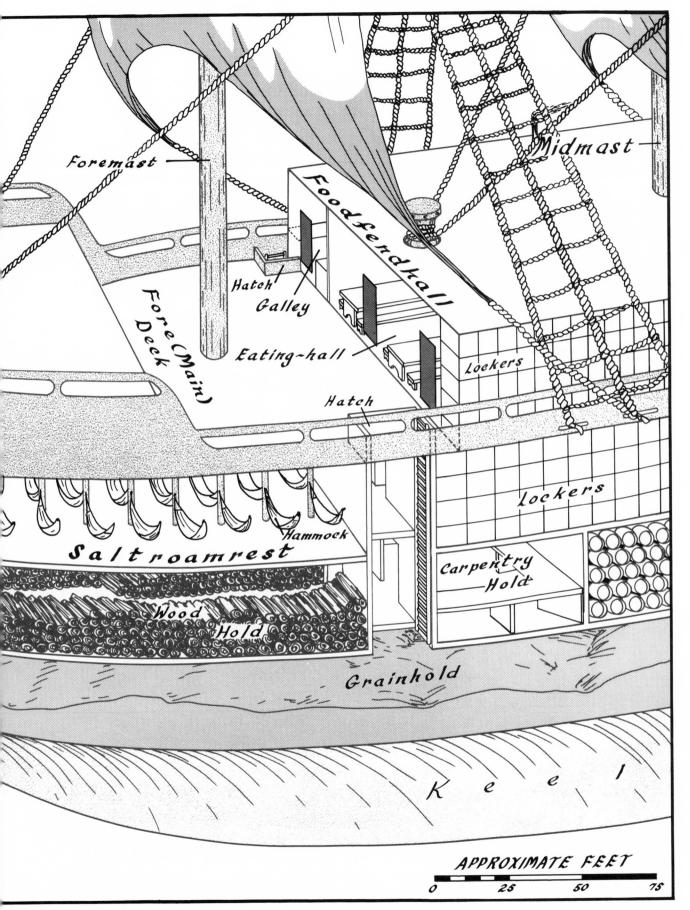

Foremast

Fore (Main)
Deck

Hatch
Galley

Eating-hall

Foodfendhall

Midmast

Lockers

Hatch

Lockers

Hammock

Saltroamrest

Carpentry
Hold

Wood
Hold

Grainhold

K e e l

APPROXIMATE FEET

0   25   50   75

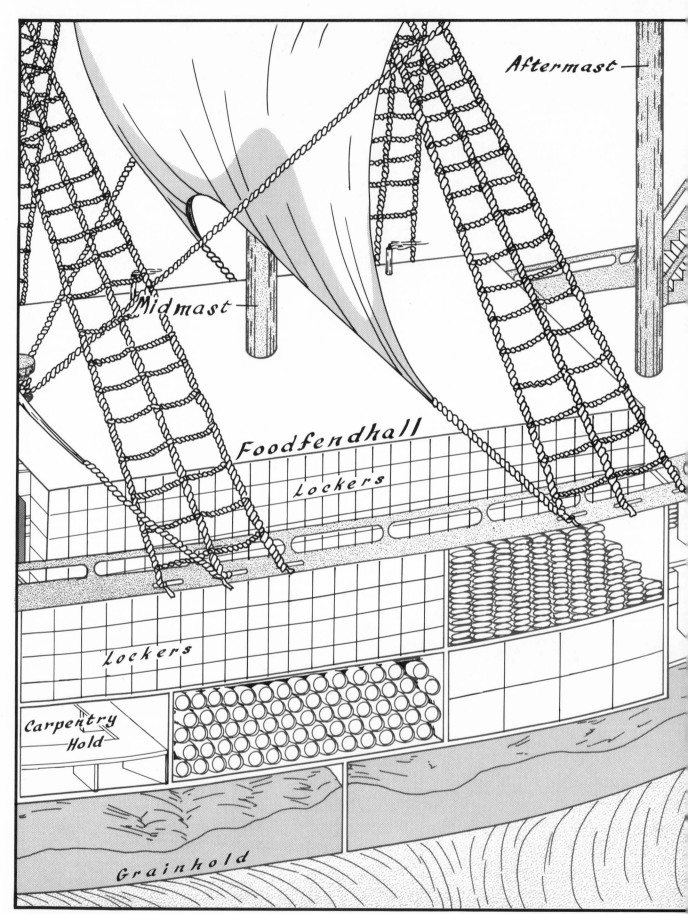

Aftermast

Midmast

Foodfendhall

Lockers

Lockers

Carpentry
Hold

Grainhold

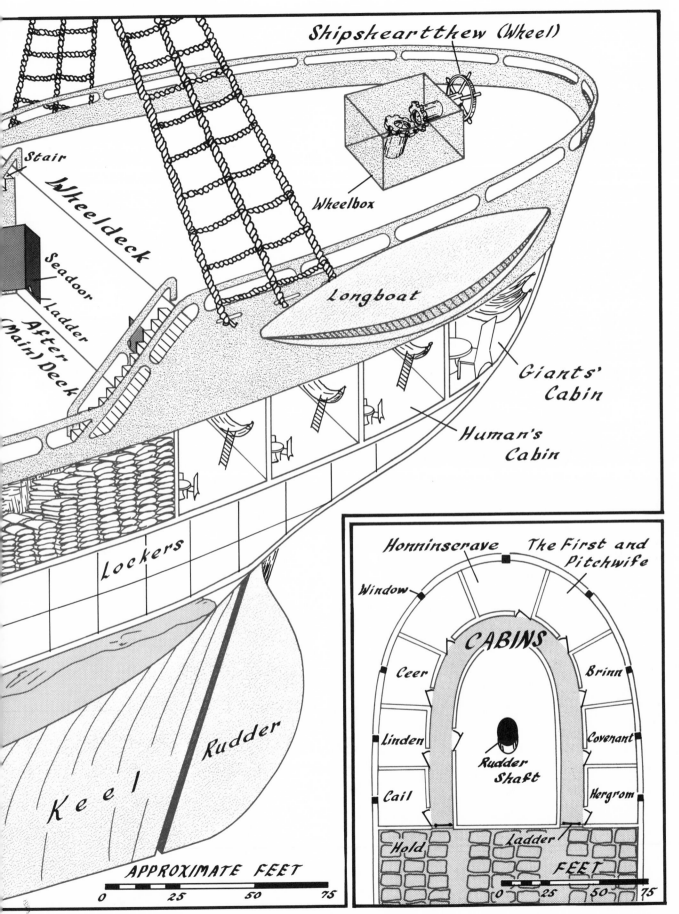

Shipsheartthew (Wheel)

Wheelbox

Stair

Wheeldeck

Seadoor

Ladder

After (Main) Deck

Longboat

Giants' Cabin

Human's Cabin

Lockers

Keel

Rudder

APPROXIMATE FEET

0   25   50   75

Honninscrave   The First and
                         Pitchwife

Window

CABINS

Ceer   Brinn

Linden   Covenant

Rudder
Shaft

Cail   Hergrom

Hold   Ladder

FEET

0   25   50   75

ELEMESNEDENE

The *Elohim* are set apart from mortal races of the world, for they are ethereal—the embodiment of Earthpower. They dwell apart as well. To gain the land of the *Elohim* Starfare's Gem first bypasses Bareisle. Sheer and rugged, its igneous peaks tower above the sea. Mostly barren, tough vegetation clings to only a few spots.[1]

The entrance to the land of the *Elohim* is the Raw, a sinuous fiord that cuts through granite mountain cliffs of Rawedge Rim for more than six leagues. The surrounding peaks rise to over a thousand feet as the fiord reaches inland. Two leagues inland the channel has become so narrow that Starfare's Gem is unable to turn. Only after a final bend does a wider area appear—a lagoon, with "a wedge of low ground between the cliffs."[2]

Shingles edge the lagoon—rubble from the melting glacier which had cut the fiord eons before.[3] Beyond the rock-strewn shore stands Woodenwold, a dense wood filled with oak, sycamore, ash, maple, and occasional willow, cottonwood, and mimosa. Through the midst of the wood, feeding into the channel of the Raw is the River Callowwail, a small, clear stream.[4]

A broad valley lies inland from the Woodenwold. The trees arc along the feet of the surrounding moun-tains, leaving a "bowl of golden grass" so wide that the mountains at the east end are purple with dis-tance.[5] The only distinctive features within the bowl are the course of the River Callowwail and its source: a fountain in the midst of the valley. The water of the fountain wells up like a greyser through the top of the travertine mound which its chemicals have formed. It then collects in the trough around the base before beginning its journey to the sea.[6]

The grassy area is known as the *maidan* of *Ele-mesnedene*, while the fountain in its midst has the abil-ity to translocate visitors to the *clachan* of the *Elohim*. *Maidan* is defined as the open area around a town, while *clachan* is the town itself.[7] These are only fig-urative in the case of *Elemesnedene*, however; the foun-tain acts only as a point of metaphysical transfer to reach the actual *clachan*—that part of *Elemesnedene* physically occupied by the *Elohim*.[8]

The *clachan* appears like a wonderland, but its fea-tures are manifestations of the *Elohim*. Once the *Elo-him* leave, the area becomes "a vaguely undulating emptiness under a moonstone sky . . . as barren and sterile as a desert."[9] The only distinctive location is the eftmound: a hill encircled by a broad ring of dead elms.[10]

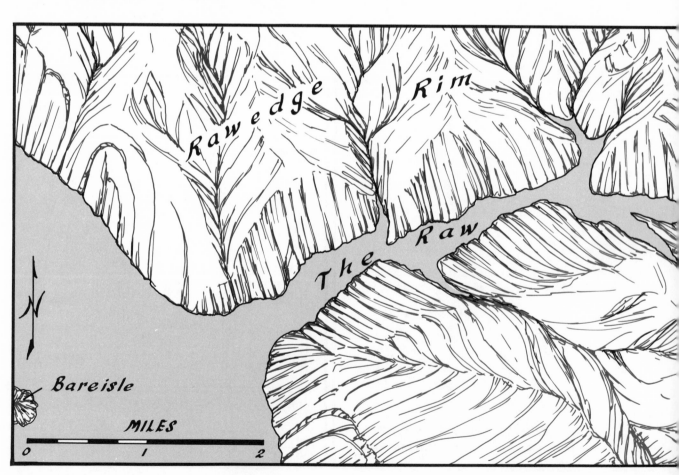

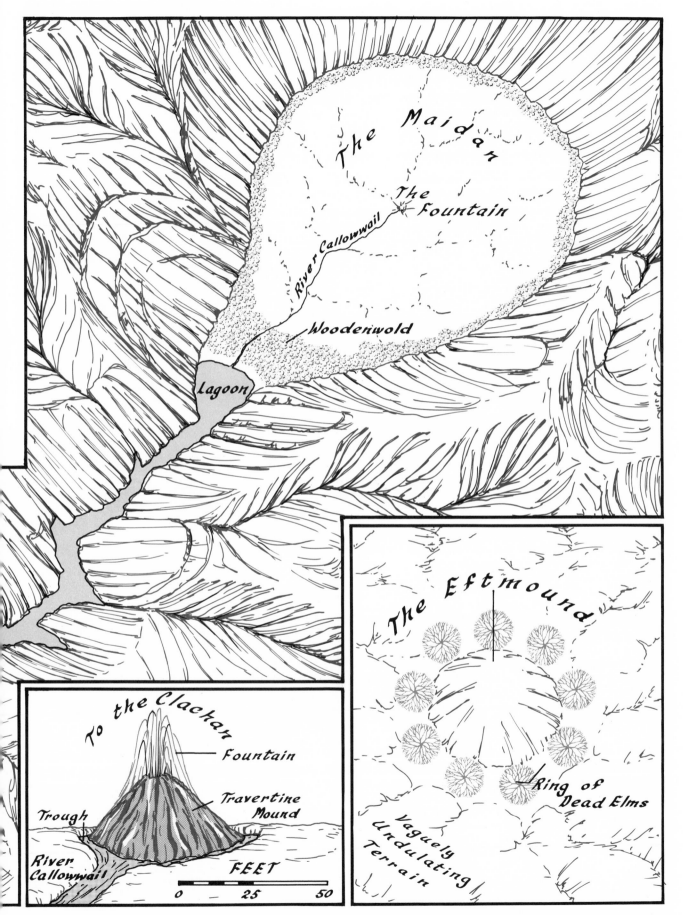

The Maidan

River Callowwail

The Fountain

Woodenwold

Lagoon

To the Clachan

Fountain

Trough

Travertine Mound

River Callowwail

FEET

0   25   50

The Eftmound

Ring of Dead Elms

Vaguely Undulating Terrain

BHRATHRAIR TOWN AND HARBOR

Bhrathairain has a deep natural harbor, large enough to dock hundreds of ships at its many piers and berths, protected from the sea by low pale-colored sandstone cliffs which end in twin watchtowers called the Spikes. The towers overlook the canyon-like gap which gives access to the harbor within.[1] The immense stone Sandwall is thirty to forty feet high, and over a hundred feet thick, protecting the harbor and its adjoining town from both the Great Desert and the warlike neighboring peoples.[2]

The coastal cliffs face roughly north.[3] On the harbor side, the cliffs arc around the east and west faces of the harbor, but on the south shore the land rises more gently. There lie the buildings of *Bhrathairain* Town. As space is at a premium, the buildings are densely packed and streets are narrow. Close to the harbor are the warehouses and supply shops dealing with the many and varied needs of the merchant marines. Farther from the harbor, warehouses and merchantries still predominate, but their products are oriented to the needs of the inhabitants and visitors rather than the needs of the ships: luxury-goods stores, weapons shops and taverns are frequent. As the town rises toward the homes, the businesses become less common, but are physically more sumptuous in keeping with the area.[4]

The far end of the fortress town is occupied by the Sandhold. Like most keeps, it is separated from the town by additional walls. Functionally, the town Sandwall encloses the innermost end of town, while the Sandhold has a Sandwall of its own (mapped as the "inner" Sandwall). The town wall is pierced by three massive stone gates, and is lined on its inner face by banquettes—the platform on which the defenders stand behind the parapet.[5]

The eastern curve of the town wall and the western curve of the inner Sandwall leave an open area between, forming two roughly triangular courts. In the center of each court is a spring. To give access to the fields and the three additional springs outside the town, a gate is cut through each of the arms of the outer Sandwall.[6]

The inner Sandwall is a perfect circle. It stands free on the town-side, next to the springs, but joins with the outer Sandwall at its southwestern edge, so only a single massive wall separates the Sandhold and the Great Desert. Two gates cut through the inner Sandwall, so there is no central gate directly opposite the one from the town. Anyone moving from the town to the Sandhold must veer left or right from the town gates to gain entry to the keep.[7]

The inner Sandwall encloses a sandy area, some fifty feet wide between the wall and the Sandhold.[8] Two broad stairs give access to the top of the Sandwall from the open sand; and underground tunnels from the Sandhold lead to passages within the wall which serve the banquettes.[9] Towering high over the Sandwall is the multistoried keep: the Sandhold.

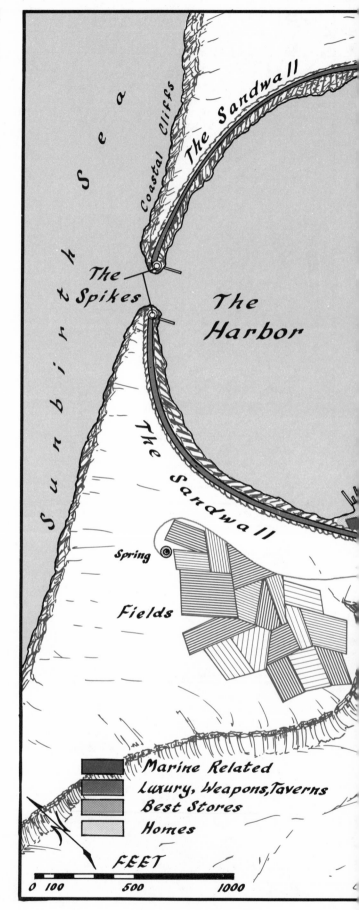

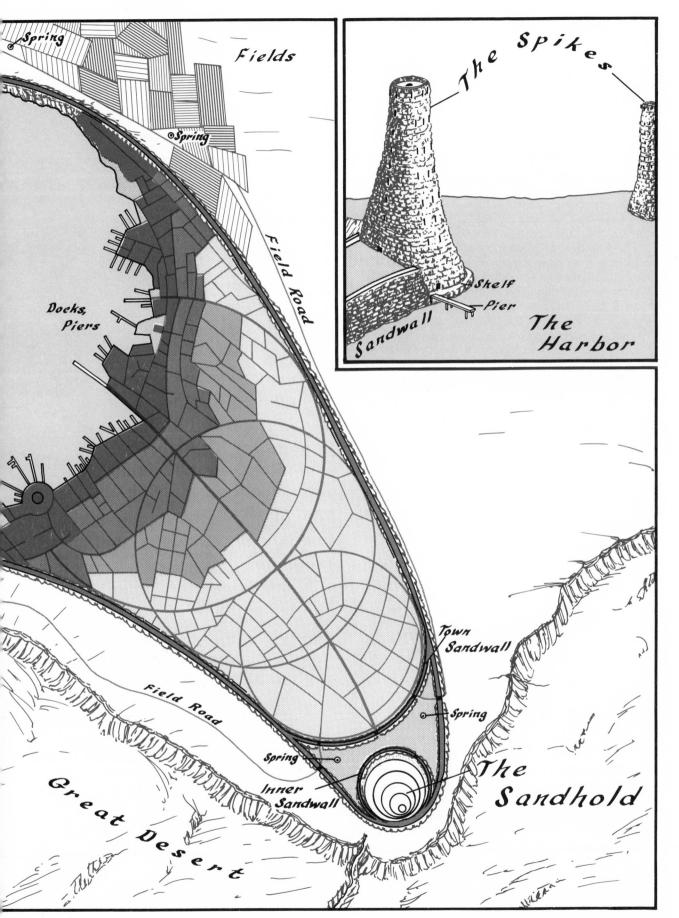

Spring

Fields

Spring

The Spikes

Docks,
Piers

Field Road

Shelf
Pier
Sandwall
The
Harbor

Town
Sandwall

Spring

Field Road

Spring

Inner
Sandwall

The
Sandhold

Great Desert

The Sandhold

In five tiers the Sandhold rises 350 feet above the outer court,[1] each tier is distinct in use and name. The prison level lies belowground, reachable via the stairs near the guardroom in the southwest,[2] and little is known of its passages.[3] All the company are eventually fettered there in a single room.[4]

The First Circinate is the warrior level and contains all the rooms necessary to eight thousand guards.[4]

The Second Circinate serves the courtiers of the *gaddhi.* Elsewhere, the tier is filled with "bright halls and chambers."[5] A large sitting-chamber and eleven sleeping rooms are provided for travelers.[6]

The third tier of the Sandhold is the Tier of Riches, and in it are displayed the treasures of the realm. The partitions give a maze-like appearance to this level.[7] A spiral stair leads to the fourth tier: the Majesty. Most of the level is filled by the *gaddhi's* throne room, whose architecture of circular tiles and downward curving ceiling focuses on the throne; the Auspice.[8] A hidden stair leads to Kasreyn's chamber in Kemper's Pitch.[9] Above, another stair climbs to Kasreyn's laboratory.[10]

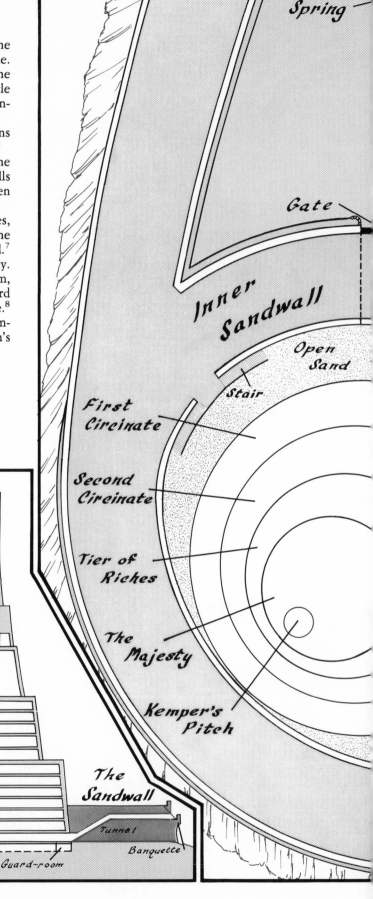

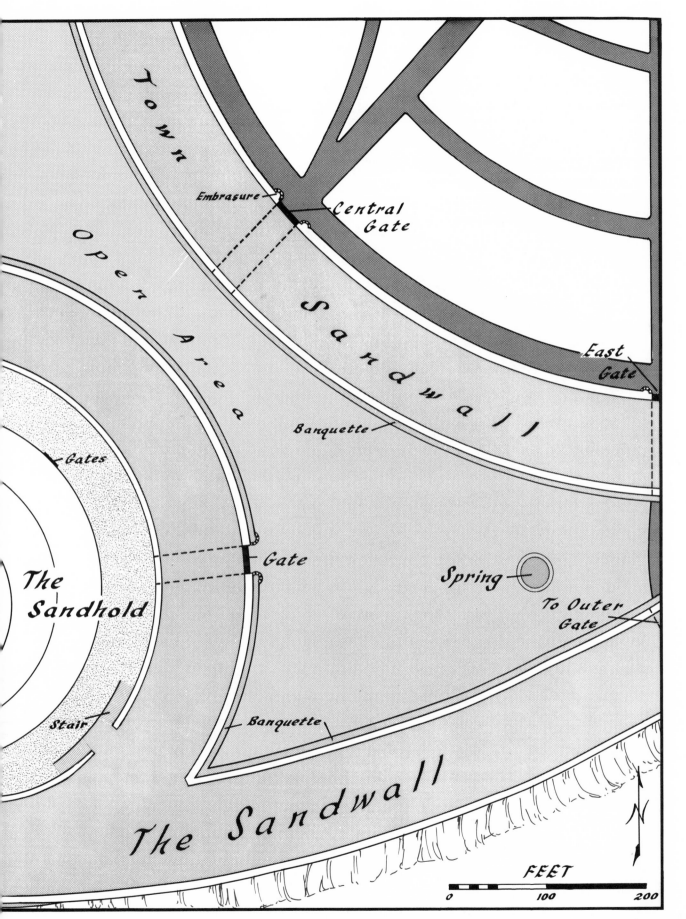

Town

Embrasure

Central Gate

Open Area

Sandwall

East Gate

Banquette

Gates

The Sandhold

Gate

Spring

To Outer Gate

Stair

Banquette

The Sandwall

N

FEET

0   100   200

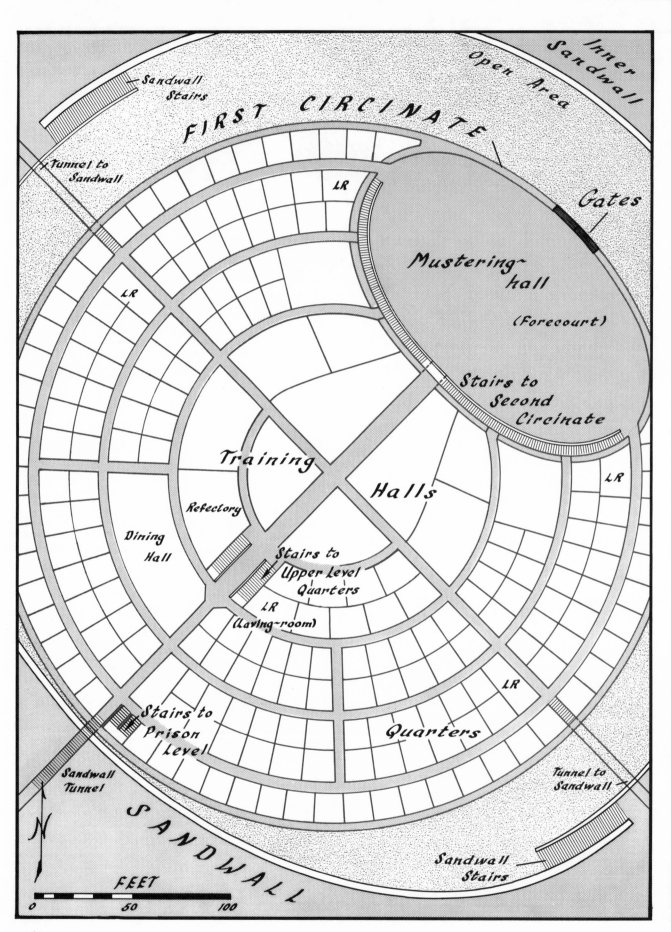

FIRST CIRCINATE

Inner Sandwall

Open Area

Sandwall Stairs

Tunnel to Sandwall

LR

LR

Gates

Mustering-hall

(Forecourt)

Stairs to Second Circinate

LR

Training

Refectory

Dining Hall

Halls

Stairs to Upper Level Quarters

LR (Living-room)

LR

Stairs to Prison Level

Quarters

Sandwall Tunnel

Tunnel to Sandwall

SANDWALL

N

Sandwall Stairs

FEET

0   50   100

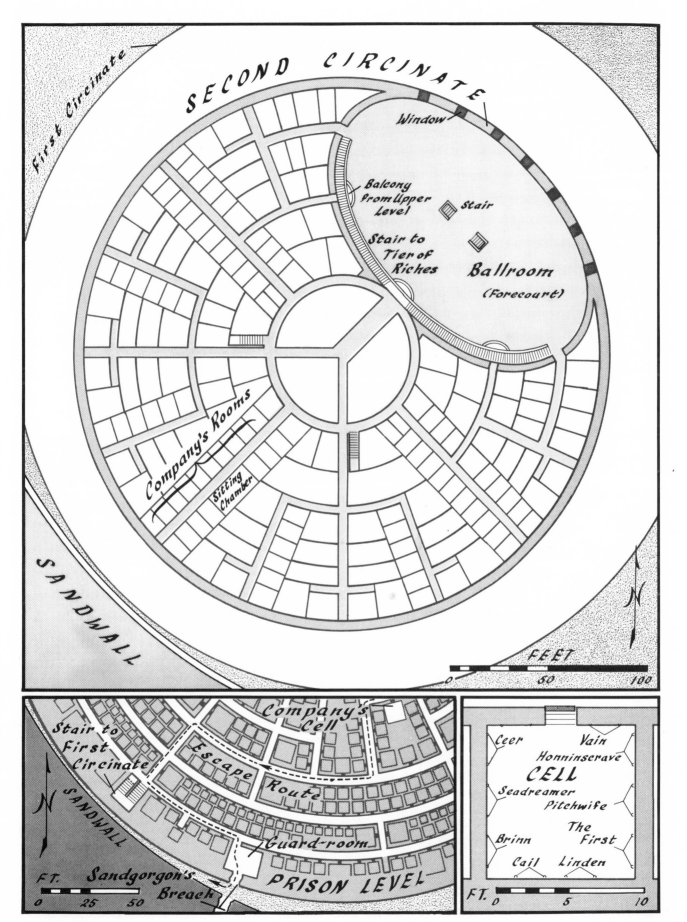

SECOND CIRCINATE

First Circinate

Window

Balcony from Upper Level

Stair

Stair to Tier of Riches

Ballroom
(Forecourt)

Company's Rooms

Sitting Chamber

SANDWALL

FEET

0   50   100

N

Stair to First Circinate

Company's Cell

Escape Route

SANDWALL

Guard-room

N

FT. Sandgorgon's Breach

0   25   50

PRISON LEVEL

Ceer   Vain

Honninscrave

CELL

Seadreamer
Pitchwife

The First

Brinn

Cail   Linden

FT. 0   5   10

THE SANDHOLD

169

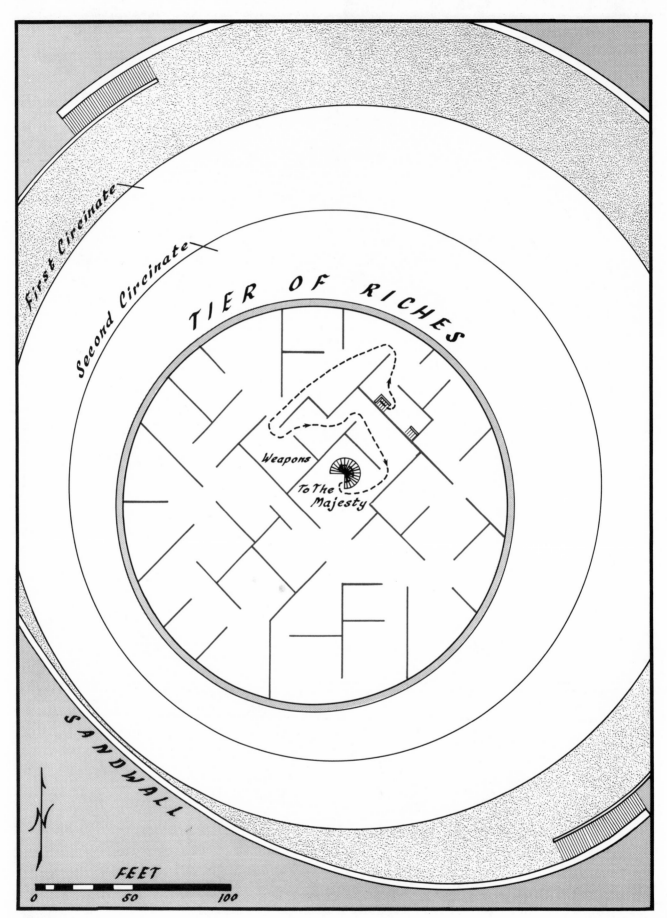

First Circinate

Second Circinate

TIER OF RICHES

Weapons

To The
Majesty

SANDWALL

N

FEET

0   50   100

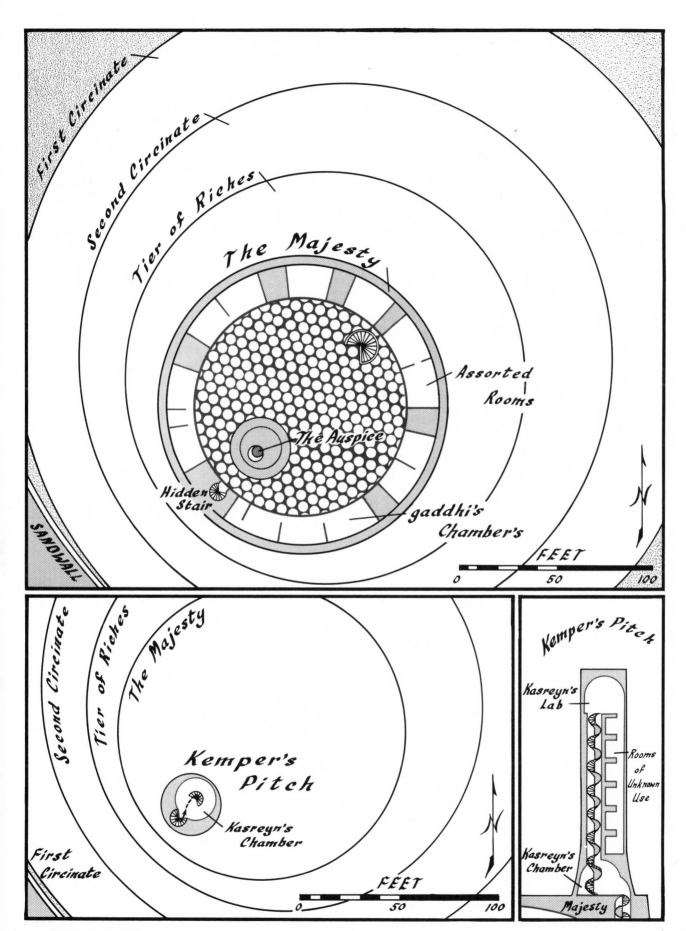

First Circinate

Second Circinate

Tier of Riches

The Majesty

Assorted Rooms

The Auspice

Hidden Stair

gaddhi's Chamber's

SANDWALL

FEET

0   50   100

Second Circinate

Tier of Riches

The Majesty

Kemper's Pitch

Kasreyn's Chamber

First Circinate

FEET

0   50   100

Kemper's Pitch

Kasreyn's Lab

Rooms of Unknown Use

Kasreyn's Chamber

Majesty

THE SANDHOLD

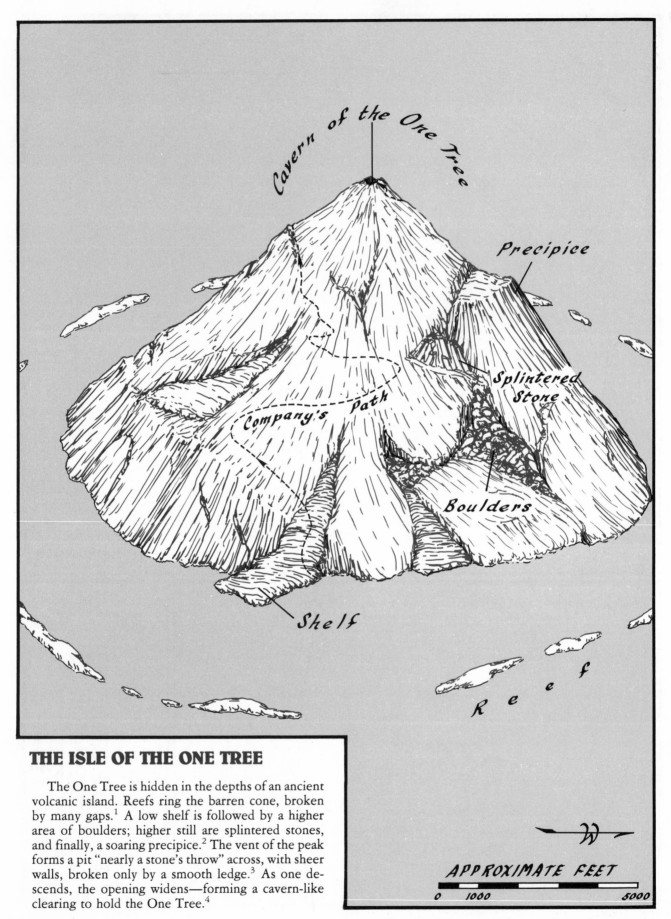

Cavern of the One Tree

Precipice

Splintered Stone

Boulders

Company's Path

Shelf

Reef

APPROXIMATE FEET

0   1000   5000

THE ISLE OF THE ONE TREE

The One Tree is hidden in the depths of an ancient volcanic island. Reefs ring the barren cone, broken by many gaps.[1] A low shelf is followed by a higher area of boulders; higher still are splintered stones, and finally, a soaring precipice.[2] The vent of the peak forms a pit "nearly a stone's throw" across, with sheer walls, broken only by a smooth ledge.[3] As one descends, the opening widens—forming a cavern-like clearing to hold the One Tree.[4]

172

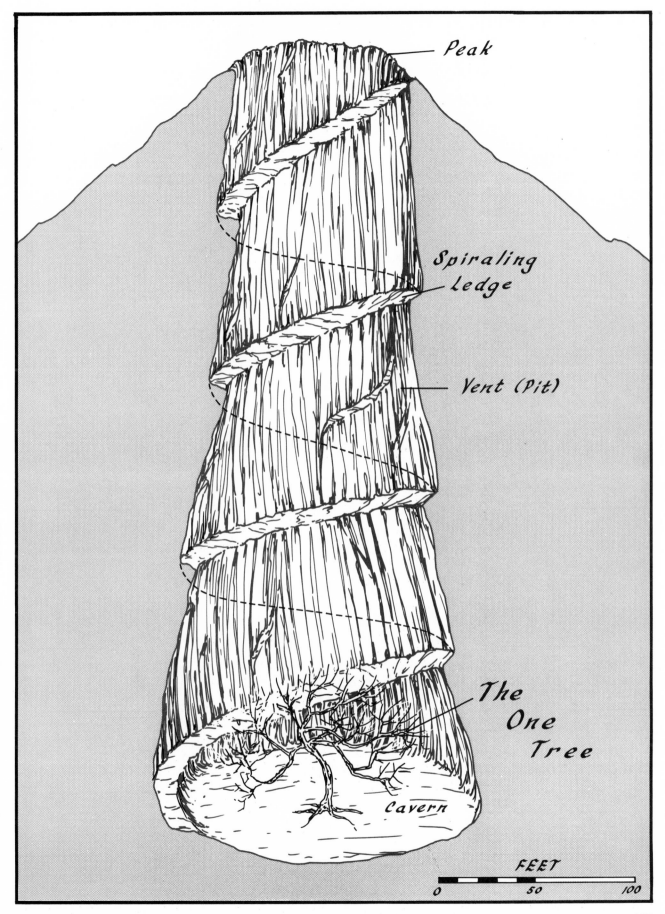

Peak

Spiraling Ledge

Vent (Pit)

The One Tree

Cavern

FEET

0   50   100

173

PATHWAY TABLES

It is during the journeys through the Land that its breadth, beauty, and tremendous variety are evident. The discoveries he makes are an important element in Covenant's gradual realization that he wants to aid the Land and its inhabitants. It is therefore helpful to the reader to trace the travels of Covenant, and other important characters, so we may more fully understand the chronology and descriptions of the tales.

The First Chronicles

Lord Foul's Bane

Day	Comments	Campsite
1	Covenant found by Lena on Kevin's Watch. Healed in Hidden Valley. Arrives at Mithil Stonedown in evening. Crosses Mithil after gathering. Rapes Lena.	Across and just downriver from Mithil bridge.
2	Atiaran comes to Covenant at dawn. Leads him into hills just north of Kevin's Watch. Triock intercepts in afternoon and tells of Lena.	North-running valley north of Kevin's Watch.
3	Leave valley.	In hills
4	Atiaran notices unquiet. Stop in late afternoon.	1st Waymeet
5	Unnatural storm.	2nd Waymeet
6	Covenant begins to perceive *health*.	By small creek
7	Find dead Waynhim in midafternoon. Walk late.	In hills
8	Uneasiness continues, but no worse.	In hills
9	Reach Soaring Woodhelven at dusk. Covenant tested.	Soaring Woodhelven
10–14	Hasten through central Andelain.	Andelain
15	Reach bowl at dusk. *Banas Nimoram* attacked. Travel all night.	———
16–20	Continue north in central Andelain. On 18th Covenant sees crescent moon rise red.	Andelain
21	Reach Soulsease River near noon. Foamfollower takes Covenant. Atiaran returns south.	Soulsease R.
22–23	Continue on river, passing confluence of the White and Gray on 22nd.	On river
24	Reach Revelstone about noon.	Tower room, Revelstone
25	Council of Lords.	Keep, Revelstone
26–31	Quest departs after dawn on 26th. Go southeast. Full moon on 29th.	Plains
32	Cross Soulsease. Find abandoned Waymeet beyond river.	South of river
33–34	Travel southeast along margin of Andelain. Foamfollower carries Covenant on 34th.	Near Andelain
35	At moonset Quest warned of *kresh* attack. Set ambush under Korik and depart. Korik leads *kresh* into hills.	Near Andelain
36–38	Quest hastens southeast at 15 leagues per day. Korik encounters marauders on 37th and is driven out of way.	Near Andelain
39	Quest reaches Mithil and turns east. Korik rejoins. Soaring Woodhelven attacked in evening.	By Mithil
40	Quest senses burning of Soaring Woodhelven. Reaches village in afternoon. Attacked in evening.	Soaring Woodhelven

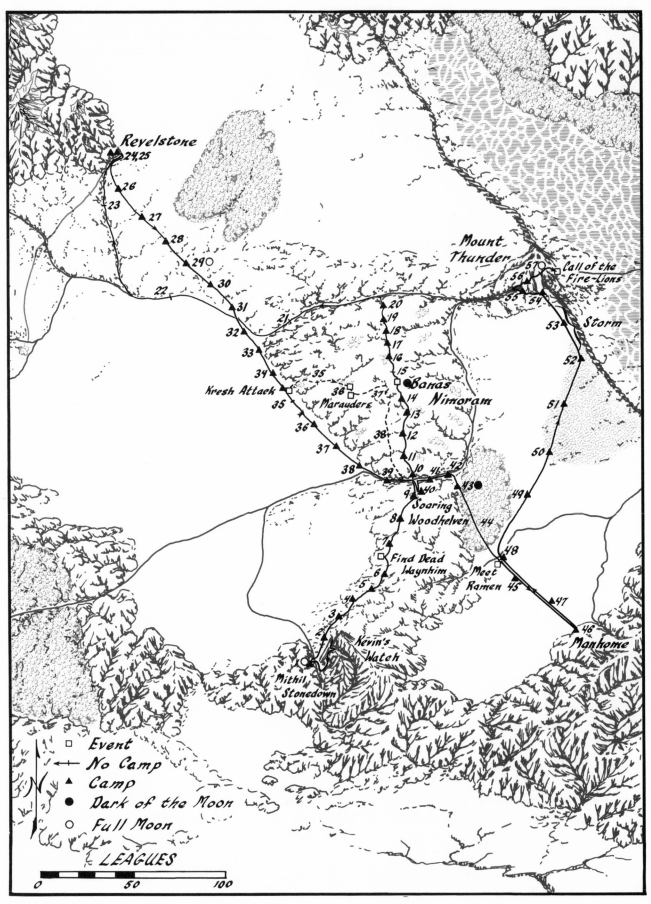

Revelstone
24,25
26
23
27
28
29
30
22
31
21
32
33
34
35
Kresh Attack
35
36
37
38
Marauders
36
37
38
39
40
9
8
Soaring
Woodhelven
Find Dead
Waynhim
6
5
4
3
2
1
Mithil
Stonedown

Kevin's
Watch

Mount
Thunder
57
56
Call of the
Fire-Lions
55
54
53
Storm
52
51
50
20
19
18
17
16
15
14
13
12
11
41
42
43
44
49
48
Meet
Ramen
45
47
46
Manhome
Sanas
Nimoram

☐ Event
↦ No Camp
▲ Camp
● Dark of the Moon
○ Full Moon

N

LEAGUES

0   50   100

Day	Comments	Campsite
41–43	Quest returns to Mithil, travels east along south bank.	Along Mithil
44	Quests passes through Morinmoss without stopping.	——
45	Quest leaves Morinmoss at noon. Cross Roamsedge Ford and rest. Ramen surround. Lead for several leagues. Ramen destroy *kresh* pack.	On Plains of Ra
46	Reach Manhome at dusk. Covenant summons Ranyhyn in late evening.	Manhome
47	In morning Mhoram chosen by Ranyhyn. Quest leaves in afternoon, rides late.	On Plains of Ra
48	Reach Roamsedge River.	Roamsedge Ford
49–52	Pass through ancient battleground.	Landsdrop on 52nd.
53–54	Storm begins at noon on 53rd; continues to afternoon of 54th.	Landsdrop
55	Quest struggles west along base of Mount Thunder. Hear drums of Drool's departing army during day. Reaches Look of Treacher's Gorge as army still departs. Camp in evening, and enter Mount Thunder during night.	Ravine near Gorge
56	Cross Warrenbridge. Brief rests. Attack in catacombs. Birinair dies. Second Ward found.	Near room of Second Ward
57	Pass through Rocklight Cavern. Covenant falls into crevice and is taken to Drool. Full moon. Battle with Drool and seizure of Staff of Law.	Kiril Threndor
58	Escape from Drool. Quest reaches ravine on east side of Mount Thunder at dawn. Drool pursues. Calling of Fire-Lions. Covenant calls Ranyhyn, then fades.	

The Illearth War

Summoning to Covenant's Departure

Day	Comments	Campsite
1	Foul's Army departs Shattered Hills. Manethrall departs. Mhoram has prescient dream of Giants' doom.	Spoiled Plains
3	Korik's Mission to Seareach departs at dawn.	E. of Revelstone
5	Attack on Mission in Grimmerdhore (*see* "Gilden-fire")	Grimmerdhore
11	Mission descends Landsdrop; enters Sarangrave; races from Lurker. Ride all night.	——
12	Mission reaches Defiles Course at midmorning. Builds raft.	Defiles Course
14	Shetra falls. Runnik sent to tell Lords.	Defiles Course
20	Hyrim revives. Mission escapes Lifeswallower. Manethrall Rue arrives in late evening. Bloodguard, Verement and Callindrill depart at night.	N. Lifeswallower Revelstone ——
21	Korik's Mission reaches Boundary Hills of Seareach. Quaan and several Eoward depart at dawn. Rest of Warward, Lords and Covenant leave in morning.	Below hills Rafts on White West of White River
22	Lords and Troy turn southwest in afternoon. Army continues south at 10 leagues per day.	Rough grassland West of White
24	Lords pass through Rock Gardens. Runnik arrives during night.	South of Maerl
25	Korik's mission reaches *Coercri*. Giants killed. Tull and other Bloodguard depart.	*Coercri*

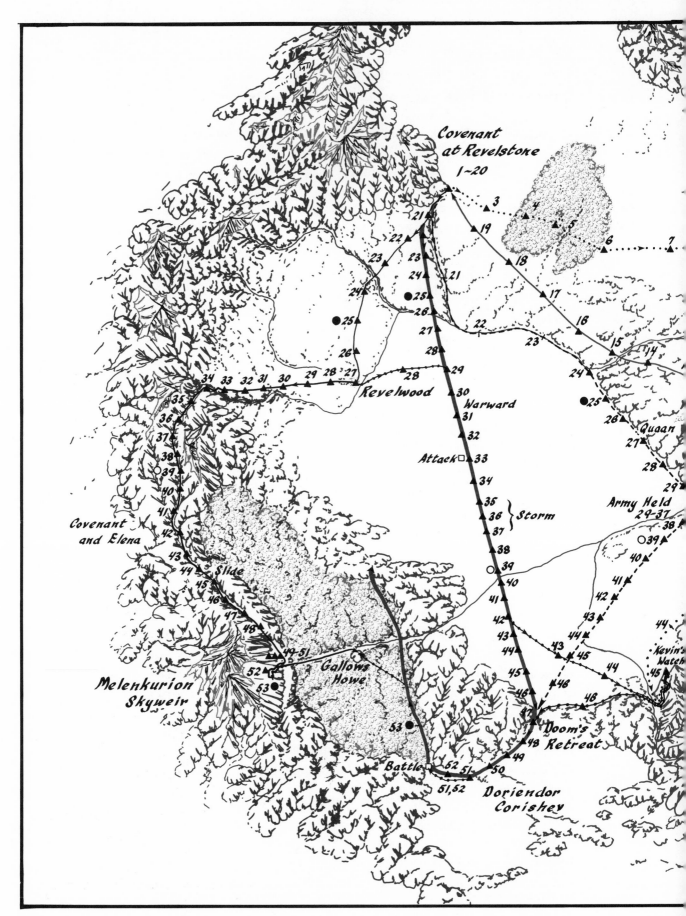

Covenant
at Revelstone
1~20

Revelwood

Warward

Attack□

Storm

Covenant
and Elena

Slide

Melenkurion
Skyweir

Gallows
Howe

Battle

Quaan

Army Held
29-37

Kevin's
Watch

Doom's
Retreat

Doriendor
Corishev

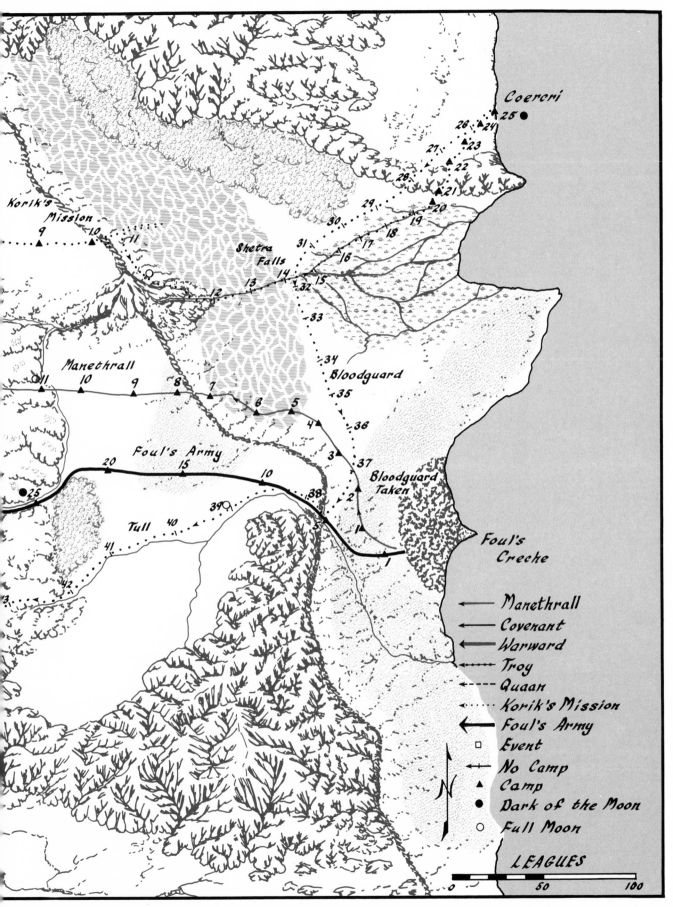

Coercri

•25

26 ▲24

27 ▲23

▲22

28 ▲21

29 ▲20

30 19

18

31 17

Shetra 16

Falls

14 15

13 32

12 33

34

Bloodguard

35

Manethrall

11 10 9 8 7 6 5

4 36

Foul's Army 3 37

20 15 10 38 Bloodguard

•25 2 Taken

39 1

Tull 40

41 Foul's

Creche

42

3

→ Manethrall

→ Covenant

→ Warward

Troy

Quaan

Korik's Mission

Foul's Army

□ Event

No Camp

▲ Camp

● Dark of the Moon

○ Full Moon

N

LEAGUES

0 50 100

THE ILLEARTH WAR

179

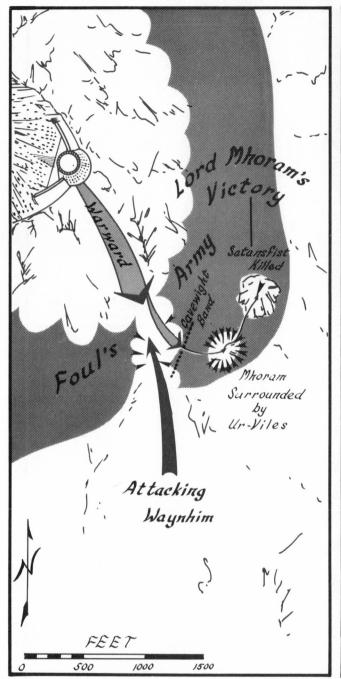

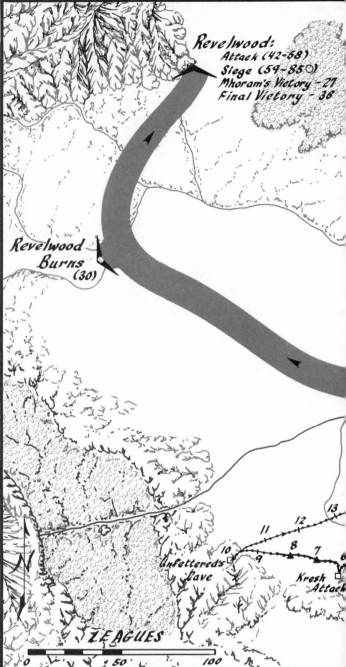

Day	Comments	Campsite
27	Lords arrive at Revelwood. Amok reappears.	Revelwood
28	Elena and Covenant follow Amok toward mountains. Troy and rest of company turn east toward Warward.	Trothgard Central Plains
29	Foul's Army reaches Mithil valley at west edge of Andelain. Bloodguard battle Army. Troy meets Warward in midafternoon.	SW Andelain Central Plains
30	Quaan and Eoward reach Mithil; join battle.	SW Andelain
33	Elena and Covenant reach gorge of the Rill. Warward attacked by *kresh* during night.	SW Trothgard Central Plains
35–37	Unnatural storm directed at Quaan.	————

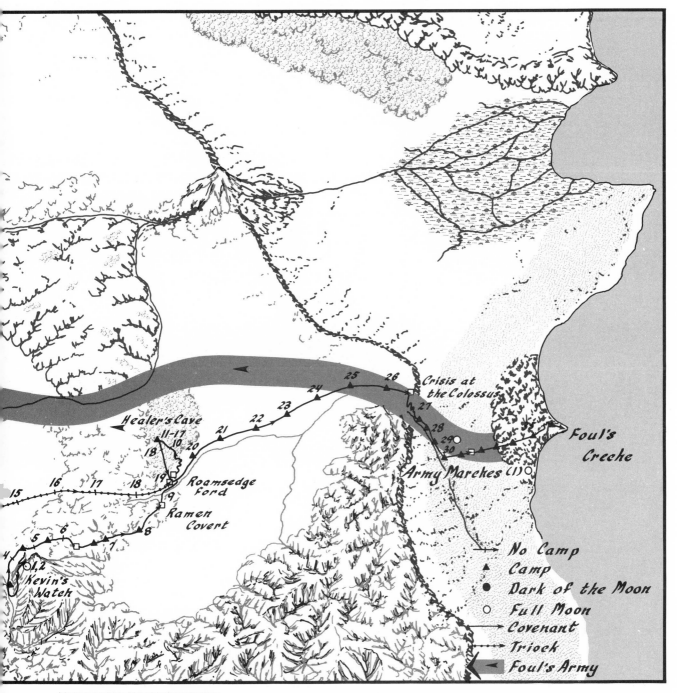

THE POWER THAT PRESERVES

Day	Comments	Campsite
	Two Bloodguard captured. Tull escapes.	
38	Quaan starts retreat 1 day early.	SW of battle
40	Warward swims Black River.	South Plains
42	Troy and Mhoram leave Warward at dawn.	South Plains
45	Elena and Covenant encounter rockslide. Myrnha dies.	Westron Mts.
	Troy and Mhoram reach Mithil Stonedown at dusk.	Kevin's Watch
	Ascend to Kevin's Watch. Tull reaches Watch in night.	
47	Troy, Quaan, Warward, and Foul's Army all reach Doom's Retreat in afternoon. BATTLE OF DOOM'S RETREAT.	Doom's Retreat

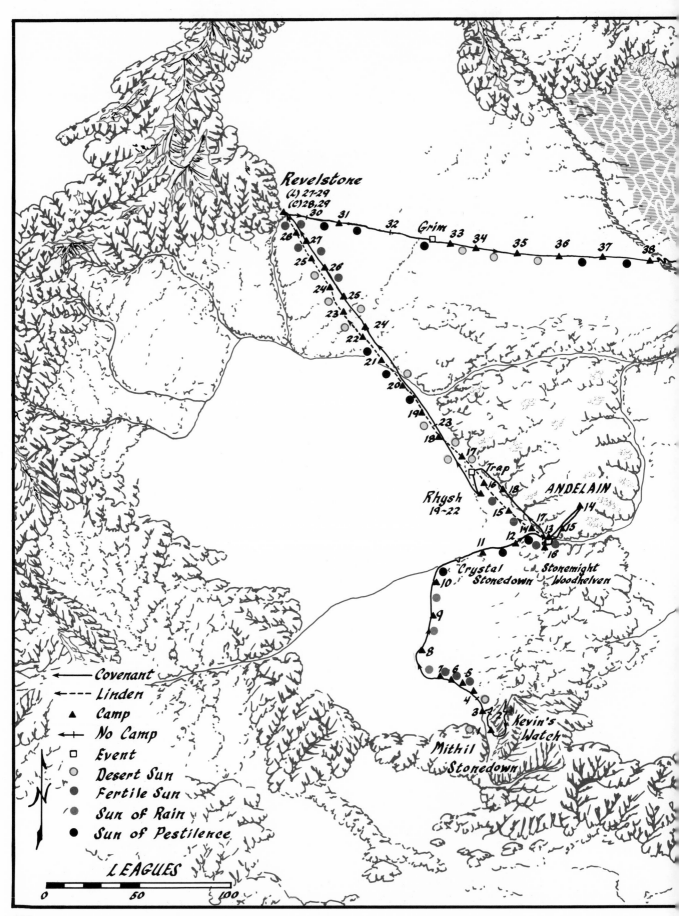

Revelstone
(L) 27-29
(C) 28,29
30 31   32   Grim 33 34   35   36   37   38

Rhysh
19-22

Trap

ANDELAIN

Crystal
Stonedown

Stonemight
Woodhelven

Kevin's
Watch

Mithil
Stonedown

→ Covenant
--- Linden
▲ Camp
+ No Camp
□ Event
● Desert Sun
● Fertile Sun
● Sun of Rain
● Sun of Pestilence

N

LEAGUES
0   50   100

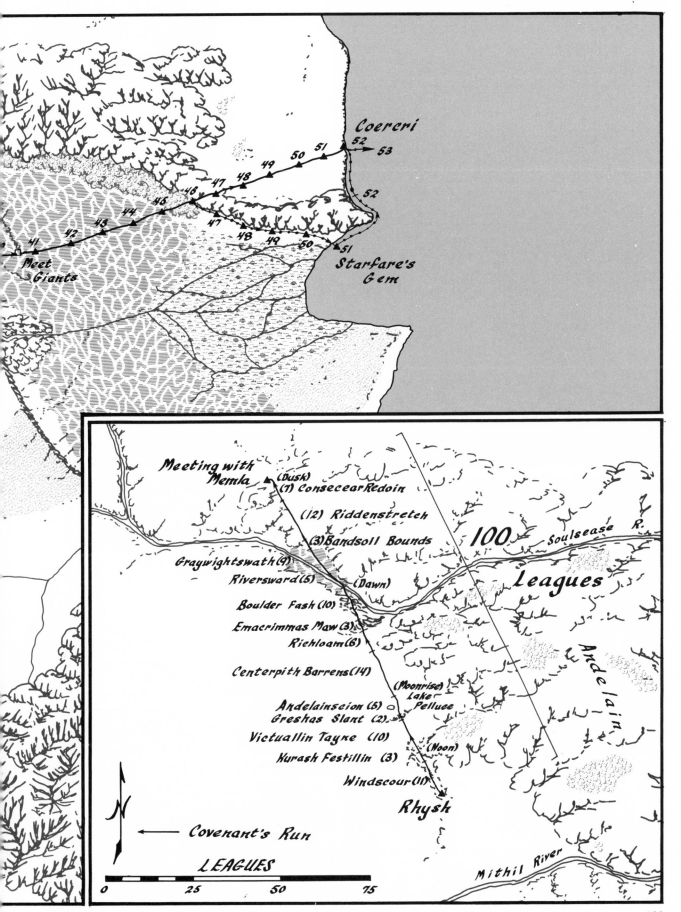

Coercri

52
53
51
50
49
48
47
52
46
45
44
47
52
43
42
48
49
50
41
51
Meet
Giants

Starfare's
Gem

Meeting with
Memla   (Dusk)
        (1) Consecear Redoin
        (12) Riddenstretch
        (3) Bandsoll Bounds   100
Graywightswath (9)   Soulsease R.
Riversward (5)   (Dawn)   Leagues
Boulder Fash (10)
Emacrimmas Maw (3)
Richloam (6)
Centerpith Barrens (14)
                (Moonrise)
Andelainscion (5) Lake
Greshas Slant (2) Pelluce
Victuallin Tayne (10)
Kurash Festillin (3)   (Noon)
Windscour (11)

Rhysh

Mithil River

N

⟵ Covenant's Run

LEAGUES
0   25   50   75

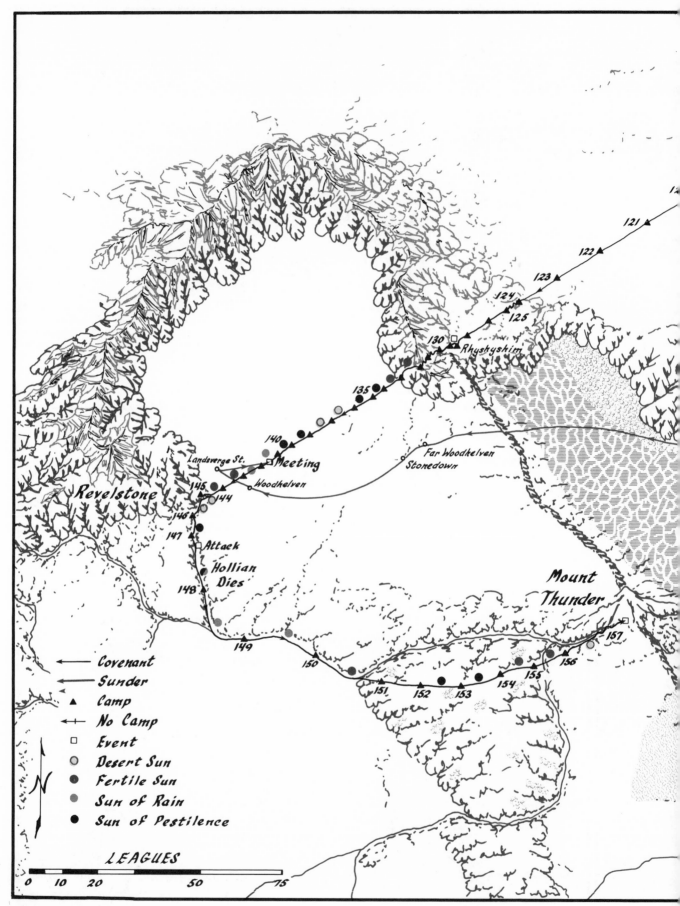

121
122
123
124
125
130
Rhyshyshim
135
140
Landsverge St.
Meeting
Woodhelven
Far Woodhelven
Stonedown
145
144
Revelstone
146
147
Attack
Hollian
Dies
148
149
150
151
152
153
154
155
156
157
Mount
Thunder

Covenant
Sunder
Camp
No Camp
Event
Desert Sun
Fertile Sun
Sun of Rain
Sun of Pestilence

N

LEAGUES
0   10   20   50   75

184

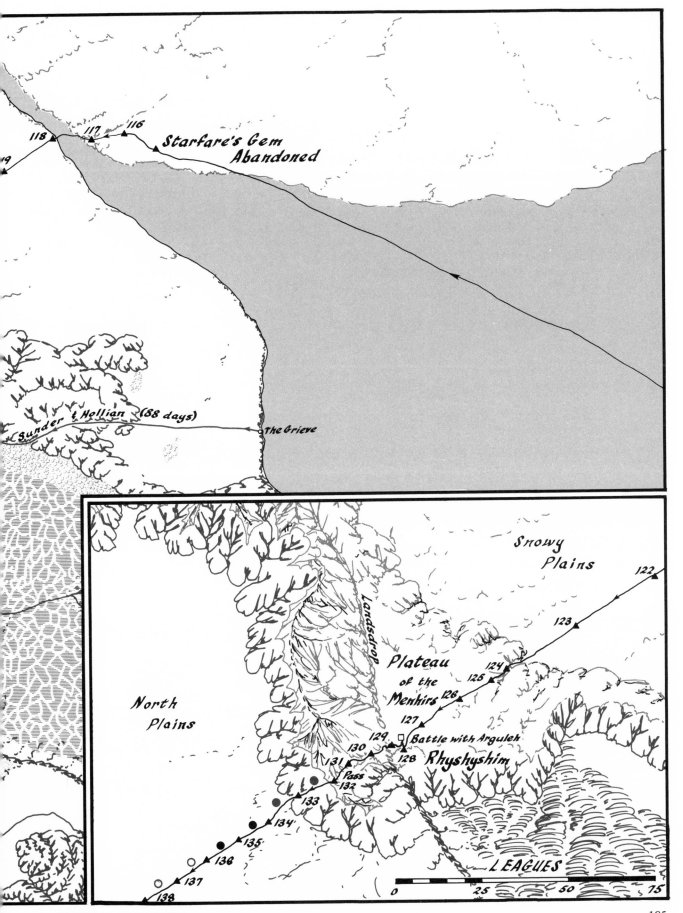

Starfare's Gem
Abandoned

(Sunder & Hollian) (88 days)   The Grieve

Snowy
Plains

North
Plains

Landsdrop

Plateau
of the
Menhirs

Battle with Arguleh

Rhyshyshim

Pass

LEAGUES

0   25   50   75

Day	Comments	Campsite
48	Verement seals Retreat. Foul's Army trapped on north. Warward marches west.	Doom's Retreat SW of Retreat
49	Foul's Army clears path through Doom's Retreat. Elena and Covenant reach Rivenrock.	Doom's Retreat Rivenrock
51	Warward reaches Doriendor Corishev in afternoon with Foul's Army close behind.	Doriendor Corishev
52	Troy sends most of Warward west. Fleshharrower summons tornado. Troy blinded. Elena and Covenant enter *Melenkurion* Skyweir.	Doriendor Corishev *Mel.* Skyweir
53	DARK OF THE MOON Troy found and escapes with rest of Warward to Cravenhaw. BATTLE OF CRAVENHAW. Forestal allows passage of Warward; destroys Foul's Army. Elena reaches EarthBlood; summons Kevin.	Garroting Deep *Mel.* Skyweir
54	Warward sent out north of Garroting Deep. Troy, Quaan, and Mhoram brought to Gallows Howe. Covenant and Bannor escape along Black River. Kevin kills Elena. Covenant fades.	Gallows Howe

The Power That Preserves

Prior to Covenant's Second Summoning

Day	Comments	Campsite
1	Full moon. Foul's Army issues from Shattered Hills. Preternatural winter initiated.	
30	Revelwood burned. Mhoram summons Covenant, but is refused.	
42	Foul's Army arrives at Revelstone. Begins direct attack.	
44–58	Satansfist attacks with Illearth Stone fragment.	
59–85	Siege.	

From Beginning of Covenant's Second Summoning

Day	Comments	Campsite
1	FULL EMERALD MOON glimpsed through clouds. Triock and Foamfollower begin attempt to summon Covenant. Covenant catches glimpse of moon. Marauders sense power and turn toward Mithil Stonedown. Foul's Army given signal to attack outer gates. End siege.	Kevin's Watch South Plains Revelstone
2	Outer gates fall. Tower taken. Inner gates attacked.	Revelstone
3	Covenant finally succumbs to summons; and is taken to Mithil Stonedown. Battle against marauders. Trell immolates the Close; but Mhoram overcomes. Attack on inner gates fails.	Mithil Stonedown Revelstone
4	Covenant heads east through hills. Foamfollower carries him until near dawn. Triock starts toward Unfettered One's cave. Sleeps a few hours in evening, then continues through night.	N. of Mithil Stonedown N. end of mts. beyond Mithil
5, 6	Triock and Covenant both continue night journeys.	———
7	Triock uses *lomillialor* to defeat *kresh* attack. Descends to plains and walks all day. Covenant found by Ramen and Bannor at dawn. Walk until afternoon, rest; then continue until late at night.	——— Nearing Ra

Day	Comments	Campsite
9	Triock encounters unnatural blizzard. Yeurquin lost at night. Triock continues without rest.	North of Doom's Retreat
	Covenant reaches Ramen covert at dusk. Covert attacked. Covenant and Lena escape north.	———
10	Triock is found by Unfettered One. Raver kills Unfettered One, captures Triock. Mhoram senses Unfettered One's death.	Last Hills
	Covenant and Lena led by Pietten to Roamsedge Ford before dawn. Lena and Pietten killed. Covenant wanders into Morinmoss and is found by Healer.	Morinmoss
11–17	Covenant in Healer's Cave.	Morinmoss
18	Covenant leaves Cave near dusk. Travels all night.	———
19	Covenant reaches Roamsedge Ford. Meets Triock-raver and is drugged.	Roamsedge Ford
20	During deep night, Covenant's ring is taken.	N. of Roamsedge
	Krill goes dead in Revelstone. Mhoram summons Ranyhyn. Tells Quaan to prepare an attack.	Revelstone
21–26	Covenant carried toward Colossus.	N. of Roamsedge
27	Waynhim destroy Foul's Army's food supply. Mhoram and Warward attack. Satansfist killed—"Lord Mhoram's" Victory.	Revelstone
	Covenant brought to Elena's specter at the Colossus. Bannor, Foamfollower, and Ramen find Covenant and attack; but are overpowered. Covenant regains ring and destroys Staff of Law. Unnatural winter ends. Covenant and Foamfollower descend Landsdrop.	Below Colossus
30	Ruinwash floods. Covenant and Foamfollower turn east.	Gully by river
31	Ascend ridge in Spoiled Plains.	Ridge
32	Attacked by fire in thicket. After seeking refuge in mud pit, are pulled below by *jheherrin*.	Tunnels of *jheherrin*
33–34	Travel for leagues through tunnels.	Tunnels
35	Ascend into Shattered Hills at night. Foamfollower swims Hotash Slay; heaves Covenant rest of way.	———
36	Covenant awakes in gully near Hotash Slay. Works toward entrance. Foamfollower overtakes him near entrance; overpowers Warder.	Foul's Creche
	Covenant and Foamfollower locate the Thronehall. Foul is reduced and Covenant destroys Illearth Stone.	
	Foul's Army routed. Mhoram gives *krill* to Glimmermere.	

The Wounded Land

Day	Comments	Campsite
1	RAIN—Covenant and Linden arrive on Kevin's Watch. Meet Nassic in Hidden Valley. Nassic leaves for Stonedown and is murdered by Marid-raver. In evening Covenant and Linden discover body; leave for Stonedown. Are captured and imprisoned by Stonedowners.	Mithil Stonedown
2	DESERT—Test of silence just after dawn. In evening Marid is bound far north of the village. Covenant convinces Sunder to lead them from Stonedown. Walk all night.	N. of Stonedown
3	DESERT—Covenant and Linden search for Marid, but fail. Covenant bitten.	Mithil riverbed
4	DESERT—Continue in riverbed. Walk part of night.	Mithil riverbed
5–7	FERTILE—Leave river. Walk in daytime only.	Near riverbed
8–10	RAIN—Build a raft and ride the river during day.	Riverbank
11	PESTILENCE—Continue on raft. Reach confluence with Black River. Bees attack Covenant. Reach Crystal Stonedown at dusk. Covenant frees Hollian. Raft east.	E. of Crystal Stonedown
12–13	PESTILENCE—Continue east on river to southwest corner of Andelain.	Wastes across from Andelain
14	FERTILE—Covenant walks all day and into night. Meets Caer-Caveral and dead. Receives Vain.	Knoll in Andelain
	Linden, Sunder, and Hollian captured by Stonemight Woodhelven. Clave Rider takes them and the Stonemight.	NW of Woodhelven
15–16	FERTILE—Covenant reaches SW Andelain in morning of 16th. Crosses river to search for Linden. Captured by Woodhelvennin.	Stonemight Woodhelven
17	DESERT—Covenant escapes after dawn with Vain's help. Crosses into Andelain and walks all night.	———
18	DESERT—Covenant sleeps in evening. Is awakened by dead who walk with him until dawn.	West Andelain
19	DESERT—In evening Covenant sees fire west of Andelain. Frees captured Waynhim, but is attacked. Is found by Hamako and Waynhim and taken to *rhysh*.	Near *rhysh* of the Waynhim
20–22	PESTILENCE—Covenant recuperates.	*Rhysh*
	Rider with Linden six days ride ahead.	N. of Soulsease
23–24	DESERT—With blood-speed from the Waynhim, Covenant runs 100 leagues without stopping. Reaches Soulsease at dawn 24th. Finds Memla na-Mhoram in same evening.	23—No camp; 24—60 lgs. SE of Revelstone
25	DESERT—Covenant journeys with Memla.	Plains
26–27	FERTILE—Covenant continues with Memla.	Plains
	Santonin reaches Revelstone. Linden and Stonedowners imprisoned.	Revelstone
28	FERTILE—Covenant and Memla reach Revelstone. Vain refused entrance.	Revelstone suite
29	RAIN—Vain scales Revelstone. Covenant shown Banefire. Vain finds heels of Staff of Law. Covenant and Vain imprisoned.	Dungeon
30	RAIN—Covenant taken to Soothtell at midday. Frees himself, those in dungeons. Goes to Glimmermere for *krill*. All escape Revelstone,	E. of Revelstone

	and with Memla go east. Ride all night. Gibbon begins raising the *Grim*.	
31–32	PESTILENCE—Quest continues east from Revelstone. Hollian foretells sending of *Grim* in afternoon of 33rd, so guest rides without stopping night of 32nd.	———
33	PESTILENCE—*Grim* reaches Quest in afternoon at same time as an on-slaught of Sunbane victims. Memla draws attack of creatures and *Grim* to herself and dies. Attack ends at dusk. Linden and Cail in convulsions.	Boulder Mound on North Plains
34	DESERT—Heat turns plain into graveling. Sunder calls Coursers and they escape.	North Plains
35–38	2 DESERT, 2 PESTILENCE—Reach Landsdrop in evening.	Landsdrop
39	PESTILENCE—Linden notes Sunbane ends at Landsdrop. Quest descends old Giantway path, enters Sarangrave. Quest is surrounded by acid-creatures; Coursers destroyed and attack ends.	Sarangrave
40–41	RAIN—In afternoon of 41st, Sunder captured by serpent. Covenant frees him using white gold. Acid-creatures reappear. Quest meets Giants' Search, escape, but are reattacked. *Sur-jheherrin* destroy creatures. Covenant convinces Search to accompany him.	Sarangrave
42–46	*Sur-jheherrin* lead Quest and Search through Sarangrave.	Boundary Hills
47–51	Honninscrave walks to Starfare's Gem. Quest and Search go NE to *Coercri*.	N. of Delta Seareach
52	Company reaches *Coercri*—The Grieve. Covenant tells of Giants' demise, gives *caamora* to the dead.	*Coercri*
53	In morning Starfare's Gem reaches *Coercri*. First agrees the Search will bear Covenant to *Elohim*. Sunder and Hollian take *krill* and return west.	Sunbirth Sea

The One Tree

53	Linden realizes Raver aboard.	Starfare's Gem
54	Raver-rats attack, bite Covenant.	
55	Call of the *Nicor*.	
58	Covenant's fever breaks.	
69	Sight Bareisle	
71	Reach *Elemesnedene*. Covenant silenced. Honninscrave learns path to Isle of the One Tree. Escape *Elohim* and leave Raw at dusk. DARK OF THE MOON.	
75	Findail appears aboard ship. Linden attempts to enter Covenant.	
77	Hurricane hits. Ship flounders.	
78	Midmast is removed. Ship rights and sails south.	
83	Starfare's Gem reaches *Brathairain*. Covenant and Linden go to Sandhold. Kemper takes Covenant at night. Hergrom rescues and kills *hustin*.	Sandhold
84	Hergrom killed by Nom. Company attempts escape and are imprisoned. Covenant taken again by Kemper.	Dungeon

Day	Comments	Campsite
85	Covenant freed from silence. Summons Nom. Company escapes Sandhold, then *Brathairain*.	Ship
90	*Haruchai* plunge after *merewives*, but are rescued.	
99	Quest reaches Isle of the One Tree in midafternoon. DARK OF THE MOON. Brinn defeats Guardian.	Isle of the One Tree
100	Quest climbs Isle, descends to Tree. Seadreamer dies. Return to ship at dusk. *Nicor* beset ship.	Ship

White Gold Wielder

Day	Comments	Campsite
ca. 108	Starfare's Gem encounters Soulbiter.	
115	Ship trapped by ice.	80–100 lgs. from coast of Seareach
116	Covenant, Linden, Search Giants start for shore. Travel 20 leagues northwest.	Ice ridge
117	Attacked by *arghuleh* at midmorning. Rest only briefly in evening, then continue.	Ice ridge
118	Climb ridge. Cross 1 lg. of water to coast.	Shore
119–123	Cross plain.	
124–125	Climb foothills of Northron Climbs to plateau-like area.	
128	*Arghuleh* attack. Waynhim rescue.	*Rhyshyshim*
129	*Arghuleh* defeated. Company journeys after battle.	Landsdrop
130–132	Climb pass of Northron Climbs.	Pass
133	FERTILE—Descend from mountains.	Foothills
141	RAIN—Company met by Sunder, Hollian, and *Haruchai*.	North Plains
144	FERTILE—Company reaches Revelstone.	Outside Revelstone
145	DESERT—Battles at gate. Covenant summons Nom. Honninscrave kills Gibbon, and Nom destroys Honninscrave-raver.	Revelstone
146	DESERT—Nom delves water channel and quenches Banefire. Company departs at noon for Mount Thunder.	White River Channel
148	PESTILENCE/RAIN—Company attacked. Hollian moves next day's sun of Rain forward, but is killed. Company swims rest of day.	Bank of river
151	FERTILE—Company reaches northwest Andelain. Sunder destroys Caer-Caveral.	NW Andelain
152	No aura. Sunder and Hollian say farewell. Findail imprisons Vain in oak. Linden leaves in evening and meets Kevin. Returns, then travels east alone most the night. Rest follow.	Stream by Gilden
157	DESERT—Andelain dies. Company descends to Treacher's Gorge and enters Mount Thunder.	Catacombs
158	Vain and Findail fall into magma pool. Covenant and Linden captured by Cavewights.	Wightbarrow
159	Giants rescue Covenant and Linden. Reach Kiril Threndor. Foul destroyed. Linden forges new Staff of Law and heals the Land.	

NOTES

The following abbreviations have been used:

I   *Lord Foul's Bane*
II   *The Illearth War*
III   *The Power That Preserves*
IV   *The Wounded Land*
V   *The One Tree*
VI   *White Gold Wielder*
Interview   Donaldson Interview
G   "Gilden-Fire," *Daughter of Regals*

Page numbers for all the Thomas Covenant books refer to the Del Rey paperback editions. For information of the book titles cited, see the Selected References section, by author.

INTRODUCTION

1. I, 96, 97; III, 131
2. I, 196
3. I, 193
4. I, 393
5. II, 104
6. I, 45
7. II, 176, 186, 267
8. II, 273
9. II, 402
10. II, 443
11. II, 511
12. II, 94
13. II, 297
14. VI, 81

HAVEN FARM

1. I, 10; Interview
2. I, 4; II, 13
3. I, 3
4. III, 23; IV, 12
5. I, 20
6. I, 10, 20; III, 24; Interview
7. II, 5
8. IV, 12; Interview: The layout of Haven Farm and Covenant's House is based on Stephen Donaldson's home at the time he wrote *Lord Foul's Bane.*
9. IV, 43
10. I, 21
11. III, 9; IV, 27, 43
12. IV, 28
13. IV, 45, 46

THE TOWN

1. I, 3
2. I, 3; IV, 5
3. III, 11; IV, 4
4. III, 13
5. IV, 3, 8, 11
6. I, 29

7. I, 2–5
8. IV, 11
9. I, 29 (Probably a bank with offices upstairs.)
10. I, 4
11. I, 7
12. I, 26
13. I, 29

THE LAND

1. I, 45, 46
2. II, 143; G, 90
3. Espenshade, 229
4. I, 96, 97; II, 94
5. II, 300; III, 431
6. I, 393

THE SOUTHWEST

1. IV, 184
2. III, 143
3. I, 100
4. I, 99
5. I, 102, 117
6. IV, 124
7. II, 325, 355
8. II, 351
9. II, 354
10. II, 420
11. II, 421
12. II, 420, 427–429
13. II, 272, 486, 489
14. II, 442, 443

CRYSTAL STONEDOWN

1. III, 143
2. Stein, 120
3. IV, 184–185
4. Interview

STONEMIGHT WOODHELVEN

1. IV, 243, 244

2. IV, 232; Interview
3. IV, 234
4. IV, 234
5. IV, 245, 247
6. IV, 234
7. Interview
8. Interview
9. IV, 241

MITHIL VALLEY

1. I, 59, 61; IV, 89, 90
2. II, 285
3. IV, 72
4. I, 59–61
5. III, 123; IV, 149
6. I, 84
7. I, 99–101, 117

KEVIN'S WATCH

1. I, 39
2. I, 101; II, 274
3. I, 38
4. I, 41; II, 285; Interview
5. I, 41; IV, 67
6. IV, 69, 70
7. IV, 72
8. Donaldson describes this image as based on a feature in India.
9. The stream course is determined by the path's turning west away from the stream, and curving south along the west face of the mountain—yet never crossing the stream.

THE HIDDEN VALLEY

1. I, 52
2. I, 52
3. III, 102
4. IV, 72, 73, 89
5. IV, 74, 86
6. IV, 73

MITHIL STONEDOWN

1. I, 59
2. Interview
3. IV, 95
4. I, 78
5. I, 61
6. Interview
7. IV, 94
8. III, 115–117
9. I, 61: IV, 93
10. Strahler, 312
11. II, 282; Interview
12. IV, 91
13. I, 62
14. IV, 94
15. I, 61, 62

TRELL'S HOUSE

1. I, 62, 63
2. I, 66; Interview
3. I, 67

DOOM'S RETREAT

1. II, 184, 185, 277
2. II, 325
3. II, 355
4. II, 326; Interview
5. II, 332
6. II, 332
7. II, 343
8. II, 349

DORIENDOR CORISHEV

1. II, 354, 355
2. II, 355
3. II, 356, 357; Interview
4. Interview
5. II, 358
6. II, 365, 370; Interview
7. II, 365, 368, 369

THE ROCKSLIDE

1. II, 427
2. II, 429
3. II, 429, 430
4. II, 430–432

MELENKURION SKYWEIR

1. II, 442, 443
2. II, 440; Interview
3. II, 443
4. II, 442, 443
5. II, 443
6. II, 486, 487
7. II, 444
8. II, 465, 467

MELENKURION SKYWEIR—INTERIOR

1. II, 469
2. II, 465, 467
3. II, 467, 469
4. II, 471
5. II, 472
6. II, 485, 488
7. II, 502, 503
8. II, 504

DAMELON'S DOOR

1. II, 467
2. II, 468
3. Lobeck, 139
4. II, 468, 469
5. II, 469
6. II, 469, 470

THE AUDIENCE HALL

1. II, 470, 471; Lobeck, 139
2. II, 470
3. II, 470, 471

EARTHROOTSTAIR

1. Lobeck, 137
2. II, 473

EARTHROOT

1. II, 474
2. II, 475, 478
3. II, 485
4. II, 502, 503

CAVE OF THE EARTHBLOOD

1. II, 487
2. II, 488
3. II, 499

GALLOWS HOWE

1. II, 395
2. Stein, p. 689
3. II, 506; Interview
4. II, 395
5. II, 395, 507

THE NORTHWEST

1. VI, 177, 178; G, 95, 98
2. II, 237
3. II, 265
4. II, 265
5. I, 272; G, 109, 112
6. I, 171
7. IV, 224, 225
8. IV, 275, 282, 283
9. II, 207
10. II, 208–210
11. II, 236, 263
12. II, 414, 420
13. I, 193; G, 90
14. G, 90
15. IV, 381
16. IV, 288
17. G, 113
18. IV, 387, 388; VI, 161
19. I, 205; VI, 306

BANAS NIMORAM

1. I, 157
2. I, 158
3. I, 160
4. I, 161
5. I, 162

THE *RHYSH* OF THE WAYNHIM

1. IV, 274
2. IV, 278, 286
3. IV, 278
4. IV, 270, 278
5. IV, 278, 279
6. IV, 279, 280, 283

REVELWOOD

1. II, 236; Interview
2. II, 236; III, 37
3. *Encyclopedia Americana,* "Banyan"
4. II, 236; Beckett, 47
5. Interview
6. II, 240
7. II, 242; Interview
8. Interview
9. II, 240; III, 37
10. II, 242, 243

THE PLATEAU OF REVELSTONE

1. II, 48; III, 301; VI, 205; Interview
2. I, 205
3. II, 120, 142
4. IV, 302; VI, 206; Interview
5. II, 143, 144; VI, 205
6. I, 209
7. I, 211; II, 202
8. IV, 301, 302

REVELSTONE

1. I, 187; IV, 480
2. VI, 205
3. II, 97
4. IV, 306; VI, 217

THE CREVICE

1. I, 435
2. I, 436
3. VI, 427
4. VI, 427
5. I, 441, 442; VI, 435

KIRIL THRENDOR

1. VI, 436
2. I, 442; VI, 437, 439
3. VI, 436
4. I, 447
5. I, 451

THE MANETHRALL'S PATH

1. I, 454, 456
2. I, 457
3. I, 458

THE RAVINE OF THE FIRE-LIONS

1. I, 458, 459
2. I, 460, 461
3. I, 465
4. I, 466, 467. Note: the elevation of the shaft exit is based on a sketch by Donaldson during the interview.
5. I, 470

COERCRI—THE GRIEVE

1. VI, 476; Interview
2. II, 300
3. II, 301
4. II, 302
5. I, 187; II, 300; Interview
6. II, 303
7. IV, 476
8. II, 303
9. Interview
10. II, 304, 309; IV, 478

THE FAR NORTH

1. VI, 70, 81
2. VI, 109
3. VI, 110
4. VI, 111
5. I, 393
6. VI, 119
7. VI, 145
8. VI, 148
9. VI, 148
10. VI, 153

THE SOUTHEAST

1. I, 345
2. I, 349; III, 299
3. III, 282
4. I, 45
5. I, 357
6. II, 482
7. II, 479
8. I, 363
9. I, 364
10. III, 193
11. III, 381
12. I, 390
13. Interview
14. III, 395, 398, 400, 403
15. III, 390
16. III, 390; Interview
17. The lava flows south of Albuquerque, New Mexico, are an excellent example, standing several feet thick, yet with tortuous passages on and within, due to the cooling process.

SOARING WOODHELVEN

1. I, 132
2. I, 476; Collingwood, 188
3. I, 133
4. I, 132
5. I, 143, 144
6. I, 145, 149

THE HEARTWOOD CHAMBER

1. I, 137, 145, 149
2. I, 133, 136
3. I, 137

BARADAKAS' HOME

1. I, 144
2. I, 144
3. Interview

MANHOME

1. I, 364
2. I, 371, 372
3. I, 364
4. I, 364, 376
5. I, 366
6. I, 364; Interview
7. III, 185, 193

RAMEN COVERT

1. III, 193
2. III, 193, 194
3. III, 196

4. III, 198
5. These formations are fairly common in central Utah.
6. Interview
7. III, 211
8. III, 212, 217

THE HEALER'S CAVE

1. III, 280, 283
2. III, 283, 284, 286

THE COLOSSUS OF THE FALL

1. II, 51; III, 358; V, 392
2. IV, 331, 333, 334
3. III, 367, 375
4. Interview
5. III, 382, 385, 387
6. III, 389
7. III, 390
8. III, 393
9. Strahler, 320
10. III, 393, 395

THE TUNNELS OF THE *JHEHERRIN*

1. III, 403, 405, 407
2. III, 413, 414
3. III, 410; Interview
4. III, 411
5. III, 419
6. III, 418

KURASH QWELLINIR— THE SHATTERED HILLS

1. III, 419
2. Valley of Fires State Park, New Mexico, is an excellent example.
3. III, 391
4. III, 418
5. III, 421
6. III, 420
7. III, 424

HOTASH SLAY AND THE PROMONTORY

1. III, 431
2. III, 390
3. III, 391, 425
4. III, 431
5. III, 432
6. III, 433
7. III, 431
8. III, 433, 434

FOUL'S CRECHE

1. III, 390

Selected References

Books and Periodicals

Beckett, Kenneth A. *The Love of Trees*. New York: Crown Publishers, Inc., 1975.

Collingwood, G.H. *Knowing Your Trees*, Washington: American Forestry Association, 1945.

Curran, H. Allen, et al. *Atlas of Landforms*, 2nd Edition. New York: John Wiley & Sons, Inc., 1974.

Donaldson, Stephen R. *Daughter of Regals*. "Gilden-Fire." New York: Del Rey Books, 1984, pp. 85–107.

—————. *Illearth War, The*. New York: Del Rey Books, 1977.

—————. *Lord Foul's Bane*. New York: Del Rey Books, 1977.

—————. *One Tree, The*. New York: Del Rey Books, 1982.

—————. *Power That Preserves, The*. New York: Del Rey Books, 1977.

—————. *White Gold Wielder*. New York: Del Rey Books, 1983.

—————. *Wounded Land, The*. New York: Del Rey Books, 1980.

Encylopedia Americana, 1968 Edition. S.V. "Banyan," "Warships."

Espenshade, Edward B. Jr., Ed. *Goode's World Atlas*, 14th Edition. Chicago: Rand McNally & Co., 1974.

Hora, Bayard, Ed. *The Oxford Encyclopedia of Trees of the World*. Oxford: Oxford University Press, 1981.

Humphries, P.H. *Castles of Edward the First in Wales*. London: Her Majesty's Stationery Office, 1983.

Lobeck, A.K. *Geomorphology: An Introduction to the Study of Landscapes*. New York: McGraw-Hill Book Company, Inc., 1932.

O'Hara, John Cosgrave II. *Clipper Ship*. New York: The Macmillan Company, 1963.

Phillips, Alan. *Caernarfon Castle*. London: Her Majesty's Stationery Office, 1961.

Snead, Rodman E. *Atlas of World Physical Features*. New York: John Wiley & Sons, Inc., 1972.

Stein, Jess, Ed. *The Random House Dictionary of the English Language*. New York: Random House, 1981.

Strahler, Arthur N. *Physical Geography*. Second Edition. New York: John Wiley & Sons, Inc., 1963.

Thornbury, William D. *Principles of Geomorphology*. New York: John Wiley & Sons, 1954.

Tunis, Edwin. *Oars, Sails and Steam*. Cleveland: The World Publishing Co., 1952.

Miscellaneous

Interview: Stephen R. Donaldson, August 6–9, 1985; assorted letters.

Index of Place Names

This index includes an alphabetical list of the place names of the Land and outlying sites. A few of the locales have two or more names, some of which do not appear on any map. The alternate forms have been listed in parentheses. Each name important enough to be found on world and/or regional maps is preceded by an index coordinate of the approximate location. Features within major sites are further identified by the site within which they are located. Abbreviations for major sites are:

BT—*Bhrathairain* Town
EL—*Elemesnedene*
FC—Foul's Creche
MS—*Melenkurion* Skyweir

MT—Mount Thunder
RS—Revelstone
RW—Revelwood
SG—Starfare's Gem

All names are followed by the page or pages on which the term can be found. Occasionally the term will not appear on the primary map, but in an inset map or cross section. The page containing the primary locational reference is shown in italic, while that of the site map is in **boldface**. Whenever a feature spans a large area, two coordinates may be given: e.g., F-14/25 (indicating a spread in only one direction), or F-19/I-25 (indicating a multidirectional expanse).

ABOUT THE AUTHOR

Originally an art major, Karen Wynn Fonstad earned her B.S. in physical therapy, hoping to become a medical illustrator. But then she chose instead to do maps, receiving her M.A. in geography at the University of Oklahoma. After teaching briefly at the University of Wisconsin—Oshkosh, where she also acted as Director of Cartographic Services, she "retired." The results were two children, and an increasing desire to channel her energies into other creative endeavors. Her avocation has always been reading—especially in the SF/fantasy genre—so her Atlas creations have finally made her vocation and avocation one.

Karen Wynn Fonstad is also the author of *The Atlas of Middle-Earth* and *The Atlas of Pern*. She lives in Oshkosh, Wisconsin.